The Cambridge Companion to David

This collection of specially written essays offers both students and theatregoers a guide to one of the most celebrated American dramatists working today. Readers will find the general and accessible descriptions and analyses provide the perfect introduction to Mamet's work. The volume covers the full range of Mamet's writing, including now classic plays such as *American Buffalo* and *Glengarry Glen Ross*, and his more recent work, *Boston Marriage*, among others, as well as his films, including *Homicide* and *The Spanish Prisoner*. Additional chapters also explore Mamet and acting, Mamet as director, his fiction, and a survey of Mamet criticism. *The Cambridge Companion to David Mamet* is an introduction which will prepare the reader for future work by this important and influential writer.

THE CAMBRIDGE
COMPANION TO

DAVID MAMET

EDITED BY
CHRISTOPHER BIGSBY

PUBLISHED BY THE PRESS SYNDICATE OF THE UNIVERSITY OF CAMBRIDGE
The Pitt Building, Trumpington Street, Cambridge, United Kingdom

CAMBRIDGE UNIVERSITY PRESS
The Edinburgh Building, Cambridge, CB2 2RU, UK
40 West 20th Street, New York, NY 10011–4211, USA
477 Williamstown Road, Port Melbourne, VIC 3207, Australia
Ruiz de Alarcón 13, 28014 Madrid, Spain
Dock House, The Waterfront, Cape Town 8001, South Africa

http://www.cambridge.org

First published 2004

Printed in the United Kingdom at the University Press, Cambridge

Typeface Sabon 10/13 pt.   *System* LATEX 2$_\varepsilon$ [TB]

A catalogue record for this book is available from the British Library

Library of Congress Cataloguing in Publication data
The Cambridge companion to David Mamet / edited by Christopher Bigsby.
p.   cm. – (Cambridge companions to literature)
Includes bibliographical references and index.
ISBN 0 521 81557 6 – ISBN 0 521 89468 9 (paperback)
1. Mamet, David – Criticism and interpretation.   1. Bigsby, C. W. E.   II. Series.
PS3563.A4345Z59   2004
812'.54 – dc22   2003063279

ISBN 0 521 81557 6 hardback
ISBN 0 521 89468 9 paperback

CONTENTS

NOTES ON CONTRIBUTORS

CHRISTOPHER BIGSBY is Professor of American Studies at the University of East Anglia. He has published more than thirty books on English and American culture including *A Critical Introduction to 20th Century American Drama* (3 vols.), *Modern American Drama: 1945–2000* and *Contemporary American Playwrights*. He is co-editor, with Don Wilmeth, of *The Cambridge History of American Theatre*. He is also a novelist (*Hester, Pearl, Still Lives, Beautiful Dreamer*) and a regular broadcaster with the BBC.

HEATHER BRAUN is a doctoral student at Boston College, MA, and teaches English literature and writing. Her research interests include nineteenth-century British poetry, revivals of medieval romance, and the British Gothic, specifically the interplay between poetic motifs and Gothic novels. She has published book reviews in the *British Journal of Aesthetics* and the *Woman's Journal* and has helped to edit the expanded edition of *An Encyclopedia of British Women Writers*. She has done editorial work for *Shakespeare Bulletin* and has worked as a graduate writing consultant while completing her masters degree. Her essay, 'Victorian Comedy' is forthcoming in *World Comedy* by Greenwood Press.

JOHAN CALLENS is Professor of English at the Free University of Brussels (VUB). He is the author of *Double Birds: Existentialist Inspiration and Generic Experimentation in the Early Work of Jack Richardson*; *Acte(s) de Présence: Teksten over Engelstalig theater in Vlaanderen en Nederland*; and *From Middleton and Rowley's "Changeling" to Sam Shepard's "Bodyguard": A Contemporary Appropriation of a Renaissance Drama*. Among his more recent editions are a double Shepard issue of *Contemporary Theatre Review*, and English-language issue of *Degrés* on intermediality in the performing arts, and a collection of essays, *The Wooster Group and Its Traditions* (forthcoming). He serves on the editorial boards of the *European Journal of American Culture*, the Flemish theatre quarterly *Documenta*, and the "Dramaturgies: Texts, Cultures, and Performances" book series published by PIE. – Peter Lang.

PHILIP FRENCH was for thirty years a producer for BBC radio and has been drama critic of the *New Statesman*, principal book critic of the *Financial Times*, and a contributor to numerous journals and newspapers, most notably the *Observer*, where he has been film critic since 1978. As editor or author his books include *Age of Austerity 1945–51*; *The Movie Moguls*; *Westerns*; *Three Honest Men: Edmund Wilson, Lionel Trilling, F. R. Leavis*; *Mall on Malle*; *The Faber Book of Movie Verse*; and *Cult Movies*. In 1972 he was a Visiting Professor at the University of Texas, and has been on the Jury at the Cannes Film Festival and a judge of both the Prix Italia for broadcasting and the Booker Prize for Fiction.

BRENDA MURPHY is Professor of English at the University of Connecticut. Among her books are *O'Neill: Long Day's Journey Into Night*, *Congressional Theatre: Dramatizing McCarthyism on Stage, Film, and Television*, *Miller: Death of a Salesman*, *Tennessee Williams and Elia Kazan: A Collaboration in the Theatre*, and *American Realism and American Drama, 1880–1940*, and, as editor, the *Cambridge Companion to American Women Playwrights*, and *A Realist in the American Theatre: Drama Criticism by William Dean Howells*.

BENEDICT NIGHTINGALE has been Chief Theatre Critic of *The Times* (London) since 1990. He has also worked as a theatre critic for the *New York Times*, *New Statesman* (London), and the *Guardian* (Manchester). He is the author of *Charities*; *50 Modern English Plays*; *Fifth Row Center*; and *The Future of the Theatre*. His work for radio includes *Kaleidoscope*, *Critics' Forum*, *Meridian*, and many other BBC radio programs, and he has also made a series on playwrights for Thames TV.

ALAIN PIETTE holds MFA and DFA degrees from the Yale University School of Drama. He is the author of numerous essays on drama, cinema, translation, and education published in the United States, Canada, Asia, and Europe, both in English and in French. Alain Piette is also the author of *The Crommelynck Mystery – The Life and Work of a Belgian Playwright* and translator of *The Theater of Fernand Crommelynck: Eight Plays*, as well as the editor of several other volumes. He has published extensively on David Mamet. He is currently Director of the School of International Interpreters of the University of Mons-Hainaut, Belgium.

STEVEN PRICE lectures on literature and film at the University of Wales, Bangor. He has published widely on David Mamet and on other American and British dramatists, and with William Tydeman is co-author of *Oscar Wilde: Salome*. He is currently working on a study of the screenplay as a textual genre.

MATTHEW ROUDANÉ is Professor and Chair of the Department of English at Georgia State University in Atlanta. His books include *Understanding Edward Albee*; *Conversations with Arthur Miller*; *American Dramatists*; *"Who's Afraid of Virginia Woolf?": Necessary Fictions, Terrifying Realities*; *Public Issues, Private Tensions: Contemporary American Drama*; *Approaches to Teaching Miller's "Death of a Salesman"*; *American Drama since 1960: A Critical History*; *The Cambridge Companion to Tennessee Williams*; and *The Cambridge Companion to Sam Shepard*. Some of his more recent work appears in Don Wilmeth and Christopher Bigsby's three-volume *The Cambridge History of American Theatre*. *He has served as a dramaturge for 7 Stages Theatre in Atlanta, where he worked with Joseph Chaikin, who directed Edward Albee's A Delicate Balance (2002) and Arthur Miller's Broken Glass (2003).*

DAVID SAUER is Professor of English and Altmayer Chair of Literature at Spring Hill College. In addition to the joint projects with Janice A. Sauer, *David Mamet: A Resource and Production Sourcebook* and the annual bibliography for the *David Mamet Review*, he has published articles in journals including *Shakespeare Quarterly*, *Shakespeare Yearbook*, *Modern Drama*, *American Drama*, and *Shaw*, and chapters in books such as *Teaching Shakespeare in Performance*, ed. Milla Riggio, and *David Mamet's Glengarry Glen Ross*, ed. Leslie Kane.

JANICE A. SAUER is a senior reference librarian at the University of South Alabama. Her writings include *David Mamet: A Resource and Production Sourcebook* and the annual bibliography for the *David Mamet Review*, both written with David Sauer. In addition she publishes on library instruction in journals such as *College and Undergraduate Libraries*.

DON B. WILMETH is the Asa Messer Professor and Professor of Theatre and English at Brown University. He is co-editor with Christopher Bigsby of the award-winning three-volume *Cambridge History of American Theatre*, editor of *The Cambridge Guide to American Theatre* (and is currently at work on a new hardcover edition), and series editor for Cambridge's Studies in American Theatre and Drama. He authored the award-winning *George Frederick Cooke: Machiavel of the Stage*. A Guggenheim Fellow and recipient of the Anthony Denning Award from the [British] Society for Theatre Research, he has recently been honored with career achievement awards by the Association for Theatre in Higher Education and the American Society for Theatre Research.

I

CHRISTOPHER BIGSBY

David Mamet

In 1974, a play set in part in a singles bar, laced with obscene language and charged with a seemingly frenetic energy, was voted Best Chicago Play. Transferred to Off Off and Off Broadway it picked up an Obie Award. *Sexual Perversity in Chicago* was not David Mamet's first play, but it did mark the beginning of a career that would astonish in both its range and depth.

The following year *American Buffalo* opened at Chicago's Goodman Theatre in an "alternative season." It was well received and opened on Broadway fifteen months later where it won the New York Drama Critics Circle Award. It ran for 135 performances, hardly a failure but in the hit or miss world of New York, not a copper-bottomed success either. Nonetheless, in three years he had announced his arrival in unequivocal terms.

David Mamet came as something of a shock, not least because his first public success, *Sexual Perversity in Chicago*, seemed brutally direct in terms of its language and subject, as did *American Buffalo*. But it was already clear to many that here was a distinctive talent, albeit one that some critics found difficult to assess, not least because of his characters' scatological language and fractured syntax, along with the apparent absence, in his plays, of a conventional plot. They praised what they took to be his linguistic naturalism, as though his intent had been to offer an insight into the cultural lower depths while capturing the precise rhythms of contemporary speech (though he did invoke Gorky's *The Lower Depths* as being, like a number of his own plays, a study in stasis). That he was highly talented seemed obvious, but what that talent might consist of was altogether less certain.

There is, indeed, a distinctive rhythm to his work but he is interested neither simply in documenting contemporary speech patterns nor in anything as self-conscious as poetic drama, despite the fact that he claimed to have written *American Buffalo*, *The Woods*, *The Cryptogram*, and *Oleanna* in free verse. The rhythm both itself contains a meaning and, like everything else, serves the plot, as does the language which may seem to shape itself into poetry, sculpted arias, but is, in fact, fully functional in terms of forwarding action and thereby revealing character or vice versa. As opposed to the cinema, the theatre, for Mamet, is a place where language dominates, where it becomes clear that "what you say influences the way you think, the way you act, not the other way around."[1] That was the essence of his work even if the critics were not yet fully registering what they were seeing and hearing.

Despite his early recognition, indeed, his was not entirely a smooth ride. Both *The Water Engine* and *The Woods* failed in New York in 1979, the former closing after sixteen performances and the latter after thirty-three. The same year *Lone Canoe* was staged at the Goodman and proved a disaster. It looked to some as if here might be another young writer thrown up by regional theatre and a forgiving Off Broadway who had been granted his day in the sun and would now disappear, as had many others before him. They were plainly wrong.

Here, in fact, was a writer uncowed by apparent failure, amazingly prolific and already diversifying into cinema, writing an accomplished screenplay for Bob Rafaelson's film version of *The Postman Always Rings Twice*. There was then, and is now, a restlessness to Mamet's talent and imagination which sees him constantly reaching out in new directions, writing a plethora of plays (not always produced), articles, fictions, screenplays.

When *Glengarry Glen Ross*, opened to much praise in London, in 1983, it seemed that he had confounded his critics. Highly successful at Britain's National Theatre, it did little business in New York until it was awarded the Pulitzer Prize, at which point lines began to form around the theatre. It ran for 378 performances.

From that moment onwards, Mamet's career opened up with revivals of his earlier work and a string of successes in the theatre and the cinema, for which he would direct as well as write. Added to this were an increasing number of essays, collected into books, which explored his early life, his theories of acting and such apparently arcane areas as poker playing, hunting, and a spell with a magazine for men, inventing captions for unequivocal photographs of women.

For some, these last seemed to chime with plays which either excluded women or concerned themselves with a seemingly unbridgeable gulf between the genders. This won him a brief reputation as a misogynist as some critics chose to extrapolate his characters' views to include their author's, and took his exploration of a contemporary sexual and social alienation as indicating his own position.

Though this view would fade with time, it received a new boost with *Oleanna* (1992), which registered contemporary debates over political correctness and the idea of sexual harassment. He was assumed by some to have his thumb securely on the scales, parodying the woman's viewpoint and vindicating the man's, though in truth audiences seem to have split along gender lines. Certainly, audience responses came as a shock both to Mamet and to Harold Pinter who directed the British production.

Oleanna is concerned with the clash between a university professor, distracted by personal concerns, a man described by Pinter as "a pretty pompous guy who loves his own authority and his own position," and a woman student initially baffled by her studies and subsequently vindictively determined to destroy her teacher, interpreting a gesture of concern as a sexual assault. The play ends as, frustrated literally beyond words, he strikes her. Pinter has recalled the first night at the Royal Court Theatre in England in 1993:

> the audience applauded. I was pretty shocked. So was the actress who was under the table at the time. When she came out she was crying. She was so shocked at what had happened. The audience thought she was crying because she had been beaten up but she was shocked by the venom, coming from men and women. In fact the leading man's (David Suchet) family were there and in the dressing room afterwards his mother said, "I'm so glad you beat her up. She had it coming to her."[2]

Rather than make any changes in his direction to obviate this response Pinter told the cast, "fuck the audience and just get on with it."

What that play, and many others, revealed was precisely Mamet's sensitivity to shifts in the cultural and political pressure that had earlier led him to write *American Buffalo* and *Glengarry Glen Ross* at a time when untrammelled capitalism was being advanced as a moral virtue. However, in *Oleanna* he seems not quite to have grasped just how vitriolic arguments over political correctness and sexual harassment had become. On America's campuses contesting languages were indeed doing battle. The nature and ownership of power was being debated precisely in the context of shifting gender roles, as he had hinted in *Sexual Perversity in Chicago*, but the stakes, it seems, were higher than even he or Pinter had assumed.

Mamet had made adjustments to the play which had originally ended not with the physical attack but with the protagonist reading out a prepared text, McCarthy style, confessing to his own guilt. It was this version that Pinter had accepted and was about to rehearse. Mamet, however, had decided to cut it on the grounds that "it didn't work." Pinter persisted, insisting to the author that "It doesn't make any sense to finish with the beating because that is the whole point. She comes back." After further negotiations he received a letter from Mamet: "Fuck it. Do it."

The fact is that the sexes are at odds in many of his plays but so they were in a culture in which they were renegotiating their roles, the nature and extent of their respective powers. What he was not concerned to do was adjudicate between positions which were, as he insisted, simultaneously both right and wrong. He was, like Sam Shepard, registering the gulf both between the sexes and between an inherited language of aggressive masculinity and needs that could barely be articulated. In truth, the men in his plays are no more assured about their own inner resources or their relationships with one another than they are about encounters across the gender divide. His is a drama in which need is as evident as the failure of experience to address it. It is the very gaps in experience which generate some of the plays' kinetic energy.

Does that make him a political writer? Plainly not in the sense that a young Arthur Miller had begun writing for the theatre believing it to be a direct agent of change, a mechanism for exposing truths which once understood would spur those who watched to transform both the agencies and philosophy of government. Mamet is not Clifford Odets, prompting audiences to shout out "Strike! Strike! Strike" and sally forth to halt the progress of capitalism, though he is an admirer of that playwright's sculpted language and is, indeed, suspicious of the commodifying power of capitalism.

He is, however, political if we mean by that that his portraits of alienated individuals, profoundly uncommunal, speaking a language often drained of human content, betraying the past and therefore the future, imply the necessity to confront what is lost, without which effort recuperation must be impossible. He is political if we mean by that that he, like Harold Pinter, whose work he admires, is concerned with power and the degree to which language is implicated in its operations. He is political in so far as he presents characters who are complicit in their own irrelevance, who compound an absurdity that is not cosmic in origin (his admiration for Beckett notwithstanding) but a product of the substitution of material for spiritual meaning.

We live, he has insisted, "in a political association," and that fact tends to abstract "individual human actions from individual consequences . . . The political system is a sad conundrum. In the name of history, reason, and loyalty, we debase and are debased . . . Our politicians seem to be the hirelings of raptors."[3] An "incorrigible liberal," he fulminates over tax cuts for the rich and a foreign policy that serves any interests but rationality:

> If the government has no ability to defend against the real threat of terrorists, but untold wealth to squander in the name of "rogue missile launch," then the organism is in irreversible decay. The fantasy wish for an opponent who would, by his military actions, *endorse* our military industrial complex by the nature of his aggression suggests a country that no longer wishes to survive . . . But this is, essentially, the error of all bloated plutocracy.[4]

There is a barely contained anger in his comments on the corruptions of power, the hypocrisies and cynicism of those who become the mere agents of corporations who disavow their responsibility for their actions and thus offer a model of human disregard. That anger is discharged, in part, in his writing, in coruscating dramas which feature those who inhabit a world gifted by such dereliction. These are vaguely aware of the betrayals in which they collaborate. They are, though, unsure how to find their way back to a language and a way of being that speaks of human necessities abandoned in the name of nothing more than the nostrums of a bankrupt culture forgetful of the past which once made it seem a great experiment.

Increasingly, he explores the idea that the vacancies he identifies in the lives of his characters might prompt a recovery of spiritual, even strictly religious beliefs. Part of his fascination with the past, indeed, lies not only in forms, courtesies, secular ceremonies which have been allowed to decay, but in beliefs seemingly traded for a mess of potage, spiritual truths surrendered in the hope that such surrender might render the world more fully into the hands of those who thought the material world to hold its own satisfactions.

It is not for nothing that he chose to make a film version of Terence Rattigan's *The Winslow Boy* in which questions of justice and moral integrity were proposed as central to private and public life alike. This is not to suggest that he is a solemn moralist. Like Bernard Shaw, he is aware of the forensic virtues of humor, even, in *Boston Marriage*, offering a pastiche Wildean parlor drama in which he both revels in and consciously ironizes a wit which refuses to acknowledge the demands of social and moral function. For Mamet, the sheer pleasure of the plasticity of language offers its own rewards.

He is a man of strong political ideas (though he harbors regret at not being more active in the anti-Vietnam war movement) but his drama is not about politics, though what it is about bears on the political as on other forms of behavior. "My plays," he has insisted, "are not political. They're dramatic. I don't believe that the theatre is a good venue for political-argument" (Kane, ed., *Mamet in Conversation*, p. 125). If it be objected that *Oleanna* precisely focuses on a political issue, he accepts that this is so but insists that the real issue at stake is power and the language deployed to exert and sustain it.

It is tempting to say that this is a distinction without a difference since politics itself is quintessentially about power and the language with which it asserts and sustains itself (see Arthur Miller's *The Crucible*), but his point is that this is equally true of all relationships, that the political is merely one expression of a common truth. It is, as *Sexual Perversity in Chicago* and *The Woods* suggest, true of the relationship between the sexes. Beyond that, however, "Everybody uses language for his or her own purpose to get what he or she wants . . . No one ever talks except to accomplish an objective" (126). There is, in other words, a politics to human relationships.

Meanwhile, his reference to accomplishing an objective is a key not only to those relationships but to writing and acting. And that objective is likely to be achieved by deceit, a disjunction between word and action, motive and declared purpose.

In his plays and novels deceit seems a natural mode of behavior and though he disavows a political role, his essays are laced with comments about the cynical slogan "Manifest Destiny" (in fact code for "pillage, plunder," and theft), the crude lies of the House UnAmerican Activities Committee and of Richard Nixon (posthumously re-invented in a breathtaking piece of sleight of hand). He comments on the self-deception of Ronald Reagan, denying, in his heart, that he had traded arms for hostages, the logic whereby the fact of political corruption in the name of public good could lead alike to the Holocaust or the chaos of Central America into which America insinuates itself with bland assurances of good will.

There is, then, a politics to David Mamet and to his plays even if he does not choose to address politics as subject matter. His plays are metaphors and their resonances expand outwards from the particularities of their setting.

Is he, then, a moralist? He certainly wags a finger or two in admonition in his essays, attacking politicians and snake-oil salesmen of sundry kinds. He looks for truth from actors, rather than the self-deceiving mechanisms they are sometimes tempted to substitute for authentic action. When he became for a time a columnist for the *Guardian* he chose to celebrate Noel Coward ("as fine an actor as anyone could hope to see"), Roger Lindsay ("the British Henry Fonda . . . incapable of falsity"), and Celia Johnson ("filled with the truth of emotion withheld"). This was not Anglophilia, though it was, perhaps, nostalgia. He had his American models – Fonda himself, Ruth Draper, Robert Duvall – but the British bias (he also includes Kenneth More, Vivian Merchant, Bernard Miles, and Ray Winstone) is not without its logic. He seems to favor a certain understatement, to be suspicious of the self-consciously histrionic.

What he primarily distrusts is "acting," though this leads him to flourish yet another Britain, Lawrence Olivier, whom he characterizes as "stiff, self-conscious, grudging, coy and ungenerous." Stephen Berkoff, scarcely himself the most understated of actors, denounced such a view as "facile," not unreasonably recalling Olivier's Henry V and Richard III. He might have added Hamlet and Heathcliff. The question is not, though, who was right in a journalistic knock-about, or even why, Ray Winstone aside, Mamet chose to burrow back into the past of the British cinema, but that his remarks were consonant with his distrust of art or, more precisely, artifice. If he is biased it is in the direction of a truth which he takes to emerge from character and action. Even language is not without its deceits. Indeed, in many ways language lies at the very heart of deception and misunderstanding, either consciously or because it can never be fully transitive. What he listens for is something other than words, which are more often at odds than consonant with emotion. As he said in relation to Olivier, "I'm hungry for lunch, and all he's serving is an illustrated menu."[5] He wants actors who act, not "act." He scarcely has a puritanical distrust of excess, his own plays launching pre-emptive strikes on boundaries of all kinds. What he listens for is authenticity.

Yet this, of course, raises a question, since so many of his characters are themselves simulators of authenticity and derive their power precisely from the fact that they are seldom caught "acting." But that is his point and his skill. They succeed in their deceptions because they do not succumb to the temptation to signal their deception. They are actors not "actors." They practice to deceive. But, where the trickster has no interest in truth, Edward Albee has observed that in the theatre lies can corrupt in the direction of truth and Mamet is interested in truth from the actor as he is from the personal and political realm.

In his essays Mamet spends some time explaining what theatre is not. It is not, in particular, as we have seen, a mechanism for changing the world. He does, though, see it as a place where "we show ethical experience, it's where we show interchange." Thus what *American Buffalo* "was trying to say . . . is that once you take a step back from the moral responsibility you've undertaken, you're lost" (Kane, ed., *Mamet in Conversation*, p. 12). The play "has to do with the corruption of heartfelt moral knowledge for the sake of a mythological ideal . . . It's about the same thing Nixon and all those people were doing" (18).

David Mamet is a Jewish writer, though until recently few accounts of his life or work suggested as much, except in so far as they sketched in his early years. Saul Bellow, Bernard Malamud, Philip Roth have all been discussed at least in part in terms of their double identity but Mamet has been discussed primarily in terms of his distinctive linguistic facility, his fascination with the brittle relationship between the sexes, the figure of the confidence trickster, his concern with the moral vacuity at the heart of much experience. All these things are clearly observable in his plays, but there is another dimension to him that presses on his work and is important to him as an individual. It may be, indeed, that his fascination with deracinated characters, with those who perform rather than live their lives, is itself a comment on the consequence of surrendering a grasp on certain inner truths having to do with identity.

The question of identity, after all, has a special resonance for those who have historically chosen to set themselves apart and have been set apart, those who in moving from one country to another have been invited to make subtle, and not so subtle, adjustments to the new world, sometimes at the price of losing a purchase on the old. The dream of inclusion may be shadowed by the nightmare of surrendered meaning. New freedoms may erode the frontiers of the self, sever the very roots which sustained. And what message do they pass to their children as they negotiate the terms on which they enter a culture determined to announce its indivisibility?

David Mamet's grandparents on his mother's side arrived in America before the First World War; on his father's side, in 1921. His mother's family derived from Warsaw, his father's from Hrubieszow, a village on the Bugg River near the Russian–Polish border. They were Ashkenazi Jews, and his father was born "right off the boat" and raised during the Depression. His grandparents brought nothing with them from the shtetl (except soon-to-be-despised languages), not objects (they were poor) nor a style. His maternal grandfather was a salesman, selling underwear. His paternal grandfather left his wife, Calara (the name of Mamet's third daughter), who therefore had to bring the family up as a single parent, in retrospect, it seems, foreshadowing a series of broken marriages which would include Mamet's own first venture.

His family life, like that of many other immigrants, was built on denial of the past, seemingly the quickest avenue to the future: "My parents generation was in the naked pursuit, first of education, and then, of success."[6] Acculturation, assimilation, was the agreed price for becoming American and in the process much was lost, though hardly counted as lost by those who were still validating the decision to leave the irrelevance of Europe and to some degree the faith which seemed to set them apart from what they would become.

They still thought of themselves as Jews but the religious content of that identification was hollowed out. They might rehearse the rituals, perform the rites of the faith but not without some embarrassment. They were Jewish by birth. Theirs was a Jewish community. They shared, as he has explained, Jewish food, "the comforting codes, language, jokes, and attitudes which make up the consolations of strangers in a strange land" (Kane, ed., *Mamet in Conversation*, p. 8). They shared, indeed, the experience of discrimination. What they did not share was a confident inner conviction expressed through an equally confident assertion, and in *The Old Religion* he would recall how fragile was their grasp on the world they believed their own, how ready their new society to force them into a role they had chosen to deny.

Yiddish and Hebrew were finally to be eschewed, for what did they mean but a willful attachment to other times and other places? They were what held apart rather than brought close. They implied a separateness that had always been the essence of the Jewish claim and the Jewish suffering. This generation staked its claim on America by seeking some basis on which they could move into the mainstream by modifying, omitting, suppressing, acting. They did not deny they were who they were but looked for ways in which difference could be de-emphasized, subtly adjusting themselves as though walking into the face of the wind.

Mamet has accused himself of doing much the same, and for too long. As he explained, "The Jewish child . . . is often torn between the desire to belong to the dominant culture and the desire to remain true to his or her heritage, religious observance, and cultural identity."[7] Assimilation still seemed a natural response to national myths and metaphors of inclusiveness. He might rebel against aspects of his parents' values but he felt the same seductive pressures that had pulled not only his father's generation but the so-called New York intellectuals into the mainstream not least because they could persuade themselves that they had, by their very presence, redefined it. Assimilation has its seductive attraction, whether it be Jewish actors concealing their origins or the gangster, Meyer Lansky, whose life he would dramatize on film and who slid into the American consciousness by way of crime, fleeing to Israel in a gesture whose ambiguity is revealing if perplexing.

As Mamet has explained:

> it pleased me to think that I was putting something over in myself . . . living in Vermont and doing things that it seemed were not acceptable behaviour for a nice Jewish boy whose family had the gene for liberalism – spending a lot of time gambling, hunting, fishing etc. And I spent a lot of time in pool rooms, and I enjoyed the life there.

Then he went to his niece's Bat Mitzvah and "I realized I hadn't been inside a synagogue for 30 years, and I started wondering why." He was "chagrined and shocked to find that it had something to do with a sense of not only assimilation, but perhaps a self-hatred that was nobody's fault but my own. And I thought perhaps I could remedy that" (Kane, ed., *Mamet in Conversation*, p. 172).

It was not simply a question of placing Jewish characters at the center of his work, though he would do that, but of acknowledging that the collapse of values that he documented, the sense of dislocation, abandonment, self-deceit which defined these characters, might have a correlative in his own experience. If America had lost its communal instinct, its sense of validating myths and authoritative principles, so, too, he suspected, had he. He had let something go, believing that to do so was a virtue, only subsequently to realize the extent to which it threatened something he came to believe was of primary importance.

Mamet has spent some time working his way back to what was, perhaps, too readily surrendered: *Homicide*, *The Old Neighborhood* and *The Old Religion* offering a reflection of that process. He would ask, in particular, how far faith is implicated in identity, what the price of propitiation might be. Thirty years on from his childhood he could say, "God bless those in all generations who have embraced their Jewishness," insisting that "We are a beautiful people and a good people" (*Some Freaks*, p. 13), while proclaiming that "I am very proud of being a Jew, and I have a growing sense of the reality of God" (20). It became increasingly important for him to challenge whatever struck him as anti-Semitism, less because he thought this might change the person concerned than because he was himself discharging a responsibility in which he had once failed.

In *South of the Northeast Kingdom*, he identifies himself: "I am a Jew, born in Chicago" (10), like Saul Bellow's Augie March laying his credentials on the table. The first chapter begins, "September, this is when the year begins. So say we Jews" (3). In an interview about *The Winslow Boy* he referred to "All of us American Jews," described his distaste for David Hare's *Via Dolorosa*, "speaking as a Jew,"[8] and warned against attempts to engage the Holocaust in art quite as if he were acknowledging a responsibility to speak on behalf of those from whom he feared he may have distanced himself.

In a poem, "Song of the Jew," he wrote:

> I would die where my grandfather died –
> In that country we were banished from,
> Even knowing it was not our home.
> We came to the New World and we throve thereby,
> In the equivalent of heresy,
> Fleeing the only home we ever saw
> In the two wandering millennia,
> Which is to say, the study of the Law.[9]

The remaining two stanzas express a preference for dying where his ancestors lived and died, rather than in a place where the poet had achieved wealth and power alongside the comfortable people who envied and feared him. But they acknowledge, too, the fact that he is an outcast, that he has opted for another fate and is caught within those contradictory impulses, having become what he affected to despise. In verse, in drama, and in a novel, he has endeavored to work out what he is and what he would be and the price to be paid for both.

Passover, he reminded himself, was "supposedly the longest continuously celebrated ceremony in the world." That fact had a meaning beyond the existence of a tradition to be honored merely for its longevity. To "cut oneself off from one's identity," he has said, "is a terrible, terrible thing" (Kane, ed., *Mamet in Conversation*, p. 183). In 1995 he published a book called *Passover*, the story of a grandmother and her granddaughter preparing for the feast. As the older woman readies the ingredients, so she recapitulates a history and in particular recalls the time when her own grandmother had survived a pogrom by smashing her own house so that those who sought her life would assume she had been visited already. The story of the sweet ingredients unfolds in parallel to the bitter truths laid before the young girl.

Passover is a story of survival – nor is it remote from those who now gather to celebrate it. As the story ends, so there is the sound of a key turning in the lock. It is, presumably, a returning family member but for Jews the memory of threat is never purged nor Passover drained of its immediate relevance. And perhaps that hints at another reason for the sense of contingency in Mamet's work, what might otherwise be seen as evidence of an urban paranoia. In *Passover*, grandmother and granddaughter hold one another, in love but also in a shared sense of apprehension. To deny "what you are, to deny who you are, to deny what you want, to live a life of hypocrisy," Mamet has insisted, "has got to have an ongoing effect of self-loathing" (183).

Nor did this seem a truth only to be embraced by Jews. In this context it is tempting to see his characters – projecting socially useful versions of themselves, fictions with little substance – as not wholly unrelated to his sense of an ungrounded life and his stress on theatre as a place to engage with spiritual issues.

He is not inclined to blame his parents for his early failure to hold on to what he would later feel to be essentials. As he has said, "it's the nature of human beings to say, 'I'm going to give my kids what I didn't have.' In the case of my parents that was economic stability. In the case of myself it's community. And identity" (218). He was, anyway, brought up in the 1950s, "when America as the melting pot with one-for-all and all-for-one was the stuff of every text-book and much of every day in the public schools." It was, though, he insists, "never true. And I think that looking back what it meant was, on the part of the majority culture, everything will be okay if you'll be like me" (223).

Conformity was not only the tax to be paid by Jews as he grew up in the 1950s; it was proposed as a national virtue. To be sure, the Beats were restlessly searching for something they could not define but even they seemed to find it in a mythicized America as much as in a reconstituted spiritualism. They were rebels but they lacked a cause. The Civil Rights movement had a cause but its objective lay in inclusion in the American enterprise, the justification for which lay in the constitutional documents of America's past.

Memories of his upbringing seem ambivalent in several respects. He submitted to religious education and, at the age of thirteen, underwent his Bar Mitzvah, but his, it seemed to him in retrospect, was a watercolor Jewishness, "American Good Citizenship . . . with some Unfortunate Asiatic Overtones." He and the family were Reform Jews determined to be "so stalwart, so American, so non-Jewish."[10] It was a faith which simultaneously declared itself and adjusted, evaded, the implications of that declaration. In an attempt to slide unnoticed into the American psyche, they collaborated in allowing faith to become a lifestyle, a mere modification of some central cultural truth born out of a supposedly secular but patently Christian culture.

It was understood that there were those who changed their names, who passed, and were suitably rewarded, their drive for success suddenly and apparently unaccountably purged of presumptions about its racial and religious origin. In an essay called "Jews for Export" he lists those Hollywood stars who have traded in their Jewish identities not simply for fame but on the assumption that audiences will not credit a Jew as a model of the universal, and this in an industry that was the invention of Jews. When Homer Simpson, in the cartoon series, discovers that Krusty the Clown ('real' name Hershel Krustofsky) is Jewish he gasps, "A Jewish entertainer? Get out of here!" – a joke which turns on the unsecret secret of both Jewish talent and its concealment. When Fanny Brice had her nose altered Dorothy Parker remarked that she had cut off her nose to spite her race.

There were those, too, who sought to distinguish themselves from those others who were seemingly determined to sustain a purer model of their faith and its practices. These strategies were to be understood because they served a seemingly higher purpose, to belong and to belong not to some supranational spiritual consciousness but a place and a culture which announced, if it did not always practice, its inclusiveness, one nation supposedly indivisible.

It took him time to ask questions and for those questions to lead to resentment, anger, and some guilt. Perhaps there is a shadow of his concern for the effacement with which his parents, and others of their generation, had sought acceptance to be found in his essay on Superman in which he describes the comic book hero as "living among aliens to whom he cannot even reveal his rightful name."[11] Superman, after all, was the product of two Jews, Jerry Siegel and Joe Schuster. Jules Feiffer once suggested that the superhero came not from Krypton but from Minsk.

In an essay entitled "Poor But Happy," he denounces the pressure to distance oneself from a meaning assumed to exist at a tangent to national concerns, pressure which invites equivocation as a means to treat with superior power:

The phrases "I am a Jew, but I am not a practising Jew," "I am a Jew culturally but not religiously," "My parents were Jews, but I am not a Jew," "I am a Jew, but I disagree with the conduct of Israel," et cetera – these phrases, while uttered as a declaration of autonomy, are, to the contrary, a ritual of subjugation to the dominant culture[12]

It is not, he insists, that such statements are illegitimate but that they are a means of putting oneself outside the group. They are a concession to power and the potential source of self-hatred and denial. To let a racial slur pass is thus not only to compound ignorance and bigotry but to accept the legitimacy if not of the charge then of the right to make it.

Membership of the group thus emerges as a virtue to a playwright, many of whose plays propose the factitious nature of America's supposed communality. And yet there is an ambivalence to groups since in most of his plays they are no more than temporary alliances as people come together to commit crimes, sell real estate (not remote from theft), make or plan movies, teach or be taught. The most intimate of communities, families, relationships between men and women, seem to lack precisely the distinguishing marks of intimacy and relationship. In other words, he proposes the virtue of communality by demonstrating the effect of its absence or corruption. There is a felt absence in his plays, an absence of genuinely shared values, of a sense of transcendence, of, in one form or another, love.

The characters in *American Buffalo* and *Glengarry Glen Ross* meet in the semblance of a community, acknowledging a need, yet they never connect, being driven by other imperatives, imperatives which are the product of a society whose myths and social virtues have to do with the self. Their principle is that of Arthur Miller's Uncle Ben in *Death of a Salesman*: never fight fair with a stranger. And the world is full of strangers. The characters in *American Buffalo*, Mamet later realized, in effect are the portraits of a family, but, in so far as that is so, such a family goes beyond the dysfunctional. It actually breeds its own dissolution.

Betrayal, desertion, abandonment are immediate and real possibilities. Mamet may celebrate community in the context of a Jewish identity, yet in his work and, it has to be said, in his own early life he found little evidence of it. Even his account of a dinner party is interrupted, as the dinner party itself was, by an anti-Semitic slur, delivered with the assurance not just of ignorance but of a seeming total unawareness of offence.

Mamet has spoken of a recurring dream. It is that he has killed someone and is on the run. He is waiting to be tapped on the shoulder. His own interpretation of the customs official, border guard or policeman he summons up is that such a person is "simply looking at someone he knows does not belong."[13] That sense of not belonging may derive in part from his role as a writer who inhabits a border territory, not quite incorporated in the culture he addresses. It is tempting, though, to see another sense of contingency, displacement, exile, deriving from his own awareness of being part of a people for whom threat has always been a present possibility and incorporation a suspect goal, a neutralizing of the self in the name of social identity and national destiny.

Mamet has written of good times with his father, a labor lawyer (*Hoffa* is in some senses a displaced celebration of his commitments) and amateur semanticist (whom he credits with firing an early interest in language, though his sister recalls his insistence on linguistic precision as a form of intimidation). He remembers family holidays in Jewish resort hotels – Jews being banned from many establishments in the 1950s, the very experience that had fired Arthur Miller to write his angry novel about anti-Semitism, *Focus*. The hostility which this implies seems not to have registered at the time but surely informs his attitude to a society with the power to exclude, and power, as we have seen and as he has acknowledged, is a central theme of his work.

Yet if there were good times, there were also bad. He was the child of divorced parents and something of the impact of that is apparent in *The Cryptogram* which was, he confessed, an attempt "to decode the message of one's childhood" (Kane, ed., *Mamet in Conversation*, p. 151). His parents separated in 1957–8, when Mamet was ten. As he has explained, "I didn't know anybody who'd been divorced . . . let alone have it happen to my family. So there was a lot of trauma in my childhood" (168).

You hardly have to be a Freudian to understand that the emphasis on "belonging" in his work (the word itself recurs in his essays), his celebration of the coterie of poker players, hunters, theatre groups, movie crews, which he created or joined, could be seen as a response to a sense of his own early experience of a fragmented family life. Perhaps significantly, he has called rehearsing, "working with my family" (173). The "nice thing about being . . . a writer," he has said, "is you get to work a lot of things out" (169).

He lived with his mother (a teacher), sister and stepfather for six years before rejoining his father for two. So if he speaks nostalgically of visits to Wrigley Field, Comiskey Park, and Soldier Field (to see the Bears), he also recalls being raised in a new suburban development, stripped of character, a place with neither roots nor meaning, in a family which was itself a new invention, his mother having remarried.

In a chilling account, the more so because of the restrained nature of the prose in which he offers it, he itemizes his stepfather's cruelties and acts of casual brutality. It is the story of a life without love, in which barely detectable offenses were punished with disinterested precision. There are moments of sudden violence from a stepfather whose implacability is matched by his irrationality, but it is the human dereliction that is most disturbing, a family broken apart leaving edges sharp with disregard.

It is, indeed, sheer absence that seems to cut a bloodless line in his psyche, an absence of human consideration. Even the middle-class environment seemed to define itself in terms of what it was not so that his later blue-collar jobs gave him a sense of reality lacking from a world from which he would effectively flee. Threat, meanwhile, required no histrionics. It inhered in relationships at once distant and ominously close. For all Mamet's later admiration of Harold Pinter, he needed no lessons in menace, the shock consequent upon the opening of a door. He never knew when the blow might come or what its reason, if reason there might be. His sister was sent sprawling downstairs as a consequence of some minor infraction of rules which were themselves arbitrary and at times impossible to fathom. And the lack of love, at least on one side, reached back a generation (his grandfather refusing to acknowledge love for his daughter while she sobbed in desperation) as though this were a family, or, rather, two families, balanced between warmth and an estrangement that could seem a condition of existence to a young boy desperate for something in which to earth himself. Perhaps his time as a child actor gave him alternative realities within which to hide.

Perhaps, indeed, as for Tennessee Williams, art itself would be a retreat, offering its own contingent coherences and completions. The content of his plays might stress desolation, discontinuities, random acts, but their form was the guarantee of a containing order.

His worst memory was of himself hitting his sister in an anger instantly regretted and denied by both of them, who found a solidarity in their mutual fear and protectiveness. That air of imminent, if seldom actual, violence in his plays does, then, have its parallel in his private life as does that gap between his characters, in need of a trust and a love they can never find. He may say that "our society has fallen apart and *nobody* knows what he or she should be doing,"[14] but he had had experience of this sense of disorientation and vertigo long before he was ready to acknowledge it in the culture.

Perhaps this was an early intimation of his conviction that "we are a savage species," his recognition of "our capacity to dominate."[15] Then, again, he was also aware that he was part of the first atomic generation, living with the knowledge that brute power, a technological savagery constructed not out of passion but out of reason, could snuff out not only his own life but everybody's. Suddenly a Jewish knowledge became a common condition, not that he was happy with those who wished to deny the Holocaust its particularity nor, indeed, wished himself to break the stunned silence provoked by that never-to-be-healed wound.

He dismissed, in particular, *The Diary of Anne Frank* and *Schindler's List*, describing the latter as "emotional pornography," "*Mandingo* for Jews,"[16] as if these were no more than exploitative gestures, an offense against an experience that could only be traduced by utterance. And this, of course, implies a sense of the moral responsibility of art rather than simply its complicated etiquette.

There are even moments when his Jewish commitments override his sense of camaraderie with fellow writers. It was for this reason that he attacked David Hare's *Via Dolorosa*, his thoughts on a visit to Jerusalem, saying, "I don't consider it my place to talk about other people *qua* writers, but speaking as a Jew, it is an appalling piece."[17]

Years later, he recalled the walk home from school through still largely open country, a description significant not for what it says but for what it does not, not for what was felt but for what was not: "From the remove of years, I can see how the area might have been beautiful. One could have walked in the stubble of the cornfields, or hunted birds, or enjoyed any of a number of pleasures naturally occurring."[18] He could have done these things, but did not. In a sense this process was a key to his upbringing. It was not a case of what his family were but what they were not; not a case of what was offered but what was withheld. The conditional tense prevailed. They were always in the making, never secure, fixed, assured in a culture committed to the pursuit rather than the possession of happiness, the latter implying a state of stasis at odds with the imperative to become – itself, ironically, not without its Jewish antecedence.

Later, a negative social truth would become a positive artistic principle. In 2002, he wrote an article about music. He had struggled to learn the piano as a young child, not realizing that his failure lay in part in an undiagnosed myopia that left him incapable of reading the notes with any clarity. Later, he tried again, hiring a practice room at $5 an hour, and learned that the ear can hear notes that are never played. This was equally, he insisted, a key to drama. The essence was "how much can one remove, and still have the composition be intelligible. Chekhov removed the plot. Pinter removed the history, the narration; Beckett the characterisations." Omission, he insists, "is a form of creation."[19] Even silence is replete with meaning which is perhaps why his characters so often fill the air with speech, speech often designed less to communicate than to avoid communication, less to express meaning than to evade it.

Certainly this is the operative principle of much of his prose whose subject is rarely stated, whose characters reveal themselves in their actions, and whose broken language expresses what is seldom uttered. We step into an action already underway and leave with that action still incomplete, the spaces at either end exerting a pressure on what is presented. And since loss is one of his principal themes, by definition it speaks itself through its absence. Yet there were other absences in his early life which he has spent some time in filling, to do with religion, to do with love, to do with a sense of a secure past, his actual past having been in thrall to denial. His primary lesson as a child was to do with who he and his family were not, who it was better they should not declare themselves to be.

His essays, though, do not recall simply a bleak upbringing. Indeed a surprising number of them seem dedicated to recuperating another kind of past to do with street games; chocolate sodas; playing Kick the Can on summer evenings; watching a horse-drawn truck with a rag picker calling, "Rags, Old Iron"; seeing an organ grinder and his monkey; lining up in the school yard, boys on one side, girls on the other; being a patrol boy on the school crossing; watching fifty cartoons on a Saturday for a quarter; listening to *The Midnight Special* on WFMT, or *Suspense* on CBS when radio itself was already a part of the past, nostalgia within nostalgia.

He remembered going on family holidays in Wisconsin, Tucson, and Miami Beach, flying there on a four-engine TWA Constellation that thrilled. It is tempting to hear a Whitmanesque pleasure in the sheer itemizing of experience, in the summoning into existence of a country by celebrating events, each with the same claim on his attention. But there is something, too, in his burnishing of the past which speaks of a desire to claim retrospective contentment, to reassemble pain and betrayal into something more acceptable, a pre-history to current satisfactions.

These may not be the false memories seeded into the brains of the imperfectly perfect biological machines in *Blade Runner*, but they are, perhaps, an alternative history to that which otherwise haunts him with the thought of a bleak and distressing childhood in which he had not been able to summon up the resistance he might have wished. To be a victim was to be relieved of guilt. To re-invent the past is to give it a retrospective grace, present need and memory dancing a subtle gavotte.

And if this seems remote from the public image of a man seemingly concerned to stage deracinated characters, adrift in a world not of their making, barely able to articulate feelings or thoughts which seem to collapse of their insubstantiality, that is because the image is not entirely accurate. Many of his characters are aware of their insufficiencies, the weakness of their grasp on experience, choosing to fill the voids in their lives with fantasies, sounds without clear meaning. But the need is manifestly there in the stories they tell, the consolations for which they blindly reach or which they perversely refuse. Something has been lost: a sense of the past, of community, of connections broken by aspects of a world which offers to provide satisfactions for needs incommensurate with such distractions. As he has said, "America is in a sorry state. We're at a very difficult time. Our culture has fallen apart and is going to have to die off before something takes its place" (Kane, ed., *Mamet in Conversation*, p. 49). Perhaps that is in part what he is doing with his plays – clearing the deck.

His career as a playwright, after all, began in the "me decade" of the 1970s and continued in the 1980s in which greed was sanctified as a value. The old American pieties might be invoked but they were, he insisted, simply pieties, camouflage for self-interest at a time when there appeared political and cultural sanction for the abandonment of social responsibilities and transcendent values alike. The American past was invoked as though it were continuous with a callously self-regarding present, as though Enlightenment values which once underlay the rhetoric if not always the reality of the Republic's foundational documents could seriously be accommodated to a harshly pragmatic present.

This past did, though, once, it seems, have integrity, a code, a sense of moral order. Perhaps that is why, unlikely as it seems, he was later drawn to *The Winslow Boy*, set, of course, in England, but which turns on the need to sustain something more than the proprieties. "Let right be done," is written across a petition to the Crown (ironically the same phrase as that used by Henry J. Hyde in concluding his case against President Clinton), as if right were then knowable and, if knowable, to be embraced in the court case at the center of that work. In a society contaminated with its own prejudices and inequities there is still, it seems, a sense of right action, even if it is the self-announced code of a class dismissive of its social applicability beyond themselves.

In an American context it is there in the figure of the lawyer in *The Verdict*, of Eliot Ness in *The Untouchables*, the quiet shoemaker in *Things Change*, and Chief of Police John Price in Mamet's television script, *Bradford*. There is, or rather was, a still center, not described or defined but there, if only as a fading shadow, a tenuously surviving value, perhaps always threatened by irony. There is a powerful sense of nostalgia evident in Mamet's essays which recreate his childhood, adolescence, first jobs (waiting, cooking, selling, cab driving, dancing, working in the merchant marine), and early career. And from these jobs came a sturdy belief in the working man (also most real and affecting in the past), a faith which came in part also from turn-of-the-century Mid-Westerners like Theodore Dreiser and Frank Norris, registering the accumulating weight of a city dominated by the making of money, along with Willa Catha who both celebrated nostalgia and treated it with a degree of suspicion.

For all of them, though, something had been lost, some animating sense of freedom along with a national purpose which pressed beyond the merely material. In like manner, he derived some of his social and political views from another Chicagoan, Thorstein Veblen, equally suspicious of a new America which found its energy in the circularities of production and consumption and abandoned ideas of honest toil and the autonomous moral self.

Not that he is unaware of the fact that dreams of the past may be mechanisms of evasion. One of the books he most admires is by another Chicago author, Richard Wright. *Native Son* addresses not merely the issue of race but its connection with sexuality. Mamet is under no illusion that a past which saw segregation and a withering violence against black Americans is in some way evidence of a lost innocence. *Edmond*, indeed, was designed to address the curious residue of that past even in an America that has transformed itself. Its protagonist goes on a journey not only into his own psyche but into that of a culture still at odds with itself.

Edmond leaves a largely sexless marriage believing he can regenerate himself through a world of sensation, access to which, he believes, may be granted by those he assumes to hold the keys. He approaches a black pimp, whom he kills, his violence giving him a new sense of his own identity, as Bigger Thomas had believed himself similarly empowered in *Native Son*. The play concludes, as Mamet himself has explained, "in prison where he finds actual love with the African-American cell mate who began the relationship by raping him." It was, he confessed, a harsh play but "I thought it was accurate. I still do."[20]

Nonetheless, for all his awareness that the past contains evidence of the very betrayals, cruelties, human derelictions which he identifies in the present, Mamet still has a taste for a world already slipping away, for bespoke tailors, shoe-repair stores, bric-a-brac, the campaign buttons of long-ago elections or celebratory events: "I do not want to be at the desk. I want to be at a place and in a time alluded to by these mementoes . . . The buttons are not reminders, they are survivors, the archaeological artifacts of the dream kingdom where . . . I spend what I suppose must be called my working hours."[21] They speak of another civilization; they are "the dream material of 'another time.'"[22]

A button from the World's Fair of 1933, alluded to in *American Buffalo*, recalls a moment when technology was grace rather than threat, when the future seemed charged with possibility even as the Depression offered evidence of the opposite. It is, in part, the space between that moment and his which has the power to generate nostalgia and irony in equal proportions and which provides something of the energy of his drama. There is, he confesses, romance in these objects. It is a romance that comes from their intimation of a time when everything seemed more rooted, more individualized, when such objects implied a sense of order and purpose into which they integrated and of which they were an expression.

It is not that human nature has changed. After all, *The Water Engine*, with its thread of violence, is set in the 1930s, as were *The Postman Always Rings Twice* and *The Untouchables*. *The Old Religion* was set in the unreconstructed South of 1913. Yet there is a pleasure to be derived from a style, a form, a language which has the patina of another time.

In a utopian society such as America only the past and the future offer a true form, often, as Fitzgerald noted in the concluding paragraph of *The Great Gatsby*, fused together in a way which explains that blend of assumed innocence and lust for the new which is a characteristic of the culture. In between is a provisional world in decline, reaching for a perfection beyond immediate reach, existing between impure nostalgia and importunate hope. If Willy Loman feels "kind of temporary," so, surely, do Mamet's characters in a society with its eyes on the prize, sure that it can only exist in the future, only consist of a materiality raised to spiritual essence.

Nonetheless, he himself is drawn to old apartments and hotels, the shadow of a lost world when the *Carpathia* nestled into a pier along the Hudson and the Mercury Theater broadcast on the radio. He celebrates the Golden Age of Television when programmes were "honestly done" before the "whorehouse mentality" had prevailed and "the pimps and hucksters" took over.[23] He confesses to being overfond of the few difficulties he encountered on what he ironically calls his "travels toward substantiality," almost as if he were still trying to account for the success which has come his way, noting the stepping stones across which he passed to the present. In some sense these seemed more real than that present which, according to a central national myth, is no more than a pre-condition for the future.

His love of Vermont lies in part in the fact that it is home to "accomplished blacksmiths, woodworkers, potters, weavers . . . an artisanal reversal, or *repeal* of the Renaissance – a dissatisfaction with the urban and industrial, and a true return to the land."[24] There is a Jeffersonian sound to this. The very remoteness of this land from the centers of power is a guarantee of its authenticity, as if here nature reassumed its supremacy breeding a sense of respect not only for the products of nature but for those who seek less to impose themselves than to adjust to diurnal rhythms.

He discovered Vermont when he went to college, and the small village of Cabot in 1965 when he taught French at the Cabot School. Vermont offered both the solitariness required for writing and a sense of real community encouraged by shared necessities away from the casual conveniences of urban life. Where the city disposed of the past, impatient for the new as if it were an undiscovered secret, here was a place that held the past close in the knowledge that it lived on the pulse.

Yet in truth the contrast is not between an urban and a rural world. It is a matter of the spirit, a sense of what is valued and what rejected. Mamet, who rushes from project to project, has respect for a certain stillness, a quality he admires in the great comedians – Chaplin, Keaton – but also in those who take time to consider. The craftsman has a different sense of time, as does the hunter. The quality of an object or an experience requires respect for its demands. The rush of language in his plays, as characters spill out words with a seemingly random but often calculated speed, is an evasion of a silence which they fear for the knowledge it might bring, a knowledge of vulnerability, of needs they forbear to confront.

Life in rural Vermont, in which time is slowed by seasons and topography alike, encourages attention to detail, the disregarded, and thereby the discovery that truth may reside precisely in the particular, in what is lost in the smear of the general. Mamet cutting goose quills into pens and fashioning wooden toys for his children has, as he confesses, an element of the consciously artisanal but it is also a reminder of individual skills, a refusal of that passive consumerism which makes the individual an extension of industrialism, subordinate to the taste of others, disabled by the sheer ease of mass production.

There is no virtue in drawing water from a hand-dug well rather than paying one's dues to the water company but it is a reminder that there is a connection between individual need and the human capacity to meet such a need out of a mind and body in harmony. The rural life breeds a certain honesty of action and purpose not least because these are not a people moving on and this is not a place in which falsity can flourish for long, much less be admired as evidence of sanctioned cunning.

Language, too, cuts a straighter furrow where deceit is not admired and irony is left to nature: "In the cities words are used to charm, to seduce, to misdirect. Here we are expected to say what we mean" (*South of the Northeast Kingdom*, p. 72).

He takes pride in having built dry stone walls, not least because, like his plays, their strengths and weaknesses must, inevitably, reveal themselves, because they are invested with himself. Whether they last or not depends on the integrity with which they are constructed, on their fusing of form with function.

For Mamet, nothing is lost. It works its way either into his plays or his essays, as if the processing of experience was itself a way of preserving it, of denying its ephemerality. He revisits in his own mind the theatre of his youth, with its long-gone productions which flared and faded. He recalls Delsomma's Restaurant on 47th Street in New York, a restaurant just across the street from where *American Buffalo* had opened, a restaurant now closed, only to be replaced by another which itself opened and closed with the rhythm of New York's blinking eye. Gone are the pool halls, the coffee shops, the green-backed Penguin books, the libraries, and with them something intangible but germane to his work and his life in that they were implicated in the making of the man and the writer.

In one essay he recalls a local store owner offering a dollar prize for anyone who can explain the function of an object he places on display. There is a sense in which he revisits his own past in the same spirit, to see what utility it turned out to have, what was encoded in experiences which once seemed no more than mere events piled arbitrarily on one another. His essays have a way of being built from accumulating reminiscences, anecdotes, stories within stories, strung together looking for a point, except that the point lies precisely in the slow accretion of such details. It lies in tales which stand as their own justification in a world retrieved to be measured against a diminished present in an attempt to identify the significance of what seems to have disappeared.

Sometimes that nostalgia is sharpened with a sense of loneliness, of someone watching the party from afar; sometimes it is warmed as he celebrates the group that meets in the back of a store around a wood-burning stove, or in a poker game, or readying themselves for hunting or fishing in a countryside that will demand skills handed down through the years, prompting a respect that can only be earned by attention to detail and an acceptance of nature's authority. What he loves about Vermont is its "commonality" (15), just as he thrills to the "communion of tracking an animal" (xv). He is looking for connection, he whose works are about precisely the absence of such, if also, on another level, its felt need.

Mamet has a love not of jargon as such (though it has its dramatic function) but of the precise word to describe an object or an action, as if this in itself offered an induction into a community going back through time, as if it pinned down the real with some absolute if arbitrary assurance, as Vermont houses are held together by a trunnel, a tree nail or peg of wood (21). That love of arcane vocabulary is a distinguishing feature of his work, from *Glengarry Glen Ross* to *The Village*. Even his home in Vermont, and his hunting cabin and the shared conversation of those who sit in the snow to watch the wary approach of a deer, are gestures of continuity and rootedness on the part of a man whose upbringing was in part to do with the denial of roots in that anonymous suburb where violence was not part of a ritual but a glimpse of pure chaos.

He may have come to suspect his motives, as though in laying claim to one tradition he were betraying another, but his respect for the past clearly goes beyond this. There is an integrity to fact and action, as there is to the precise vocabulary that it generates, which seems to deliver the world more securely into his hands. Hemingway knew as much and made it the basis of his aesthetic. The best teaching is by example. Mamet himself has sought out those who would teach him how to fire a gun, throw a pot, a whole panoply of rural crafts, the rural to him always implying a natural connection between past and present as well as an integrity born out of shared experience: "Is the geometric increase in rascality between the village and the empire," he asks himself, "simply a matter of the square of the distance from the afflicted to the official?" (100).

Reclaiming his Jewishness never involved him in laying aside his national identity, indeed he resents those who propose a tension. So he describes his home town Fourth of July parade, albeit one with a touch of irony about it. That irony, like the humor which characterizes so much of his work, derives from his position both inside and outside the world he describes. This is a world which equally includes town meetings (in which people vote in public, putting their name to their convictions) and blunt negotiations with Hollywood producers. In that home town, people do business, he explains, by giving their word. The need for trust is strong. It is precisely what happens when it is abrogated that becomes the subject of much of his work.

His love of field sports, still more his love of deadly weapons, can seem disturbing, as if John Milius and Charlton Heston had been fused together to form a playwright. He is a member of the NRA, which would seem to put him beyond the liberal pale. But this appears to have less to do with Second Amendment rights, the musket by the fireplace to defend America against the British or itself, than with the pleasure he derives from craft and skill, from laying claim to an American tradition that gives authority to the past.

Doing something well has gone out of fashion. He celebrates its satisfactions. He is an admirer of those with craft skills in part because, as he quotes Sherwood Anderson as saying, "a man who has a trade is a man who can tell the rest of the world to go to hell" (Kane, ed., *Mamet in Conversation*, p. 52). Such a man is not a commodity. In this he seems close to Arthur Miller who builds his own furniture from native woods, and services a Land Rover first purchased forty years before. The making of art and the making and care of functional objects derives from the same source. The mechanic commands respect for his integrity but he is also related to a sense of an integral world.

Mamet favors weapons with a history or made by an individual in the back room of a Vermont house. In a disposable culture, which at times objectifies people, discarding them as the petty criminals have been flung off to the periphery in *American Buffalo* and the salesmen are threatened with dismissal in *Glengarry Glen Ross*, he values both continuity and uniqueness.

He celebrates the past through its style of living, its attitude to time, through the individualized products of craftsmen, whether they are fashioning clothes, wood, or metal. He admires the nineteenth-century roll-top desk, finds himself in antique shops and at yard sales. He is, he has confessed, "by nature and profession, a browser." And every object contains a history and deserves the respect of precise identification. A knife is a Sloyd knife. A shotgun is a Parker, circa 1915. A revolver is a .22 Ruger "SingleSix." It is, he has said, "invariably the overlooked, the seemingly innocuous, the dismissed 'connective' term, which is the clue to the mystery."[26] This is simultaneously a comment on history, on relationships, and on the aesthetic of his plays and films, from *American Buffalo* and *Glengarry, Glen Ross* to *House of Games* and *Heist*. What is invisible, omitted, concealed, gains particular power, as does the gap between what things appear to be and what they perhaps are.

In one sense that is an entirely familiar truth. *House of Games*, as he has pointed out, is in one regard a classic *film noir*, and *The Spanish Prisoner* a romantic thriller of a kind perfected by Hitchcock. Reality is a construct in *The Spanish Prisoner* just as it is in *Vertigo*. Thus, even his films are in some respects themselves acts of homage and therefore to a degree nostalgic gestures, though he was not, he insists, responsible for the reference to Eisenstein in *The Untouchables*. *The Winslow Boy*, like his play *a Boston Marriage*, recapitulates aspects of the past for which he has respect, whether it be the sense of honor, the pursuit of truth at all costs of *The Winslow Boy*, or the relentless wit of his pastiche turn-of-the-century comedy, *a Boston Marriage*, a play written, he has said, as an act of homage to Vita Sackville-West.

He is a collector, then, of memorabilia, of guns and knives, each identified by its maker and given meaning by the man who holds it. He resists aspects of the modern, from stainless steel through to television and computers, not because they are corrupting but because they homogenize, fail to please the eye or the soul. When he buys a house he wants it furnished with arts and crafts objects and furnishings. What he seems to admire is that these objects were once organically related to everyday life. They combined form and function, like a work of art.

He even set up his own clothing company – The Joseph Morse Company, Cabot, Vermont – to sell outdoor clothes as they used to be when they appeared in the catalogues of another age. He put his own money into it. It failed. This was a serious investment in nostalgia and a warning as to its limits. Even its failure, though, seemed right in its way. The past, after all, can be respected but not repeated. You can never really go home again.

This was not a mere style statement, however. It was born out of a sense of the integrity of the old designs, materials, craft skills, and hence out of a sense of integrity as a principle of living. Enron, he noted, used to distribute to its employees – those it would defraud along with everyone else – polished stones emblazoned with such words as "Integrity," "Trust," "Loyalty." Assuming this not to be an inside joke by insider traders, it was stealing language along with everything else and then offering it back as a reward and keepsake secure in the knowledge that it had done its bit to degrade civility and belief itself.

When he speaks of whisky it is of single malts, each with a unique history, not a blend, and he speaks of them in the context of an almost secret meeting of connoisseurs come together to celebrate not only the whisky but its sharing. He has a liking for such groups, with their sense of intimacy and agreed values, shadows of that lost family life, itself never fully retrieved. For the same reason, he has a fondness for the secret codes and signals, the private language of coteries, because they are signs of membership, of a fraternity of shared beliefs and ways of being. Even confidence tricksters trust one another's signs, exemplifying the very needs of which they take such consummate advantage.

Now all this would seem to take us a long way from the urban brittleness and alienation of *Sexual Perversity in Chicago*, *American Buffalo*, and *Edmond*; the real estate salesmen in *Glengarry Glen Ross*; the fast-talking, non-teleological Hollywood executives of *Speed-the-Plow*; the Escher-like logic of *The Spanish Prisoner* and *Heist*. But in part that is the point. Something has been evacuated from the world. His characters are people who have lost the plot in the sense of being distracted from real as opposed to proximate meanings. "What is missing," Mamet has said of the contemporary world, "is the feeling of knowing our place and a sense of belonging. It's the theatre's job to address the question of 'What is our place in the universe' and 'How can we live in a world in which we know we are going to die," (Kane, ed., *Mamet in Conversation*, p. 54).

In *The Old Neighborhood*, Bobby Gould has lived a life without interrogating it as to its meaning while Joey, the other half of this sad vaudeville of a misremembered self, tries to connect himself to his Jewishness by retrospectively inserting himself into a history he barely understands. What emerges is a sense of loss, of paths not taken, truths not embraced, a life not lived. The third part of the triptych which is *The Old Neighborhood* features a woman damaged by lack of love who has built her life on resentment and a kind of uninspected courage, getting by without ever quite reconciling herself to the cost of this necessary re-invention.

It is in that sense that he suggests that the purpose of the theatre is "not primarily to deal with social issues" but "spiritual issues." The function of drama, he insists, quoting Stanislavsky, "is to bring to the stage the life of the human soul so that the community can participate there" (Kane, ed., *Mamet in Conversation*, p. 63). And that is a reminder that by its nature the theatre depends for its existence on the survival of a sense of community that was not merely slipping away but, from the 1970s onwards, at least, increasingly dismissed as a source of values. In what Mamet has called his "gang tragedies," *American Buffalo* and *Glengarry Glen Ross*, venality, self-concern, the values of the market place, all but destroy a sense of connection beyond the pragmatics of survival. But there is a yearning for something else, a vague sense of what is being betrayed.

As he observes, "The air and the water and the cities grow worse every day, and the electronic answer, the anodyne, is not their amelioration but a narcotizing of the mind and will."[27] His parents may have compromised with their values in order to succeed but they "worked hard." The 1960s came close to taking a free ride, living out "a hallucination of entitlement and license."[28] Then came the '70s, and a retreat from the commitments which had been the counterforce to licence, which in turn devolved into the Reagan years in which self-interest was elevated as a value, not least by means of attaching it to American myths which the President himself occasionally seemed to find it difficult to distinguish from reality.

It is such an analysis that prompts his respect for the past, his love of those novels "about the prairies that never end, about an emptiness in the stomach, about a certain feeling, almost a love, of pain,"[29] a pain deriving from an awareness of what Willa Cather would call not so much a country as the material out of which a country might be made. And if a book can draw him back so can the smell of cigarettes, cigarettes as they used to be, a Proustian prompt not by way of a madeleine but tobacco roasted in the American way. And the truth is that like Sam Shepard he is simultaneously drawn to American myths and aware of their potential corruptions.

The past, then, has an irresistible pull. It is a place of good and bad memories but it has a feel of the organic, a sense of a society yet to be eroded by bad faith, bad conscience, a failure to distinguish the real from the simulated. For him there is no global village, pulled together by shared electronic images. That is an artificial community, like the coercive propinquity of performance theatre. A village, by contrast, is a real place. And if his novel *The Village* indicates his awareness that moral anarchy can infect both past and present, nonetheless things were in place which are no longer there.

There is another distinguishing mark to that past. It has a masculine feel to it, consisting as it often seems to of "The Lodge, Hunting, Fishing, Sports in general, Poker, Boys Night Out." Yet, he insists, "It's All Right." It is an environment "where one is understood, where one is not judged, where one is not expected to perform,"[30] in short where one is loved or in search of grace. In other words, those enrolled are engaging in communal experiences and thereby constituting the sense of community whose loss he otherwise laments. And it is a seemingly uncomplicated world free of the interference pattern caused by gender difference, or the anxieties provoked by social striving.

He is hardly unaware, of course, that it is also a retreat and, at a time in which male–female relations seem hedged around with doubt and confusion, an evasion. What is especially missing in male–female relationships is trust but then trust has been one of Mamet's central concerns, a moral and social issue, occasionally a political one, but also the basis of his dramatic strategy. Whenever anyone literally or metaphorically says "Trust me" in his work they are almost certainly practicing deceit, as the writer himself takes pleasure in deception, thus involving himself in the processes he stages. Trust, spectacularly broken and betrayed in most of his works, is a matter of power in whose name deceptions are elaborated. There are shadows of Herman Melville's Confidence Man and Ralph Ellison's Rinehart in Mamet's characters whose Protean skills are at once contaminating and compelling. He has, he has explained, "always been interested in the continuum that starts with charm and ends with psychopathy. Con artists deal in human nature, and what they do is in the realm of suggestion. It is like hypnosis or, to a certain extent, playwriting" (Kane, ed., *Mamet in Conversation*, p. 127).

That last remark offers a clue to his ambivalent attitude to deceptions which may forge a link between social behaviour – which itself is invested with performance and criminality – and the artistic enterprise. The "con game," after all, "is what people do, most of the time, with few exceptions" (127–8). What he is dramatizing, then, is not aberrant individuals but those who consciously refine normal human behavior to achieve specific ends. What he is staging is at one level the lives of all.

And since story telling is the elaboration of seductive lies, we are so many moths thrilled at the thought of the flame that may sear and even engulf. Why else do children insist on tales whose horrors flood their dreams while in the process they are prepared for the pleasures and pains of deception which are their human inheritance?

There can be a price to be paid, however, in that the morphing skills of some of his characters leave them without a still center. When men die, as they do in *House of Games* and *Heist*, the blood seems artificial. The action scarcely skips a beat. There is no mourning because there is no one for whom to mourn. When the protagonist in the latter film sends his wife to seduce someone he wishes to deceive, it is not a moral decision but a move in a chess game to be judged purely by its effect. Even moral affront is a pose, an act to ensnare the unworthy. The audience, meanwhile, have been seduced into admiring the trickery, thereby willing their own deception not least because those are the terms of the contract between writer and reader, film maker and audience. The characters are merely the agents of the magic by which we wish to be enthralled.

When Bobby is beaten in *American Buffalo*, however, the betrayal has a human face, as it does when Levine's life spirals down in *Glengarry Glen Ross*, though the scene written into the film version, and played by Alec Baldwin, compellingly brilliant though it is, introduces a figure as immune to pain as those Mamet would create in the films he would write and direct. Like Bernard Shaw or Oscar Wilde, Mamet can be seduced by the sheer pleasure of his own inventiveness, and *Boston Marriage* is evidence that he can meet such writers as equals on this ground. But he is most disturbing when, as in his early plays, and in *The Cryptogram*, the pain shines through and the game-playing has a human consequence.

In the latter he tries to break the cipher of a family which should offer comfort and consolation but instead is the site of betrayal. Need is evident but not the capacity to address it. The past is inauthentic, the present uncertain, the future the source of apprehension. Desertion is merely a natural extension of the estrangement which characterizes relationships. It is a play in which speeches rarely extend beyond a single sentence because there are secrets and privacies to be protected out of a mixture of fear and guilt. The characters tell stories not out of the pleasure of invention but because of a kind of terror at impending desolation, evidence of that very isolation which they dread.

One curiosity of *The Old Religion* is that the man who dies at the hands of a lynch mob himself seems so curiously detached from his own life that his death appears no more than an extension of a habit of self-abnegation. In his case, however, he is not a conscious fantasist. He has simply turned himself into a construction, denying himself in search of an identity he can embrace. The process of redemption may be underway but he has not yet found his way back to the self he had so readily sacrificed and hence dies more as a symbol than a man, a symbol not to Mamet but to a society which preserves news of his death because he dies as what he had liked to believe in some fundamental way he was not: a Jew.

Gore Vidal makes a distinction between his historical novels and what he calls his "entertainments." There is, perhaps, a similar distinction in Mamet's films between those which are avowedly the latter (*Wag the Dog*, *State and Main*, *The Spanish Prisoner*, *Heist*) and those which pursue anxieties which surface in his plays. To be sure, it is possible to see *The Spanish Prisoner* raising questions about the status and nature of the real. Indeed, one character obligingly remarks, "We don't know what's real," but the primary pleasure lies in the unravelling of a mystery to which there is a solution, though in contrast to *North By Northwest* the protagonist never becomes the agent of his own salvation. The truth is revealed rather than unravelled.

Nonetheless, there is clearly a continuity between this film and many of Mamet's plays. As Susan remarks, in *The Spanish Prisoner*, we "never know who anybody is."[31] These are a series of performed selves. Who, after all, is the protagonist of the film when returned to himself at the end of the film, stripped of illusions? Since we never see him outside the context of the illusions which he takes to be an adequate account of the real, he effectively only exists through the deceptions practiced upon him.

Susan claims to be "Loyal and True," when she is neither or, if so, to something or someone other than the man she conspires to destroy. "I promise you won't regret it" (*The Spanish Prisoner*, p. 38), she says, seemingly offering him an authentic relationship while having no intention of fulfilling her promise and determined that he will regret it. "You can't go through life mistrusting everybody" (25), says the person deceiving him. In the world of *The Spanish Prisoner*, *Heist*, *The Shawl*, *House of Games*, you would do well to mistrust. The protagonist carries a boy scout knife engraved with the motto, "Be Prepared," while failing precisely to take such advice to heart.

There is no space in his films for the random. Every word, every image is freighted with significance, even if that significance is grasped only in retrospect. The background is also the foreground. There is no air not processed through the machine of the plot. And that is something they have in common with his plays – the sense of being trapped within a system of meaning or unmeaning. His characters sense some coherence, promising or threatening, that they can never fully bring into focus. There are rules beyond the contingent demands of social or business etiquette but they are, for the most part, not sure what they might be. The protagonist of *Homicide* works within the parameters of police procedure, only to discover that there are other rules, hidden, disturbing in their demands not least because they by-pass rationality.

There are aspects of these "entertainments," however, that threaten the apparently untroubled waters of their own landscape. What matters in *The Winslow Boy* is not simply that justice is done, in a case so insignificant that its moral implications alone elevate it to a debate over principle, but that the lives of everyone are shaken. The false assurance of a smug society is disturbed, but so, too, are the casual assumptions which had seemingly smoothed the way of the characters towards a future voided of human significance.

The suffragettes are on the move, but only to shore up the factitious democracy of a country ruled less by the public will than by tradition, that is to say a culture in which class is assumed to provide the structural framework for action. The victory at the end is not for the little man, nor yet for justice over law. It is, ironically, for fair play, itself the ruling principle of a country in which the playing fields of Eton were a training ground for Empire.

A young man is indicted. He neither lied nor stole. Very well, he was what he had appeared all along, a decent member of a class whose prerogatives had always seemed the product and the guarantee of probity. Is the story, then, complete or has assurance been sufficiently shaken to leave the system no longer quite secure? This, after all, is the Edwardian period. The First World War is a breath away, a war which would expose the incompetence no less than the moral myopia of those who congratulated themselves on securing justice for a young man who would doubtless follow a generation into the trenches to serve the fantasies of two empires blind to their inanities.

Mamet came to writing via acting. A nephew of the chairman of the Chicago Board of Rabbis, he would appear, on Sunday mornings, in instructional dramas on radio and television as a child actor and was involved in Hull-House – a Chicago theatre originally born out of the social work commitment of its founders and revived in 1963 – in the 1960s. At high school he performed in a musical and studied drama. When he went to university in 1965, at Goddard College in Plainfield, Vermont, he spent most of his time in the theatre department, submitting a play (*Camel*) instead of a thesis. In New York, during a year away from Goddard in 1967–8, he worked backstage at *The Fantasticks* and studied drama at the Stanislavsky-influenced Neigborhood Playhouse School.

He was subsequently employed as a teacher of acting at Marlboro College (1969–70), writing plays at first to provide convenient texts with which his students could work, including *Lakeboat*. He then spent two years at Goddard as Artist in Residence where he wrote *Duck Variations* and co-founded the St. Nicholas Theater Company (later re-formed in Chicago as the St. Nicholas Players) that was to produce his early plays. William H. Macy, who has appeared in so many of his works, was one of his students.

His fascination with acting has never dissipated, although it has never transmuted into actual accomplishment (indeed he has confessed to being deeply unimpressive as an actor). Not merely has he continued to teach, from time to time, and written essays on his own theories of acting, but performance has become a central trope of his work.

His characters not only perform themselves but deploy performance as both strategy and tactic. Dan Shapiro in *Sexual Perversity in Chicago* plays the role of a world-wise, sexually compelling, cock-of-the-walk to hide his total failure to connect. The criminals in *We're No Angels* masquerade as priests in order to escape. The protagonist of *Heist* is effectively an actor performing a series of dramas the better to deceive but also because he seems to exist in and through performance, as do the characters in *House of Games*. There are few Mamet plays or films in which the characters do not present their lives as performances, offer stories, stage dramas in which to ensnare their audience.

He is hardly unaware, of course, that the writer is also an actor, a confidence trickster who deploys his power to capture the attention and acquiescence of those who watch. The 'cold calling' of *Glengarry Glen Ross* has its parallel in the 'cold reading' of *The Shawl*, but also, perhaps, the cold presentation of a play to an audience who do not know what it is they are buying. Drama, he has insisted, "is basically about lies, somebody lying to somebody" (Kane, ed., *Mamet in Conversation*, p. 63). For the most part, though, his fascination was and is with story, with the mind's power to create, to console, to entice, to deceive. His plays and films are full of story tellers whose lives are an extension of the stories they tell.

Mamet's story tellers are often in the service of nothing more elevated than their own enrichment, or they spin their fables to protect themselves from the consequences of their actions. But in a perverse way those skills contain the possibility of redemption in that they require precisely that instinctive understanding of the other, that ability imaginatively to leap the spaces between themselves and their apparent victims, that had seemed all but impossible. His confidence tricksters exploit the need to trust and believe, the desire for companionship, but in doing so they affirm the existence of such feelings in a world otherwise seemingly so bereft of humanizing qualities. It is not merely the communality of theatre that makes it a paradigm; it is the fact that it is a house of stories, a house of games.

What fascinates, with respect both to characters and to drama itself, is the nature of those lies, their plausibility, their power simultaneously to conceal and reveal. Stories, as comfort (*Dark Pony, The Shawl*), distraction (*The Duck Variations*), self-deceit (*Sexual Perversity in Chicago, American Buffalo*), coercive lies (*The Old Religion*), business tactic (*Glengarry Glen Ross*), confidence trick (*House of Games, The Spanish Prisoner, Heist*), are fundamental. As with Sheherazade (or, indeed, *Things Change*) they are to do with survival. Acting, therefore, fascinates Mamet as both craft and subject and not incidentally as the site of moral concern. He is aware of its potential for corruption, exploitation, careerism (*A Life in the Theatre*), but equally of its power to confront and to challenge.

He was formed as a writer in a decade, the 1960s, in which performance was seized on as a principal metaphor by sociologists and psychologists. The presentational self became a central concept. This is not to say that Mamet had any interest in, or respect for, "performance theatre," which he regarded with something approaching contempt: "I have always thought that mixed media and performance art was basically garbage, very decadent . . . the sign really of a cultural disease." It seemed to him a "search for novelty," with "no capacity to move." Though he had read Artaud, "finally it does not work" (Kane, ed., *Mamet in Conversation*, p. 61). Though he could admire the operatic qualities of Robert Wilson, it seemed to him that this was a form of theatre which invited the audience to fill egregious gaps, which urged an intellectualized, aestheticized response and which evaded fundamental responsibilities. For him, the rituals of American theatre had their roots in specifically American cultural needs and rhythms. How many of the performance works of the 1960s, he asks, have survived, exhausting themselves in the act of presentation as though surviving the moment were a form of betrayal?

In a sense, of course, this is a willful misunderstanding of phenomena that were precisely intended to serve and celebrate the moment. This, after all, was a decade in which presence was apotheosized, whether in marches for various causes, which often themselves incorporated theatre groups, or at the party which was presumed to be the newly liberated life. But his suspicion, amounting to contempt, derives from the formal weaknesses of much performance theatre and art, its easy effects, its "fascistic wish fulfilment," its invitation to abstract criticism, to an intellectualized analysis (62).

His own points of reference tend to be Aristotle, tragedy, Stanislavski (though he was equally capable of dismissing his work as "just gibberish"), Hemingway (another Chicago writer), Beckett, Pinter. His preference is, if not for the austere, then for a spare aesthetic. He works by elimination. Where Artaud had seen theatre as a three-ring circus, a genre which dealt in and celebrated excess, Mamet is concerned to pare down. Character is action; language exists to forward the plot. Nothing must be extraneous. He is apt to quote Hemingway's advice to the writer, to cut those passages of which he is most proud, the implication being that the reason they stand out is that they serve neither plot nor character but a self-regarding aesthetic egotism. "I like it, it stays in," becomes, "I like it, it goes out."

In plays and films alike, he is loath to provide characters with a back story, challenges people to break the code of conversations already underway.

When *Glengarry Glen Ross* was staged by the National Theatre in England there was a discussion as to whether the program should produce a glossary of the seemingly technical terms used by the salesmen – leads, cold calling, etc. He was understandably resistant. Such information was extraneous. Its lack was in part what compelled attention.

Mamet, like Arthur Miller, is a compulsive worker and in part, perhaps, for the same reason. Both had seen their parents financially ruined. The specter of failure was real and never fully purged by success, so seemingly easily could it be taken away. Yet he has now achieved success as a playwright, screenwriter, director, essayist, and novelist. Doubts about his own role and identity have also now apparently been put to rest, not least because he has used his art as a means to understand and come to terms with his own life no less than with the tensions which disturb his society.

Arthur Miller, an atheist, has nonetheless spoken of his sense of envy of those who can lay claim to membership of a tribe, while acknowledging the danger of exclusivity, of drawing a circle around one's own people which must leave others outside. David Mamet, not an atheist, has rediscovered a sense of what was lost and now tends to invoke the name of his rabbi – Larry Kushner – and identify his synagogue – Temple Beth El in Sudbury, Massachusetts – as a clear statement of his loyalties. But what does this have to do with the work of either man? The answer would seem to be everything and nothing.

Mamet has attacked Miller for failing to identify the characters of *Death of a Salesman* as being Jewish, an old *canard* going back to Trotskyite assimilationist Jewish intellectuals of the 1940s and the equally Trotskyite Mary McCarthy whose brother Kevin appeared in a Boston production where, with an all Irish cast, the play was assumed to be about Irish Americans. The remark is less interesting for what it says about Miller – who, after all, wrote one of the first novels about anti-Semitism in America (*Focus*) as well as a large number of plays and stories with Jewish characters (*They Too Arise, Boro Hall Nocturne, Incident at Vichy, The Price, Broken Glass*), one of which, "Monte Sant' Angelo," was precisely concerned with the rediscovery of Jewish roots – than for what it says about Mamet's felt need to make it. Indeed his complaint, as phrased, is oddly beside the point. Willy Loman, he explains, is a Jew "in a Jewish industry." It is sufficient answer, perhaps, simply to ask which industry, since none is mentioned in the play. Mamet, it seems, is providing a back story merely in order to establish the grounds for his complaint.

His own plays, after all, include those with and those without Jewish characters, the latter nonetheless sometimes containing characters whose names seem to imply a Jewishness not addressed in the text. The fact is that, for both writers, where Jewishness is the central concern the characters are so identified, and when it is not, they are not. Once, Mamet would not have identified himself as a Jewish writer. Now he is inclined to do so and, indeed, acknowledges a shift in his commitments that is registered in his private life and his work alike, though Jewish characters appear at the beginning of his career in *Duck Variations*.

Now, and it might seem despite *Oleanna*, he is to be found asking for a revision to familiar school songs so as to remove specifically Christian references which might be offensive to Jews and other religious minorities. He is now inclined to patrol the boundaries of a newly rediscovered faith as if it were a country menaced by its neighbors or, still more, by those masquerading as true citizens.

What, then, to David Mamet, is the theatre for? It is precisely to address that need for community, for trust, that perceived sense of entropy which lies at the heart of his plays. As he has explained, in perhaps his clearest statement on the subject:

> In a morally bankrupt time we can help to change the habit of coercive and frightened action and substitute for it the habit of trust, of self-reliance, and co-operation. If we are true to our ideals we can help form an ideal society – not by *preaching* about it, but by *creating* it each night in front of the audience – by showing how it works. In action.[32]

This is the bridge between his social, spiritual, and aesthetic commitments. The theatre itself is the evidence for surviving values, for that communality otherwise under severe pressure, that sense of trust betrayed which seems the common currency of the private and political world, of individual and social commerce. In a world that has substituted sensation for knowing, both in personal and civic life as well as in much of the art which offers itself as an account of that life (and theatre has been as culpable as cinema), "theatre must strive to recognize and to ratify the universality of our desire and our fears as human beings."[33]

Mamet is drawn to ceremonies. They are an expression of continuity, a refusal of the American denial of the past, the sense that identity is a product of the moment as if this in itself were an embodiment of promises of social and existential re-invention. The Jewish ceremonies about which he has written have their own resonances, reaching back beyond the denials of his parents, but other rites, some seemingly trivial, others going beyond an easily retrievable meaning, are crucial, too. When his father died, a father from whom he had been alienated for a while, he seized the spade from the gravedigger and filled the hole himself. He was not burying the past but asserting and feeling a connection to it, performing one last service to his father and thereby consolidating a link threatened by memories of absence, breaks in the human chain. The void of the grave, the blank page, invite peopling.

The theatre, too, is a ceremony with its own attendant rituals and it seems likely that it performs a similar function. A present-tense art, it nonetheless has the power to bring past and present together as though there were a persuasive continuity. It forges connections at a time when such seem broken by seemingly disjunctive experiences, by languages which pull away from human meanings.

Mamet hardly writes Greek dramas but his sense of the tragic (and I suspect he is the first playwright since Miller to speak unembarrassedly about tragedy in relation to his work) connects him to a form which once engaged the whole community as it confronted its anxieties and celebrated its shared survival on the edge of extinction. Sometimes in interview he can seem relentlessly ironic, as though protecting something more than the privacies he has a right to guard. He is calculatedly frivolous so as not to be caught being too serious, though the humor in his work is precisely fused with such seriousness. It is as though he were engaging in a game whose first and most important rule is to disclose nothing for fear of reductiveness. At times his many different roles themselves almost seem like strategies of evasion. Yes, he is a playwright, but he is equally a director, a screenwriter, an essayist, a novelist, a poet. There is something Protean about him as well as about his characters.

Of course, this is primarily the description of a man who likes to work, who constantly looks for new fields to conquer. He spills plays out at such a rate that he publishes some of them as though they were redundant, not meriting, or if meriting not likely to receive, the time and energy required of production. His novel *Wilson* is a joke elaborated at great length so that its pleasures derive precisely from redundancy. He is prolific in all fields while acknowledging that this can be mistaken for facility. Hence, too, the irony with which he protects himself from critical intrusion.

The word "rabbi" means "teacher." His nickname, like that of his character in *American Buffalo*, was Teach, having himself been such briefly. He would, I suspect, recoil in horror at the thought that there might be something didactic about his work. But, taken together, his plays and novels suggest a clear sense of what has been lost and what needs to be regained in American society and private life alike. And art is a primary agent in that act of recuperation.

The theatre, for Mamet, is in itself and its concerns a celebration of what binds together, as it is of the transient nature of experience. Theatre, in its essence, is not repeatable. Each occasion, like each life, is unique. That is part of what gives it value. That fact is in itself a value.

His early play *A Life in the Theatre* seemed to imply the near impossibility of different age groups communicating. *Sexual Perversity in Chicago* and *The Woods* suggest that the genders share little beyond desire and that even that takes different forms, generates different languages, metaphors, necessities. *House of Games*, *The Spanish Prisoner*, *Heist* imply that human relationships are calculated gestures, mere performances easily abandoned for others, as *The Shawl* registers vulnerability, hope, and trust seemingly only as stimuli to exploitation. Taken together they would seem to constitute a world of estrangement, deceit, and self-concern. Yet David Mamet's plays suggest something else as well.

He may offer diagnosis rather than prescription but the mere fact of doing so impacts upon prognosis. Trust betrayed is still trust confirmed. Story as entrapment is close to story as enchantment. A hand brushed aside is still a hand reaching out. Perhaps the primary accusation to be leveled against him is the last accusation that would come to mind: sentimentality. Yet in the end the emotion in his plays is earned. The reckless abandonment of responsibility by so many of his characters is an acknowledgment of a demand refused.

He is, of course, himself a confidence trickster, and not only in the matter of interviews in which his disingenuous tone leaves the interviewer uncertain as to what is true and what is false. As he once observed, anyone who can fool the canny moviegoer up to the last beat deserves a house in Bel Air. But beyond the sheer pleasure in subtle manipulation, he is about the business of deceiving, the better to enlighten. Even while staging a world seemingly bereft of values, he invites into the theatre an audience which must reconstitute those values in order to function at all. Form is reinvented, along with community. Communication is both method and objective. The genders, races, classes come together to share. Disbelief is willingly suspended and, whatever the financial motives of those involved, it is not suspended merely as part of a trade for material advantage.

Nietzsche insisted that, "we need lies *in order to live* . . . That lying is a necessity of life is itself a part of the terrifying and problematic nature of existence."[34] Eugene O'Neill, an admirer of Nietzsche, was liable to interpret that as a defense of what Ibsen calls "life lies" and he called "pipe dreams." It is what his characters so desperately cling to in *The Iceman Cometh*. For Mamet, though, it is something more than that. As George Steiner has pointed out, language itself deals in invention, ambiguities, ambivalences. It speaks of a yearning for something that does not offer itself up to the gaze. It is stained with needs which only imperfectly make their way into words. We thrill to it when it rises above the limited function of uninflected description. Why else do we respond to stories which take us beyond need into the territory of desire?

The child's need for bedtime stories (as in *Dark Pony*) is of a piece with the assurances we seek later in life, knowing them to be factitious but needing them nonetheless, welcoming our own deceit and taking a seemingly perverse pleasure from it. Does a person consulting a fortune teller expect anything so banal as the truth (*The Shawl*)? He or she pays to be told plausible and pleasurable lies. Those who once gathered around fires in the Great Hall of Viking warriors recounted tales which the hearers knew to be false even as they wondered at the rhythm of pleasurable deceit. There is a greater truth than mere facticity.

A story is an entertainment, a game, but it is also the perception that not all meaning renders itself up to the eye. Melville knew as much and wrote a book, *Moby Dick*, to remind us of it. Religion itself, with its master story and cluster of parables, offers the promise of transcendence, of going beyond what confronts us in its tactile opacity. And art and religion have always been coeval. Mamet's fascination with both is hardly surprising, whatever the particularities of the psychological and spiritual necessities which drive him and which are not even for him to know.

That the Devil practices to deceive, pouring honeyed words into the ear of Eve, shows that there is what Steiner, in another sense, calls the anti-matter of language. He uses the phrase to underline its counter-factual pull, its seductive alternity, though we might also think of it as language used in breech of the contract which seems implied in the act of communication. But the word "seduction" is not without its force for there is something in the performative pleasures of language which lead us away from simple description, and in our willing submission to that language, which addresses a need which is almost erotic. And there are moments, of course, when the erotic and the religious intersect. It is story tellers who know this most acutely.

Virtually all of Mamet's work can be described in these terms. It is full of inventors of alternative worlds. At the heart of his plays and films, at the most crucial moments, the action concerns two people, one of whom tells the other a story, or both of whom tell one another a story. There is a speaker and a listener. They meet, or do not, within the story. As Steiner observes, "In the creative function of language non-truth or less-than-truth is . . . a primary device. The relevant framework is not one of morality but of survival. At one level, from brute camouflage to poetic vision, the linguistic capacity to conceal, misinform, leave ambiguous, hypothesize, invent is indispensable to the equilibrium of human consciousness and to the development of mankind in society."35 Just so: this explains Mamet's withholding of moral judgment.

The fact is that we deal in such approximations, conscious distortions, playful inventions, willful deceits because they are evidently as necessary as dreaming, and Mamet has invoked the dream, for the individual and for the culture, in explaining the art forms in which he works.

We know, and Mamet has stressed, the significance of what is not said and what is not done. These represent a shadow reality, no less real for not making themselves immediately available, perhaps the more significant for that concealment, concealment even from the person who conceals them. This, too, after all, is language, perhaps the truer for not submitting itself to inspection. Steiner quotes Theodore Adorno: "The only true thoughts . . . are those which do not grasp their own meaning."36

It is in part the evasive nature of language, its power to dazzle and disorient, and, behind that, of thought, mysterious, able to evade even self-interrogation, which provides that Darwinian drive to continue. It is the gap between appearance and reality which provides the energy that fuels the journey. If everything were known, if everyone were what he or she appears, if words were no more than correlatives of an objectively verifiable world, we would be faced with stasis, the death of history, the end of a fructifying ambiguity – that is to say, Eden, the utopia from which we were summoned into consciousness and towards which we would be returned, curiously bereft.

It is within these tensions that Mamet creates his work, not out of any academic concern (the mockeries of *Wilson* are warning enough against this) but with a conviction that his characters live fictively. And if they do battle, the weapons they choose are, for the most part, words. Few of them willingly reveal their most fundamental needs, often because they do not know what they might be, but they are liable to expose them in the fictions they offer and the stories to which they respond. They look for intimacy and affect to find it in a shared language, the codes of their trade, the pre-owned words which they sometimes take for an adequate account of themselves. But in truth they discover the inadequacy of this. They do not inhabit Eden. They are the stories they tell and the words they speak, even, perhaps especially, when the words are untrue.

As to Mamet himself, he has become less guarded with time. *South of the Northeast Kingdom*, a book ostensibly concerned with celebrating Vermont, is something more than an act of homage to what, with a certain hesitation and humility, he claims as his home state. It is a statement of his beliefs, a confession of his values, an account of essential truths discovered from others and from human necessities transcending the artificial imperatives of career, status, ambition.

It is a book of some beauty and is touched with a certain unaffected modesty as he describes the process of learning which is coeval with living. It is a book which has the added advantage – not always included in the price – of seeming true. It is a reminder that the caustic analysis of human failings and social decay which he offers in his plays is rooted in an understanding of what is being betrayed, abandoned, devalued by those who have lost their grip on essentials. Like Arthur Miller before him, he is a moralist but not a moralizer.

David Mamet has purchased a burial plot. He can see it from his kitchen window. It was, he confessed, a gesture not unmarked by a certain presumption, as though his resting place would be an occasional place of pilgrimage for his family. Beyond that, though, it is surely something else. For the author of works in which his characters seem to lack a sense of home, a real connection with the world they inhabit, it is a gesture towards some ultimate inclusion. It is a gesture, perhaps, not without a certain ironic humor, with its implications of a final rootedness. Yet at the same time it is a statement of belonging by a man whose plays, novels, and essays acknowledge a desire to reclaim what he senses he is not alone in losing as one century ended and another began, a sense of who he is and how he relates to the essential mystery of being.

NOTES

1. Leslie Kane, ed., *David Mamet in Conversation* (Ann Arbor: University of Michigan Press, 2001), p. 13.
2. Interview with the author, March, 2003.
3. David Mamet, *South of the Northeast Kingdom* (Washington: National Geographic, 2002), p. 12.
4. *Ibid.*, p. 104.
5. David Mamet, "I Can't Stand Olivier," *Guardian*, April 18, 2003, p. 5.
6. David Mamet, *Some Freaks* (New York: Viking, 1989), p. 8.
7. David Mamet, *Make-Believe Town* (New York: Faber & Faber, 1996), p. 200.
8. David Jenkins, "England of His Drama," *Sunday Telegraph Magazine*, August 22, 1999, pp. 16, 18.
9. David Mamet, *The Chinaman: Poems* (New York: Overlook, 1999), p. 30.
10. *Some Freaks*, p. 17.
11. *Ibid.*, p. 179.
12. David Mamet, *Jafsie and John Henry* (London: Faber & Faber, 1999), p. 133.
13. *Ibid.*, p. xi.
14. *Some Freaks*, p. 23.
15. *Jafsie and John Henry*, p. 139.
16. David Mamet, *Writing in Restaurants* (New York: Viking, 1986), p. 140.

17. David Jenkins, "England of his Dreams," *Daily Telegraph Magazine*, August 22, 1999, p. 18.
18. David Mamet, *The Cabin* (New York: Viking, 1993), p. 11.
19. David Mamet, "Mind the Gaps," *Guardian*, July 22, 2002, p. 11.
20. David Mamet, "Misguided, Excessive and True," *Guardian*, July 17, 2003, pp. 16–17.
21. *The Cabin*, pp. 153–4.
22. *Ibid.*, p. 152.
23. David Mamet, *Five Television Plays* (New York: Grove Weidenfeld, 1990), p. vii.
24. *South of the Northeast Kingdom*, p. 46.
25. *Ibid.*, p. 70.
26. *Jafsie and John Henry*, p. 28.
27. *Ibid*, pp. 66–7.
28. *Ibid.*, p. 66.
29. *Some Freaks*, pp. 66–7.
30. *Ibid.*, p. 88.
31. David Mamet, *The Spanish Prisoner and The Winslow Boy* (New York: Vintage, 1999), p. 23.
32. David Mamet, *Writing in Restaurants*, p. 27.
33. *Ibid.*, p. 29.
34. George Steiner, *After Babel* (London: Oxford University Press, 1975), p. 227.
35. *Ibid.*, p. 229.
36. *Ibid.*

2

JOHAN CALLENS

The 1970s

When David Mamet began writing, the urgencies of the 1960s seemed to have been put to one side. The protest over Vietnam was abating. The radical experiments of Off and Off Off Broadway, which had seen the emergence of a new generation of young writers and the development of a number of theatre companies emphasizing the actor over the writer and improvisation over the text, seemed to have run their course. There appeared to be a move from the public to the private realm. Those who had made their reputations before the 1960s had largely fallen silent. The theatre itself, which had provided a ruling metaphor for a decade fascinated by the performing self, no longer seemed on the cutting edge of social, political, or aesthetic concerns, even if the opening of new theatres across America suggested a counter-current. It is true that the women's movement was having its effect and that women writers were beginning to be heard but there was no sense, as yet, that drama would play an important role in this.

The exception to what was beginning to seem like the marginalization of theatre, perhaps, was the growing recognition of Sam Shepard, who, in 1970, opened *Operation Sidewinder*, while out in the mid-west the importance of Chicago as a theatrical center was an increasingly badly kept secret.

This was the world, this the theatre, into which a new young writer emerged. Raised in Chicago, but educated, as far as university was concerned, in Vermont, he had watched the improvisational comedy at Chicago's Second City and was an admirer of Beckett and Pinter. Briefly a child actor, he confessedly spent most of his university years in and around the theatre department, before teaching theatre and trying his hand at writing scenes for his acting classes.

For all practical purposes, Mamet's professional career may be said to have begun with *Lakeboat*, an episodic play set aboard a merchant ship on the Great Lakes. Mamet had himself once worked as a sailor to raise money. Critical opinion of the play has been divided. Yet, the existence of several versions, spanning three decades, indicates his attachment to it. It is a play, too, which anticipates many of the concerns that would reappear in his work, dealing, as it does, with an all-male world in which language and power are intimately connected, a world in which story telling plays a central role for characters vaguely aware of the insufficiency of their lives.

Lakeboat was written in 1970, while Mamet was teaching at Marlboro College, Vermont, and premièred there the same year in a production by the Theatre Workshop. Almost a decade later it was rewritten with the help of John Dillon, then artistic director of the Milwaukee Repertory Theater, who revived it in April 1980 at the Court Street Theater. It is this version that was published by Grove Press.[1] Insofar as the intervening years had witnessed the decline of the freshwater Merchant Marine,[2] the play may seem more elegiac and less comic than it had a decade earlier. It is not a work, however, which encourages nostalgia in that it stages the lives of those who seem to lack a sense of direction and purpose, trapped as they are in the circularities of something more than the ship's unchanging itinerary.

Subsequent productions of the play in the early 1980s led to further, minimal changes, incorporated in the 1983 Samuel French edition. This revision then served as the basis for the 2000 screen adaptation, directed by Joe Mantegna and featuring the playwright's family members Tony (as Dale, a twenty-year-old literature student, on board as Ordinary Seaman) and Bob (who plays the piano in the sound track's jazz combo and co-arranged the suite from Tchaikovsky's *Swan Lake*). For the movie new speeches were added, seemingly on the basis of improvisations on the set, while some of the existing material was cut.

To all appearances the play's twenty-eight short scenes constitute a realistic portrait of life in the Merchant Marine. Dale is a summer stand-in for the cook who has gone missing, for reasons unknown. We learn little of the crewmen beyond their age and status. The fireman and pierman are identified only through their functions. Instead Mamet paints a collective portrait of men whose boredom, loneliness, and sense of loss are compensated for by memories, tall tales, and drinking.

Melodramatic speculations on the plight of the cook, who may simply have overslept, amount to little more than an attempt to breathe drama into empty lives. The fantasies the crew spin, as boring day succeeds boring day, seem to derive from the media. They improvise a story which sees the missing man as a victim of the Outfit who, doubtless, "beat the living fuck out of him. Left him for dead," so that "he'll never perform again" (57–8). If they seem to be killing off a fantasy, as George and Martha do in *Who's Afraid of Virginia Woolf?* (1962), it is not in the name of reality, which they fear, but as a further investment in fantasy. In the last act the missing cook is restored.

Un-phased by his reappearance and the absence of any drama they fall back into their familiar routine.

In the movie version, Joe Mantegna presents the crew's fantasies in a black and white *film noir* style, in keeping with Mamet's *House of Games* (1987) and *Lakeboat*'s cinematographic frame of reference. That these insets feature an uncredited Andy Garcia underscores the degree to which Hollywood has shaped the imaginations of those on board.

On the page, the play's episodic structure, reflective of the influence of Second City, enhances the discontinuities of the characters' lives. Few conversations last long, few involve more than two people. Such continuity as there is derives from the unitary set though this is less continuity than repetition as they sail on this ship of fools, endlessly traveling and with no final destination. Subtitles like "The Illusion of Motion" or "The Inland Sea Around Us" foreground the unchanging, even absurd nature of their lives. In the film version, Mantegna adds a prologue, showing Dale's trip to the ship whose sense of movement is maintained by rolling images, traveling shots, and aerial panoramas of the boat at full speed. Supported by an orchestral sound track, these shots seem to give the trip an epic grandeur, further enhanced by the ship's name change (from the bland *T. Harrison* to the more romantic *Seaway Queen*) and by Skippy's enthusiasm for the poetry of Rudyard Kipling. But this visual dynamic generates a sense of irony, radically at odds as it is with the lives of those on board.

It is tempting to relate *Lakeboat* to the sea plays of Eugene O'Neill and, indeed, there are perhaps echoes of a playwright fascinated by characters who prefer what in *The Iceman Cometh* he called "pipe dreams." O'Neill's characters, too, were seen as trapped in their own limitations, story tellers looking to find meaning in their own desperate inventions. And in 1975 Mamet directed O'Neill's first full-length play, *Beyond the Horizon* (1918), at the Grace Lutheran Church on West Baldwin Street.[3] Like O'Neill's characters, Mamet's want to belong, though without having any clear idea what they belong to. The ship would seem to constitute a provisional society. They do, after all, have to work together for it to function at all. But, like the wider society of which they are a part, and which they perhaps exemplify, they exist most acutely in their privacies, in needs which they hesitate to express for fear of the vulnerability this would attract. They meet, if at all, only in the stories they tell each other and themselves, stories which give them the significance for which they long but which they suspect they lack.

Their lives seem to be spiralling downward, but the Lakes themselves have lost the romance which had once been part of their appeal. The economic relevance of the lakeboats has declined, along with the industries they served. That threatening obsolescence attaches itself to those who serve on board. Like O'Neill's characters, they remember ambitions which have now foundered or, like the forty-year-old Stan, see the drink to which they have turned for oblivion as evidence of their manliness and even, parodoxically, their purity: "It's a man's thing, drinking. A curse and an elevation. Makes you an angel. A booze-ridden angel." It is also a fact, something fixed in a declining world: "I know my alcohol, boyo. I know it and you know I know it. And I know it" (30). If they are the products of irony they also generate their own. In that sense they are precursors to the confidence tricksters that will recur in Mamet's work, except that in this case they seek to deceive themselves.

Theirs is in part a Beckett-like world. They are indeed on a journey but that journey can have only one end. Meanwhile, they pass the time, talk, joke, deploy a crude language which would become a trademark feature of Mamet's plays, less for naturalistic reasons than because these are characters whose lives are shaped by secondhand images, who are spoken by a language detached from their real needs.

Mamet followed *Lakeboat* with *The Duck Variations*, which premièred in 1972 at Goddard College, in Vermont, where the play's first draft originated during Mamet's student days (1965–9). It was staged by the St. Nicholas Theatre Company founded there by Mamet, Steven Schachter, and William Macy. The play presents two doting immigrants, Emil Varěc and George Aronovitz, sitting in "A Park on the edge of a Big City on a Lake. An afternoon around Easter" (73). Traipsing back and forth between their bench and apartments, they fill their days watching ducks and telling stories. They have the air of an aging comedy team improvising, with Emil playing stooge to George's more outrageous claims.

The title, *The Duck Variations*, hints at a musical structure, and certainly rhythm was to prove of central importance to Mamet who was prone to beat out the iambs of spoken English as he directed. Behind the banality of the conversation, too, is at times a certain lyricism and it is this which in part, he suggests, gives it its power to "strike a responsive chord" in the audience. There is a truth which transcends mere verisimilitude.[4] Driven by the characters' needs, speeches at times aspire to literal poetry, as in Emil's paean to the country, receiving an appropriate layout on the printed page (101–2). It is a lyricism, however, which frequently breaks down again in non-sequiturs or incompletions. Disagreements and emotional outbursts more often than not form the dynamic that keeps the conversation and their lives going, yet run-on lines, shared by the men, suggest at least a momentary alignment of viewpoints, a brief sense of contact.

At times these two old men seem in tune, with one another and their surroundings. More often, they speak at cross purposes or observe a world with which they feel ever less connection. And when the word death is spoken a tremor implicitly runs through the text, since death is the one topic they wish to shun, the reason they fill the air with inconsequence. Disease, decay, pollution seem to force their way into these otherwise inconsequential conversations. Try as they might, the logic of their situation continually exerts itself. And plainly there is a social and political dimension to this conversation between two old men who observe outside themselves the decline which they fear within. *The Duck Variations*, indeed, is a fable, as is *Lakeboat*, as would be *The Water Engine*. David Mamet the social critic is already putting in an appearance.

The fabular dimension is underlined here by the ducks of the title. Certainly George insists that, "Historically yes . . . many human societies are modeled on our animal friends" (113). The observation may immediately be undermined by the fact that he somewhat mysteriously invokes, by way of evidence, "The French," a fact which he has derived from "Some guide to France," but the fact remains that he has underscored what is plainly a central proposition of the play.

There are just the two of them, survivors offering one another a desperate mutuality constantly threatened by truths they would rather avoid. And though there would be plays with a greater number of characters, Mamet's work tends to center on two people talking, often communicating less through what they say than, as here, through what they studiously avoid saying. As with music, silence, too, plays its role, is an essential element of his rhythms.

George is the principal story teller. He distrusts abstraction and the very idea of a future which can hold nothing but bad news. Perhaps in a parody of Wittgenstein's "Die Welt ist Alles Was der Fall is" (the famous opening of the *Tractatus Logico-Philosophicus*), he observes that, "There, here, it's like it is today. How it is *today*, that's how it is" (75). When Emil sighs, "I don't know . . ." George replies, "What's to know?" (75). What is to know is potentially too threatening to acknowledge. The present carries no threat. Tomorrow does. How much better to pass the time with word games, a conversation which lurches around, veering away from threatening questions, than confess to what they fear most. Nonetheless, the truths they would avoid have a way of seeping back into their remarks, reminding them of what they most wish to avoid.

Once again we seem not far removed from the world of Samuel Beckett. George and Emil appear close cousins to Vladimir and Estragon in *Waiting for Godot*. There is the same inadvertent comedy of characters aware of a looming absurdity they are ill equipped to address. These, too, are vaudevillians trying not to get the cosmic joke. For all the hard-boiled reputation he would acquire, however, Mamet has a less bleak perspective. Where Beckett deals in ironies factored into existence, Mamet would prove more liable to track irony to its lair in a failure of social, moral, and even political values. Unlike Beckett, Mamet would increasingly choose to locate his characters in a recognizable environment and in a society with a precise history. He would seemingly, as here, catch his characters at the end of something but that presupposed a world in which decline had had a beginning. And this would prove no less true of America than it would of those waiting out their days in apparent serenity. In *The Duck Variations*, his characters are aware of the fact that they were born astride the grave; they simply have no intention of acknowledging it. In his later work the social and even political implications of entropy would be underscored more overtly but already his is very much a world running down. His characters try to use language to contain and control their experiences but, as in his next play, *Sexual Perversity in Chicago*, they are more often the products of language than its confident users.

Perhaps, though, there is an element of redemption here. If George and Emil's plots tend towards death – as plots will do – and the play is about to end with a blackout, their conversations take place "around Easter." Plainly, their salvation does not depend upon resurrection but there is, one suspects, something more than irony in the observation that "Watching each other. / Each with something to contribute. [. . .] the world might turn another day" (125). Beckett's characters fear that the world will turn another day. Mamet's Americans are more sturdily resilient.

Mamet wrote the first draft of *Sexual Perversity in Chicago* while at Goddard College (1965–9). The finished play was premièred by Chicago's Organic Theater in the summer of 1974, and was directed by Stuart Gordon. After receiving a Joseph Jefferson Award for best new play of the year, it moved to Off Off Broadway's St. Clements Theatre in December, 1975, and six months later to Off Broadway's Cherry Lane Theatre where it won an Obie Award.

The play is a late twentieth-century comedy of manners which reflects something of the confusions over gender identity and role as the women's movement gathered momentum. At its center are two men and two women who approach one another with a mixture of lust and disdain. Indeed, this admixture generates much of the comedy in a play in which men and women consistently sabotage their own strategies as they consistently fail to achieve what they believe they desire. Both sexes seem to lack a usable language, a shared understanding, or even a rudimentary social etiquette. Bernie and Danny boast of their exploits with women who self-evidently baffle and reject them. They parade a sexist vocabulary as if it were evidence of their mastery of women and experience. They tell one another stories about their conquests which become ever more baroque and unbelievable, substituting, as they do, words for action and fantasies for truths. Bernie, who presents himself as the teacher, plainly has much to learn, lacking precisely the skills to which he lays claim. Danny, naïve, inexperienced, is hopelessly adrift and ill equipped to affect the relationship he believes he wants.

Here is another vaudeville act in which the audience can see what the characters cannot. There is a mismatch between the women of their fantasies and those they now encounter. Bernie expects submission and acquiescence. He encounters aggression and rejection. Having run through his whole repertoire, he discovers that his strategy accomplishes nothing. He sees himself as the protagonist of this urban drama but ends up on the sidelines. Danny does briefly make contact but has no idea how to function with a real woman rather than the fantasy he has been led to expect. Women are "Tits and Ass"; men are sexual threats. Beyond that, the men understand nothing of the women.

For their part, Deborah and Joan seem no more clear as to their roles, no more able to negotiate the relationships to which they are drawn but which they inherently distrust. It is not clear to any of the characters what is at stake, beyond a momentary connection which does no more than underscore the space between them. As in *Lakeboat* the scenes are brief and fragmented. Nothing can be sustained. The play effectively ends as it begins.

The men's models for sexual behavior are second-hand, spin-offs from pornographic films, products of the reductive language which seems their only available resource. Spirituality is no more than the hand-me-down rhetoric of late-night television evangelists. Even the past which Bernie invokes is a fantasy, borrowed from the media. Thus his war experiences in Korea are entirely vicarious, derived from the 1972 televison version of *M*A*S*H*, a series based on Altman's movie and itself, ironically, filmed not in Korea but at the Twentieth-Century Fox ranch in the Lake Malibu area and on a football playground in Griffith Park. The real, it seems, is no less suspect in American society at large than it is to these two sexual no-hopers. Altman's movie, perhaps not incidentally, was itself criticized for denigrating women and homosexuals.

Bernie ends the play as baffled as when he enters. He runs through the cast-list of willing women ("Pro, semi-pro, Betty Coed from College, regular young broad, it's anybody's ballgame" – 12), passing on his supposed expertise to his inexperienced friend but the actual women who confront him leave him confused and bewildered, even as he insists on his mastery of those who repel him. Joan's suggestion that heterosexuality "never *was* supposed to work out" carries the force not only of this play but also of several of Mamet's later works in which women are either conspicuous by their absence or struggle to find space in a male world.

Yet there is something exuberant about Bernie's inventions. His stories get ever more outrageous and his language ever more obscene (this was the first of Mamet's plays to send critics and audiences into a state of shock over his language) but there is something compelling about him. In later plays, too, Mamet would implicitly confess admiration for the performance skills of his characters, hardly surprisingly, perhaps, for a dramatist. And though those skills are effectively deployed to deceive, there is a sense, nonetheless, in which *homo ludens*, mankind who plays, justifies himself thereby.

Mamet returned to the relationship between the sexes in *The Woods*. It opened in November, 1977, at the St. Nicholas Theatre and starred Peter Weller and Patti Lupone. This original production, directed by the playwright himself, was revived in 1982 at New York's Second Stage, though by then Ulu Grosbard had staged the play with Christine Lahti and Chris Sarandon at the Public Theatre. The revivals notwithstanding, the play was not a major success. What it was, was a dramatization of the differing needs of men and women, a fable of sexual relationships conducted not in Mamet's typical urban environment but in the countryside. The woods of the title, however, figure as the *locus classicus* of fairy tales where the protagonists conventionally play, become lost, and acquire selfhood by coming to terms with their fears and desires. This is such a tale or fable in which that maturation process is duly enacted. Beginning at dusk and moving through the night to morning, it traces the stages of an exemplary tale of human relationships. A young woman, Ruth, hankers for the love of her friend, Nick, who refuses to give it, as if she were a "witch" (93) wishing him evil. Meanwhile, behind contested love lies the death they fear: "Fuck me, I don't want to die" (93). Ruth and Nick are presented as archetypes and *The Woods* becomes an account of the primal encounter of man and woman.

Ruth is invited to Nick's summer house where she hopes life will be breathed into their relationship. She is nervous, intense, apt to speak more than she should in an effort to conceal her fears. She urges him to accept an obligation to her, to make a commitment beyond the moment. She is looking for love, for continuity. For her, this is the beginning of a continuing story. For him, it seems, it is a relationship coming to an end. He wants no more than a temporary and essentially physical relationship. He is wary of the biological trap she seems intent upon springing. He resists her initiatives. Their incompatibility, however, implies a more fundamental disjunction.

Ruth tells a story of Vikings who, undervaluing female children, smashed their heads in. It betokens an awareness of threat and, indeed, she is assaulted by Nick and responds in kind. The two in effect share little beyond need, and even that need is different in its nature. By the same token they speak a different language, turn to different metaphors, perceive the world around them differently. The play's opening image is of a seagull which cannot tolerate the presence of others for more than the briefest moment. Ruth becomes its figural victim, anxious to hold on to a man who wants to escape. A similar tension is observable in the work of Sam Shepard (*Fool for Love*, *A Lie of the Mind*); his and Mamet's is a culture whose myths and history have had a male bias, a streak of violence. Ruth says of Nick that "there was no one *there*" (73); it is a lament heard equally in Shepard's work.

In a sense *The Woods* assumes the shape of a psychodrama or therapeutic session. In a variation on the central mentor–protégé relationship common to a number of Mamet's plays, Ruth seems to play the psychoanalyst provoking her patient into abreacting his repressed unconscious by, in her case, using the natural world as a cue for free associations. Ever more importuned by her persistent injunction, "Tell me," Nick relates a nightmare world and blurts out his fear of dying. Plainly for him commitment carries with it the idea of time which in turn leads in only one direction. On the other hand, when she seems ready to acknowledge that their relationship is over he suddenly shows interest in reviving it. We seem not that distant from the world of Sam Shepard's *Fool for Love* in which the man and woman at its center are simultaneously attracted and repelled.

There is a perversity, in short, to the relationship between the sexes as power shifts with a disturbing rhythm. They are, it seems, one another's fate. When Nick needs Ruth he is urgent in his desire. When his desire is satisfied there seems little to connect them. For her part, when she thinks she is secure she sees everything in terms of her relationship, neurotically cataloguing memories, speculations, events as if she were a unifying principle. When things seem to come to an end she explodes in anger: "You don't know *dick*. And I respected you, too. (*She snorts.*) You lure the poor babes up here in the winter and you roll around and tell them of the Indians. You fuck them and you send them home. I hope you're very happy. (*Pause*)

You don't deserve me" (88). The description is evidently not far from the truth.

She, too, recalls a past which carried with it a sense of threat, her family having suffered persecution by the Cossacks in a distant Russia. These are two babes in the wood, lost as much to themselves as to others. The play ends as Ruth recites her family history urging Nick to put his arms around her, and as he declares his love for her. It seems an ending drained of irony but she is surely pulling him into her story in order to keep him with her.

Early in the play, Nick had been the story teller, speaking of a madman in the forest who believed Hitler had been telling him things about his wife. The man had killed himself. Now Ruth is the story teller and the story she tells is of comfort and reconciliation. In a sense she seems to have won. They are still together. On the other hand it seems likely that they are doomed to re-enact their battles. This is a fable. Repetition seems factored into it.

The Water Engine (1977) originated as a short story and was subsequently turned into a movie treatment. Both were rejected but the script resurfaced as a radio play for the *Earplay* series of National Public Radio.[5] A commission from Howard Gelman provided Mamet with a first opportunity to write for a medium he had been involved with as a child when his uncle, Chairman of the Chicago Board of Rabbis, allowed him to perform in radio and television shows.[6] In Mamet's own assessment, radio drama offers the advantage of focusing on the essentials of the story, leaving the rest to the listeners' imagination. *The Water Engine* first reached the stage in May, 1977, as a St. Nicholas Theatre production, directed by Steven Schachter and featuring William Macy.

When Mamet came to transfer it to the stage, however, he retained the idea of it being presented as a radio play, with the cast members assembling around a microphone and freely switching between reading their parts into the microphone and realistically enacting scenes for the live audience. The audience, too, played a double role, sometimes being invited to applaud on cue as if they were a studio audience. The alternation between observation and participation, and between presentational and representational styles, created what Mamet, in an editorial note, has called "a third reality, a scenic truth, which dealt with radio not as an electronic convenience, but as an expression of our need to create and to communicate and to explain – much like a chainletter."

The play begins with a song and the voice-over of an announcer proclaiming "welcome to the Century of Progress Exposition," the exposition referred to in *American Buffalo* which, in the middle of the Depression, chose to celebrate America's past and future. Nor is this the only voice-over. At various stages we also hear the voice of a Chainletter, a letter which solicits money and implicitly threatens reprisals should the chain be broken. This voice offers various cautionary tales, in effect urban myths, one of which then forms the central action of the play.

Charles Lang is a punch-press operator for a company run by Dietz and Federle. He has invented, and is trying to patent and market, an engine running on distilled water. Driven by the dream of success and a concern for the welfare of his sister, Rita, he works at his invention in between fixing toy planes for the child of the local candystore owner. He is torn between securing immediate material wealth for himself and his sister, and serving humanity by gifting it a clean and more readily available source of energy, a pressing enough issue during the oil crisis which faced the Carter administration as the play was being written. Lang is, however, about to discover the literal truth of the fact that "we are characters within a dream of industry. Within a dream of toil" (23), as others move to steal and suppress his invention. The play, Mamet tells us in a subtitle, is "An American Fable." To the extent that this is so, it is an account of business as crime (a familiar Mamet trope observable in both *American Buffalo* and *Glengarry Glen Ross*), of the betrayal of trust. As such, it also anticipates his later film, *The Spanish Prisoner*, in which another invention is stolen by businessmen who betray the trust of the inventor.

Lang goes to a lawyer seeking copyright protection for his invention, paying the man a dollar before he speaks, believing, as he does, in the sacredness of a contract. The lawyer duly betrays him and slowly this innocent abroad is robbed, beaten, and, along with his sister, finally killed. A Barker at the Fair announces that "Great Wealth and Fame stand just beyond our grasp. / All civilization stands on trust. / All people are connected. / No one can call back what one man does" (61). The sentiment is unexceptionable; only its source makes it suspect, the Barker reading it from the Chainletter he has just received. Trust is thus invoked by those who seek to betray it. Even his role as Barker is to persuade and cajole. Language has plainly detached itself from its referents.

Thus, a journalist, required to produce rapid copy on the "quintessence of those things which made our country great," comes up with an encomium to capitalism:

The Century of Progress, sign and symbol of the great essential strength of the Free Market. All around the nations founder and decay . . . the East Turns Red, and senile Europe limps from day to day in search of that lost leader, that forgotten vigor never to return [. . .] The Principles which made this country made it great, as it *is* great, as, once again, it shall be great. With Trust, with power [. . .] With mutual understanding of the simple grace and the eternal power of "The Bargain Made and Kept To." (63)

As he finishes he adds to his Secretary, "Thank god I don't have to sign it," as well he might since his rhetoric accompanies the unfolding story of the betrayal of an innocent inventor and the intended destruction of the machine that would indeed have represented progress but which must now be sacrificed to greed and self-interest: the real principles, it is implied, behind the American Way.

At the same time, of course, this story is itself a dramatization of an account in the Chainletter and thus in itself fraudulent. Where is the real when newspapermen lie, Barkers exaggerate, stories are told with no basis in fact, and language is used to conceal rather than communicate truth? There is, it seems, a human penchant for deception. *The Water Engine* is a play of many voices. Though the scenes are not distinct, being intercut with one another, interpenetrating, Mamet still employs that episodic structure which typifies his early plays. Into the central story of the betrayed inventor are interspersed other stories of betrayal, real or fantasized. He presents myth as history and history as myth, all within an encompassing fiction – the Chainletter, which itself is enclosed by the radio play. Meanwhile, the irony of an Exposition celebrating progress echoes through a play in which moral regression seems the primary force, the motivating drive. An American fable has presented a dream of avarice which seems the only substantial reality available.

The metatheatrical dimension of *The Water Engine* was picked up again in *A Life in the Theatre*. This play premièred at the Goodman Theatre, Chicago, in February, 1977, with Mike Nussbaum and Joe Mantegna. It was directed by Gregory Mosher, to whom it is dedicated. Two years earlier Mosher, then heading the Goodman's Stage Two devoted to alternative theatre, had joined forces with the St. Nicholas Theatre to produce *American Buffalo*. After being relocated from Goddard College, Vermont, to Chicago, the St. Nicholas had developed into one of the leading Off Loop theatres of the seventies. Even so, in the 1977–8 season, around the time the Goodman switched its affiliation from the Chicago Art Institute to DePaul University's School of Drama, Mamet became its Associate Artistic Director and Writer-in-Residence under the overall leadership of Mosher. Until (and even after) his 1985–6 transfer to New York's Lincoln Center, Mosher would come to produce many of his friend's plays and thus prove instrumental in consolidating his artistic status.

A Life in the Theatre features two repertory actors, an old hand and a novice, seen in their natural habitat. This is a play about theatre but a play which accepts the notion of the theatre as a metaphor for the social and moral world beyond its walls. In that sense, once again Mamet seems to be interested in fable. The theatre may require no more than "Two *actors*, some *lines* . . . and an audience" (51), but life itself requires much the same. Being in the theatre means having a "job to do. You do it by your light [. . .] expertise [. . .] sense of rightness . . . fellow feelings . . . etiquette . . . professional procedure" (6), "Take too much for granted, [and we will] fall away and die. (*Pause.*) On the boards, or in society at large. There must be law, there must be a reason, there must be tradition" (56–7). At least for Robert, the older of the two actors, that reference to death has a real force. Everything which precedes it in that sentence is offered as an antidote. The theatre deals in arbitrary meanings, but so, too, he implies, does the life it shadows.

For a writer interested in dissembling, in the tension between the ideal and its degraded representation, the theatre was a plausible, if ambiguous, arena, capable alike of truth and deception, the two inevitably wedded. The play may have come into being as a consequence of writing occasional brief sketches which he subsequently brought together around two representative types, but it becomes much more than this. On one level he plainly takes pleasure in the pastiche dramas he creates for his two actors to perform, in the gap which opens up between the seriousness with which they purport to take their craft and the material they are required to perform. But these two actors represent something more than a self-referring parody. Behind it lies the Shakespearian proposition that the theatre is something more than a mirror held up to nature. We are actors performing our lives, well or badly.

There is a contrast between the two actors. Robert is, seemingly, established, happy to offer advice to his brash young colleague. The repertoire they proceed to perform, however, suggests that they are far from the center of the theatrical world. Robert, it increasingly seems, is waiting out his time, struggling to convince himself of his continuing significance. John, for his part, can barely tolerate waiting for his break. Nor is Robert a model of acting he is prepared to accept. John is ambitious. Robert is aware that the confidence he exudes is itself part of his performance. They are at the beginning and end of their careers, but for the moment share the stage, a stage which is empty for part of the time so that their words have a hollow ring and their gestures seem false. Desperate to lend significance to a career essentially lived at second hand, they look for hidden significance in the meretricious material they are required to perform. Efforts to dignify their status and the material they are given frequently collapse of their own weight. This time Mamet's characters are almost literal vaudevillians, where in the earlier plays that had been a symbolic role. All are aware of a clock ticking, a clock momentarily suspended in the factitious time of the theatre.

Robert does not always prove the most reliable instructor, despite relying on the role for a sense of his own pride. He neglects his own advice while his ponderous generalizations and mistakes elicit as much ridicule as George's puffery in *The Duck Variations*. For a man who pays lip service to the need for "an outside life" (25), his is an all-consuming, even self-alienating world of routine. More often than not he is met with the incomprehension of audiences and critics alike. To the extent that skills are passed on from mentor to protégé, learned the pragmatic way rather than through formal schooling, training becomes a life-long venture, only terminated by death: "You start from the beginning and go through the middle and end up at the end [. . .] A little like a play" (23). Robert's "way out" of the theatre, then, is an exit from life (73), though in his tenacity he risks being trapped, like the aged Firs in Chekhov's *Cherry Orchard*, a play which Mamet would later adapt for The New Theatre Company (1985).

A Life in the Theatre alternates offstage and onstage action and, like so many of these early plays, is episodic. The actors are required to jump from one performance to another, simulating emotions. Their lines are given. Their job is to give them life. The problem is that this, in itself an echo of social living, so easily descends into pure farce when Robert forgets his lines and starts to argue and improvise onstage. If John walks out on his former mentor at this time, the break had been prefigured in the rookie's repeated challenges to the senior actor's restricting directorial guidelines.

A central dramaturgical challenge of the play indeed consists in making the swapping of positions plausible without pre-empting it, given the reversal's early programmatic announcement ("Young people in the theatre . . . tomorrow's leaders," 5). Throughout the play John guards his privacy, refuses to divulge much about his audition, humors and manipulates Robert to further his career, setting up the tension between friendship and business which drives so many of Mamet's plays. The men's relationship gains interest (comic or other) to the extent that they are at loggerheads, but as with George and Emil in *The Duck Variations*, theirs is, at least briefly, a relationship of mutual dependence, with Robert needing the companionship and learning in the teaching process what he himself stands for. John's education therefore masks Robert's self-education which, judging by the number of lines assigned to him, clearly has dramatic priority.

A Life in the Theatre constitutes a personal, tragicomic tribute to the profession at a crucial moment in Mamet's career. That the playwright celebrates the magic of the theatre even as he exposes it is a mark of his consummate artistry. At the same time, the play harks back to the 1960s when the theatre possessed a paradigmatic character. Given the art's growing marginality, there is perhaps a note of doubt in Robert's assertion that "Our aspirations in the Theatre are much the *same* as man's. (*Pause.*) (Don't you think?)" (24). Conditioned by increasingly conservative times, the best he can do is to insist on the theatre's authenticity and its performers' sincerity. His hope that better "souls" will manifest themselves outwardly in better social selves is undercut by his assertion that "You can a learn a lot from keeping your mouth shut" (56). A desirable reticence is fused with the idea of social disengagement while he incautiously observes that theatre is about fending off the "bloodsuckers. The robbers of the cenotaph" (67). For Mamet, the (his)story of the theatre needs to be told to counter its ephemerality.[7] Yet, it is that very ephemerality which has a disturbing truth to tell.

In an interview with Ross Wetzsteon, conducted shortly before *A Life in the Theatre* premièred, Mamet explicitly remarked on "the degrading life of performers, especially the way, like all oppressed groups, they internalize the prejudice society holds against them."[8] What ultimately redeems the theatre to Mamet is its educational and experiential capacities. As he remarked,

> The essential task of the drama (as of the fairy tale) is to offer a solution to a problem which is nonsusceptible to reason. To be effective, the drama must induce us to suspend our rational judgment, and to follow the *internal* logic of the piece, so that our *pleasure* (our "cure") is the release at the end of the story. We enjoy the happiness of being a participant in the process of *solution*, rather than the intellectual achievement of having observed the process of construction.[9]

It can be no coincidence that John rehearses the opening of Act II of Shakespeare's *Henry V*, the play whose famous Prologue celebrates the actors' and spectators' joint capacity to people the "unworthy scaffold" in the theatre's "wooden O" with the variety and "full[ness] of life" (71). If the world is a stage, then the theatre, despite the brevity of its performances, Robert's "minute or so" of watching (71), offers countless fields of play, like the "vasty fields of France," much to the public's instruction and delectation. Through its exemplary character, *A Life in the Theatre* thus presents art as a privileged, if ambivalent, domain. Mamet's plays of the seventies, meanwhile, set the stage for the riches of a talent, fully blooming in the decades to come.

NOTES

1. All subsequent parenthetical page numbers refer to the New York, Grove Press, editions.
2. Dennis Carroll, *David Mamet* (London: Macmillan, 1987), p. 84.
3. *Ibid.*, p. 9.
4. Leslie Kane, ed., *David Mamet in Conversation* (Ann Arbor: University of Michigan Press, 2001), pp. 48–9.
5. David Mamet, *Writing in Restaurants* (New York: Viking, 1986), p. 13.
6. The one-act play *Prairie du Chien* had a reverse production history. It was first broadcast on radio by the BBC and NPR's *Earplay* in 1978, before premiering on stage, December 23, 1985, in a double bill with *The Shawl* at the Mitzi Newhouse Theatre, Lincoln Center, under the direction of Gregory Mosher.
7. *Writing in Restaurants*, p. 104.
8. Kane, ed., *Mamet in Conversation*, p. 14.
9. *Writing in Restaurants*, pp. 13–14.

3

MATTHEW ROUDANÉ

Betrayal and friendship: David Mamet's
American Buffalo

American Buffalo is at first glance a simple play about simple men who cannot pull off a simple robbery. The drama unwinds in Don's Resale Shop, located on the South Side of Chicago. The junk shop is littered with odds and ends, many of which are objects from the Great Depression and the 1933 Chicago World's Fair. As the play begins we learn that Don Dubrow has recently sold a coin collector a buffalo-head nickel for $90. Now sensing that this customer not only deceived him but somehow affronted his sense of professional competence, Don sets his sights on stealing back the coin and what he thinks must be the man's valuable coin collection.

Don initially picks his young friend, Bob, for the job. However, as Don and Teach, his associate, orchestrate the robbery plans, Teach argues that they should cut Bob out of the deal, an arrangement on which they agree. As it turns out, the heist never happens. Soon after midnight Bob returns, not with *the* but *a* buffalo-head nickel, which, he finally confesses, he simply purchased. After learning that Bob lied about seeing the coin dealer leave his apartment earlier that day, Don seems embarrassed and angry, and the paranoid Teach explodes, viciously attacking the helpless boy and trashing the junk shop. Their collective inability to execute a simple robbery only highlights their insignificance, while the only thing they have left of genuine value – friendship – is, like the American buffalo, pushed to the brink of extinction.

The play's ostensible simplicity, however, expands into a parodic version of the American dream, a social drama, and a metaphysical work of surprising complexity and genuine originality. With its echoes of another America, uncontaminated by entrepreneurial greed, a product of utopian rhetoric rather than psychotic fear and aggression, *American Buffalo* offers a portrait of the Republic in terminal decay, its communal endeavor and individual resilience all but disappeared. The trust and unity invoked on its coinage have now devolved into paranoia, the security and hope it once offered into a frightening violence. Business enterprise, in *American Buffalo*, has decayed into petty criminality while the play's metaphoric and literal setting – a junk store full of the mementos of Chicago's Exposition (motto: A Century of Progress) – offers an image of ultimate decline.

American Buffalo is David Mamet's breakthrough play. Although he had written several dramas prior to 1975, *American Buffalo* first brought critical attention to a 27-year-old playwright whose earlier works – *Lakeboat* (1970), *Duck Variations* (1972), *Sexual Perversity in Chicago* (1974) – played before small audiences in a college in Vermont and, soon after, appreciative theatregoers in Mamet's hometown, Chicago. With the première of *American Buffalo* at Chicago's Goodman Theatre Stage Two on November 23, 1975, however, Mamet began to reach a wider audience. After a twelve-show run at Stage Two, Mamet took his play to the St. Nicholas Theatre Company in Chicago, and though the play received mixed reviews it brought increased attention to this new playwright. In February of 1976 the play moved to St. Clement's Theatre in New York City and, on February 16, 1977, *American Buffalo* had its Broadway opening at the Ethel Barrymore Theatre, starring Kenneth McMillan, John Savage, and Robert Duvall. Within a few years *American Buffalo* was staged at the Cottesloe Theatre, National Theatre in London (1978), and the Schiller-Theater in Berlin (1980). It enjoyed numerous revivals in the United States, including the well-received 1981 production featuring Al Pacino, and, in one of two film versions, Dustin Hoffman. Today *American Buffalo* is considered a classic of the American theatre.

Soon after the play opened, Mamet confessed to the fact that he had been motivated in part by his fascination with American business. *American Buffalo*, he argued, "is about the American ethic of business . . . About how we excuse all sorts of great and small betrayals and ethical compromises called business. I felt angry about business when I wrote the play."[1] Indeed, Mamet is at his best when exploring the relationship between "the American ethic of business" and the ways in which such a problematic ethos affects the individual. This relationship, in *American Buffalo* as in *Glengarry Glen Ross* (1983), prompts debates about the individual's sense of public responsibility and his or her definitions of private liberties. Throughout his theatre, Mamet creates a dialectic which, on the one hand, recognizes the individual's right to pursue entrepreneurial interests, while, on the other, concedes that in an ideal world such private interests should, but do not, exist in equipoise with a sense of civic and moral duty. This underlying tension produces divided loyalties in Mamet's characters; it also gives his theatre its particular unity of vision and ambivalent intensity.

Mamet seems drawn towards certain civic issues that Alexis de Tocqueville explored in his two-volume critique of the Republic, *Democracy in*

America (1835, 1840). The heart of Tocqueville's beliefs, suggests one historian, centers on the ambiguous interconnections of public ideals and private desires:

> The great distinction, in short, between classical republics and modern democracy lay in the commercial motive . . . The problem was to make private interest the moral equivalent of public virtue. This could be achieved through the disciplinary influence exerted by society on its members – an influence embodied in the mores and in law and institutions. For Tocqueville, *Self-interest rightly understood* was the key to the balance between virtue and interest in commercial values.[2]

The delicate moral balance between public virtue and private interest which so engaged Tocqueville clearly has a purchase on Mamet's imagination. It is, in fact, central to his theatre.

> I know of no other country [than America] where love of money has such a grip on men's hearts or where stronger scorn is expressed for the theory of [the] permanent quality of property.   (Tocqueville, *Democracy in America*)

In such plays as *A Life in the Theatre* (1977), *The Water Engine* and *Mr. Happiness* (both 1978), *Lakeboat* (1980), *Glengarry Glen Ross*, *Speed-the-Plow* (1988), and *Oleanna* (1992), Mamet explores a contemporary American civilization whose public issues, often played out in the form of deceitful business transactions by suspect "associates," permeate the individual's private world. "Business," for Mamet, becomes an expansive term, including not only the individual's public, professional vocation, but also one's private, personal existence: the Hemingwayesque manner of living, the various ways in which, in *American Buffalo*, Teach, Don, and Bobby conduct themselves. Mamet discusses the connections between one's job and versions of public responsibility, and one's life and private liberties, especially in the context of the myth of the American Dream:

> [The American Dream myth] interests me because the national culture is founded very much on the idea of strive and succeed. Instead of rising with the masses one should rise from the masses. Your extremity is my opportunity. That's what forms the basis of our economic life, and this is what forms the rest of our lives. That American myth: the idea of something out of nothing.[3]

The coercive allure of the American Dream myth proves to be as powerful to Teach and Don as it had to Willy Loman in Arthur Miller's *Death of a Salesman* (1949). Mamet is, in effect, spotlighting some of the public issues animating *American Buffalo* and the ways in which those public considerations generate private, internal tensions within the play's characters:

And this [public pressure to succeed] also affects the individual. It's very divisive. One feels one can succeed only at the cost of someone else. Economic life in America is a lottery. Everyone's got an equal chance, but only one guy is going to get to the top. "The more I have the less you have." So one can only succeed at the cost of the failure of another, which is what a lot of my plays – *American Buffalo* and *Glengarry Glen Ross* – are about . . . As Thorstein Veblen in *The Theory of the Leisure Class* says, sharp practice inevitably shades over into fraud. Once someone has no vested interest in behaving in an ethical manner and the only bounds on his behavior are supposedly his innate sense of fair play, then fair play becomes an outdated concept: "But wait a second! Why should I control my sense of fair play when the other person may not control their sense of fair play? So hurray for me and to hell with you."[4]

In *American Buffalo*, we come to see that public crimes dovetail with private transgressions. Through such transgressions, moreover, Mamet removes, or at least destabilizes, the very basis of our sense of social faith and loyalty.

Mamet's Thorstein Veblen allusion is also significant in that Veblen was deeply suspicious of the privileging of business concerns over social improvements. Throughout *The Theory of the Leisure Class* (1899), he suggested that Americans reveled in waste, abundance, and showy consumption. Such conspicuous consumption of material goods was deeply offensive, not only for its crass celebration of materialism, but also for its potential for precipitating the financial collapse of the American economic system, which would consign the working class, especially, to financial oblivion. The particularly American urge to amass wealth, Veblen argued, led to the rise of the Robber Barons, who often ignored the most fundamental ethical principles of fairness and civil conduct in their maniacal pursuit of the American Dream. Their fabulous wealth fed their predatory nature.

Not surprisingly, Veblen linked the social behavior of these tycoons with the predatory instincts of wild beasts, a persuasive analogy, no doubt, to late nineteenth- and earlier twentieth-century audiences, whose views of the social contract were highly influenced by Darwinian "survival of the fittest" evolutionary theories. No wonder Mamet chooses as one of his key stage props "the dead-pig leg-spreader"[5] – a device used in the slaughter houses of Chicago – and appropriates the language of business during a telling scene in which the tool figures prominently as Teach explains why he should be the one to execute the robbery:

> *I* want to go in there and gut this motherfucker. Don? Where is the shame in this? You take care of him, *fine*. (Now this is loyalty.) But Bobby's got his own best interests, too. And you cannot afford (and simply as a *business* proposition) you cannot afford to take the chance. (*Pause. Teach picks up a strange object.*) What is that?

Don: That?
Teach: Yes.
Don: It's a thing that they stick in dead pigs keep their legs apart all the blood
       runs out.[5]

The allusions to killing, blood, violence, death, slaughter, dominance, and control suggest that, for Teach and Don, theirs indeed is a Darwinian world. Mamet ironizes the exchange, of course, for, despite the blood and dominance references, and Teach's conviction that he is the best man for the job, these men are more impotent than powerful; it is as if they, like the pigs, have been drained of their life-blood, their vitality, though they seem only dimly aware of such depletions. Edmond Wilson's reflections on the status of the American novelist, written in a letter to Maxwell Perkins five years before the Chicago World's Fair, anticipates precisely the kind of impotency afflicting Teach, Don, and Bob, whose "thoughts never pass into action."[6]

Mamet's characters are also vaguely aware of what Veblen, throughout *The Theory of the Leisure Class*, calls "pecuniary emulation." Veblen believed that the individual dwelt in a social world, and that his outward behavior to an extent was defined and accorded value when compared to that of his neighbors. These neighbors, Veblen argued, emulated each other, and when – in trying to keep up with the Joneses – they participated in "pecuniary emulation," they sought to accumulate more wealth in order to be financially like (or even better off than) their neighbors.

Hence it was essential that the individual succeed at all costs, even if that success involved breaking the law. It is scarcely surprising, then, that Mamet has always been interested in Veblen's conviction that, in the playwright's words, "sharp [business] practice . . . shades over into fraud," and that several of his plays explore "how business corrupts, how the hierarchical business system tends to corrupt. It becomes legitimate for those in power in the business world to act unethically. The effect on the little guy is that he turns to crime."[7] By exposing his characters' unethical impulses, Mamet generates some of the play's humorous if sad ironies when revealing that the men never act upon their obsessive impulses. By the play's end the men emerge more as dumb waiters than accomplished thieves.

American Buffalo thus may be viewed as an interrogation of the business ethic in America. The wayward trajectory of this business ethic is nowhere better seen than in Teach's definition of an honorable and competitive capitalist system. In Teach's Macbethean world, where "fair is foul and foul is fair," everything is negotiable. As Mamet shifts the basis of social faith, democratic pieties are rationalized and distorted to fit private interests. Thus for Teach, American (per)versions of free enterprise become a license to rob. The following rich exchange, laced with comedy and wit, reveals Teach's seemingly persuasive argument:

> Teach: You know what is free enterprise?
> Don: No. What?
> Teach: The freedom . . .
> Don: . . . yeah?
> Teach: Of the *Individual* . . .
> Don: . . . yeah?
> Teach: To embark on Any Fucking Course that he sees fit.
> Don: Uh-huh . . .
> Teach: In order to secure his honest chance to make a profit. Am I so out of line on this?
> Don: No.
> Teach: Does this make me a Commie?
> Don: No.
> Teach: The country's *founded* on this, Don. You know this.   (72–3)

Teach's argument, of course, quickly dissolves when measured against his willingness to break any law to "secure his honest" opportunity to achieve wealth. When their business opportunity – the robbery – fails to materialize, Teach responds with his ridiculous and violent tirade near the end of the play, becoming a shrill parody of the very ideals to which he aspires. The humor of watching small-time would-be thieves buffalo themselves darkens by the end of the play, but Mamet's figures dazzle audiences with their skewed philosophical debates justifying some remotely perceived ideal or truth while trying to nudge their way past a friend to close a deal in a way that plainly negates that ideal or truth. The comedy remains – as in a scene in which Teach dials a wrong number (70–1) – and audiences gaze at characters whose verbal wizardry seems to validate their shady business practices. The comedy in *American Buffalo*, however, becomes more strained, the ironies more disturbing. By the final curtain, entrepreneurial greed has devolved into a vaudevillian leitmotif, and the vaudevillian yields to a sense of emptiness, an emptiness generated by the strains the men place on their own friendship.

Teach's definitional "To embark on Any Fucking Course" speech underscores two central principles within the entrepreneurial system from which he desperately tries to profit. This sense of being *entitled* to the free market and free enterprise appeals to Teach because of his a priori beliefs that competition is central to the success of democratic capitalism, and that competition flourishes best when business practices are free of government meddling. For Teach, as for Don, the vocabulary of American democracy is directly implicated in the American capitalist system, which, as Harry N. Rosenfield suggests, "is pictured as a swashbuckling, no-holds-barred, uninhibited private-profit economy based wholly on unbridled free competition and a completely free market."[8] Precisely such a deep-rooted belief in uninhibited competition drives Teach and Don; they feel that to steal is their inalienable right since their anticipated thievery is subsumed within their unencumbered pursuit of the American Dream. Teach and Don ennoble their spirits, or so they think, through work and profit, but fall prey to the process identified by Tocqueville a century before when he suggested that private self-interest, unchecked by moral conscience, inevitably leads to self-collapse.

Interestingly, we never learn what Teach does for a living. Bob, a recovering junkie, cannot hold a steady job. Only Don has a tangible if marginal business, but it is he who abdicates his moral position. Don betrays his friendship with Bob. This is, for Mamet, self-interest wrongly understood. Indeed, in summing up Tocqueville's theories, Arthur Schlesinger writes, "Self-interest wrongly understood tilts the balance away from republican virtue and from public purpose. The individual withdraws from the public sphere, becomes isolated, weak, docile, powerless. Individualism, in the Tocquevillean sense, leads to apathy, apathy to despotism, despotism to stagnation, stagnation to extinction. The light dwindles by degrees and expires of itself."[9] Mamet places Don, Teach, and Bob in just such a dismal pattern. In *American Buffalo*, informed social or public responsibility turns into anomy. The richly symbolic allusion to The Century of Progress becomes an ironic mockery, given the regression of these characters' ethics, a regression that presses the men, Teach screams, towards pre-civilization:

> The Whole Entire World.
> There is No Law.
> There Is No Right And Wrong.
> The World Is Lies.
> There Is No Friendship.
> Every Fucking Thing.
> > *Pause*
> Every God-forsaken Thing . . .
> We all live like cavemen.
>
> (103)

Within the context of Teach's regressive logic, and all of the characters' exchanges, much of *American Buffalo* appears to be a summation of the characters' invalidated ideas. From Teach's viewpoint, legal systems and ethical boundaries give way to mendacity, and loyalty and amity are nowhere in evidence – even though he as much as anyone is responsible for such regressions.

American Buffalo, however, is much more than an interrogation of errant business ethics in America. Above all, it is a play about friendship. It is a play about (an extended) family. About loyalty. About the fragility of companionship. About betrayal and greed. It is a play about the utter precariousness of existence for those whose lives unwind in this junk shop. It is equally a play about those who deploy a language whose communicative inadequacy becomes increasingly a source of both farce and terror.

Nine months after its première, Mamet said of the play:

> I think it's concerned with the mythology of America, which is that we've always been susceptible to exhortations to do what is right, but we've never been susceptible to exhortations to *think* what is right and to arrive at our own conclusions . . . I think the theme of the play has to do with the corruption of heartfelt moral knowledge for the sake of a mythological ideal, whether that ideal is patriotism or loyalty.[10]

More specifically, *American Buffalo* is about what happens when the protagonist – Don – loses sight of that friendship and the ability to honor a set of behavioral codes that will help Bob learn how to grow into a decent man.

While America, and Mamet, were still coming to terms with the cultural and political aftershocks precipitated by Richard Nixon, Watergate, and the war in Vietnam – and the attendant debates about language, truth, and honor – the playwright in 1975 was equally

> interested in the idea of honor among thieves; of what is an unassailable moral position and what isn't. What would cause a man to abdicate a moral position he'd espoused? That's what *American Buffalo* is about. Teach is the antagonist. The play's about Donny Dubrow. His moral position is that one must conduct himself like a man, and there are no extenuating circumstances for supporting the betrayal of a friend. That's how the play starts. The rest of the play is about Donny's betrayal of the fellow, Bobby, who he's teaching these things to.[11]

Mamet stages a subtle shift, with the first hint of Don's incipient betrayal of Bob heard when he says, "I don't know *that* I want you to do [the robbery]" (42). It is not that Don is completely wrong in his decision not to use his "gopher"; it is his motivations, fueled by pride and greed – his version of hubris – that temporarily blind him to the consequences of his own action. Bob brings him food, and then a different buffalo-head nickel, gifts from one seeking solace, guidance, and acceptance. Now, Don turns on his young friend, allowing the antagonist of the play, Teach, to assault not only the boy but the very essence of their friendship.

The germ of the idea for *American Buffalo* – and especially its opening scene – came to Mamet after an incident with his friend, actor William H. Macy. Both were in their twenties, struggling to make ends meet, when Mamet stopped by Macy's "wretched hovel." As Mamet recalled two decades later:

> I opened the refrigerator, and there was this big piece of cheese. I hadn't had anything to eat in a long time, so I picked it up, cut off a big chunk, and started eating. And Macy said, "Hey, *help yourself*." I was really hurt. I went away and fumed about that for several days. Then I just started writing, and out of that came this scene, which was the start of the play. [Teach] comes in furious because someone had just said to him, "Help yourself."[12]

Hence, when Teach makes his first appearance on stage, he launches into the story about Ruthie's "Help yourself"-to-the-piece-of-toast story. His remarks, however, quickly deepen to reveal the fragile nature, in this play at least, of friendship and loyalty, and the way in which a seemingly off-handed and harmless remark to a friend turns into betrayal and rejection. Loyal and good friend Ruthie suddenly is "a Southern bulldyke asshole ingrate of a vicious nowhere cunt" (11) who has, Teach explains, hurt "me in a way I don't know what the fuck to do" (11).

Mamet fills the entire first act with debates about the importance of friendship and loyalty, but the conversations are filled with comedic inversions of logic and definitions of the social contract itself. Ideals deflect into betrayals. The smallest perceived slight is assumed to be grounds for attack; or, as Teach eloquently puts it, "Cocksucker should be horsewhipped with a horsewhip" (72). Anyone who turns on the ironically named Teach must be dealt with in absolute terms: "The only way to teach these people is to kill them" (11). Although these men are planning a robbery for that evening, Teach seethes over shop owners (like Don) who sell World's Fair memorabilia at inflated prices; he simply reduces them to "A bunch of fucking thieves" (19). When Don abdicates his moral stance towards Bob, the play, which Mamet claims "is finally a play about a family constellation,"[13] reveals its tragic textures. *American Buffalo*, whose action takes place within twenty-four hours and occurs in the same place (the playwright still believes in the power of Aristotelean Unities), is, for Mamet, a contemporary tragedy. Indeed, as he remarked, "*American Buffalo*, sneakily enough, is really a tragedy about life in the family – so that is really the play that is closest to *Death of a Salesman*, though it's something I only realized afterward."[14] Eleven years after its première, Mamet elaborated,

American Buffalo is a classical tragedy, the protagonist of which is the junk store owner who is trying to teach a lesson in how to behave like the excellent man to his young ward. And he is tempted by the devil into betraying all his principles. Once he does that, he is incapable of even differentiating between simple lessons of fact and betrays himself into allowing Teach to beat up this young fellow whom he loves. He then undergoes, as I have said, recognition in reversal – realizing that all this comes out of his vanity, that because he abdicated a moral position for one moment in favor of some momentary gain, he has let anarchy into his life and has come close to killing the thing he loves. And he realizes at the end of the play that he has made a huge mistake, that, rather than his young ward needing lessons in being an excellent man, it is he himself who needs those lessons. That is what *American Buffalo* is all about.[15]

For this one evening, at least, Don lets business trump friendship. The pressures exacted upon their friendship prove too much. Don abandons the lessons he taught his young ward at the beginning of the play, where he appears something akin to a benevolent surrogate father instructing his well-meaning yet clueless adopted son.

When I saw my first Mamet plays in Chicago in 1975, I was immediately taken by what has engaged (and offended and humored) audiences and actors alike: language. Indeed, Mamet's voracious repartee signaled a turning point in cultural taste for many American audiences, ushering in an arresting riposte that was as far as one could imagine from the kind of dialogues heard in Susan Glaspell, Lillian Hellman, and Eugene O'Neill. With *Sexual Perversity in Chicago* and *American Buffalo*, the timbre of American dramatic language was altered by a playwright whose language was as fresh in its broken poetry (and its efficaciousness) as was the language of an earlier playwright whose first major play was also staged in Chicago three years before Mamet's birth. Just as Tennessee Williams, with *The Glass Menagerie* (Chicago première 1944), introduced a lyricism that played counterpoint to the realistic stage language that had informed American drama before 1945, so Mamet, with *American Buffalo*, introduced a new form of lyricism on stage, a language that a new generation of playwrights and audiences found as refreshing as it was liberating.

And yet it would be an oversimplification to claim, as many of the first critics of Mamet did, that in *American Buffalo* Mamet's is *merely* a streetwise, gritty language, a reflection of the cadences of small-time hustlers inhabiting Chicago's South Side pawnshops. To be sure, there is, in the plays he writes, a scabrous language whose rhythms, elisions, inflections, pauses, and mangled syntax derive their mimetic energy from a realistic apprehension of outer experience. But Mamet's language is not only concerned with "realistically" replicating the banal and prosaic surface of his characters' depleted lives. Mamet's is a stage and staged language. His is a *poetic* language. When asked to clarify the role of language in his plays, Mamet replied:

> It's poetic language. It's not an attempt to capture language as much as it is an attempt to create language. We see this in various periods of American drama. And when it is good, to the most extent, it's called realism. All realism means is that the language strikes a responsive chord. The language in my plays is not realistic but poetic. The words sometimes have a musical quality to them. It's language tailor made for the stage. People don't always talk the way my characters do in real life, although they may use some of the same words. Think of Odets, Wilder. That stuff is not realistic; it is poetic. Or Philip Barry: you might say some part of his genius was to capture the way a certain class of people spoke. He didn't know how those people spoke, but he was creating a poetic impression, creating that reality. It's not a matter, in *Lakeboat* or *Sexual Perversity in Chicago* or *Edmond* or my other plays, of my "interpretation" of how these people talk. It's an illusion. It's like when Gertrude Stein said to Picasso, "That portrait doesn't look like me." Picasso said, "It will." It's an illusion. Juvenile delinquents *acted* like Marlon Brando in *The Wild One*, right? It wasn't the other way around. It was life imitating art! So, in this sense my plays don't mirror what's going on in the streets. It's something different. As Oscar Wilde said, life imitates art! We didn't have those big pea soup fogs until somebody described them.[16]

The language of *American Buffalo* is, we see, adorned, overdone, the relentless swearing exaggerated for theatrical purposes. It may appear flawed with its extensive deployment of expletives, but when audiences understand Mamet's aesthetic – that his language functions as a kind of street poetry, a deliberately embellished dialogue – then the acerbity of the language takes on a non-realistic, metaphoric cogency. These three men, Mamet would concede, talk this way in *American Buffalo* to highlight the enervating influence their "business" has on their friendship, and on the spirit of the individual.

But there is something more to Mamet's language. There is a conspicuous gap or fissure between the spoken word and the enacted deed. Within that space between spoken gesture and meaning lies the satire, irony, and sense of loss that pervades the action of *American Buffalo*. Here Mamet's language assumes its thematic and cultural importance within the play. For Mamet downloads a multivalent language that gauges the intensity of these three men's desperation, their need for friendship, for community, for understanding in a world that increasingly sees them as cosmic evacuees and that denies them full entry into a civilized *polis*. A community so conceived is a rhetorical battleground. Revolutionary calls to arms and freedom, by the time Mamet stages *American Buffalo*, lose their authentic meaning, their social resonance, drained, as such calls are in the voices of Don and Teach, of any true mythic texture, any real enabling force. The audience hears, in the fractured syntax, the twisted logic, and in the inadequate words summoned by the men, some larger, primal void in their very existences. The rupture of language reveals the fundamental breakdown of a society whose inhabitants lack the vocabulary to describe the real, to understand that theirs is a demythicized world whose life-blood has long been leeched away.

In the contemporary world of *American Buffalo*, the characters struggle to find a basic vocabulary that adequately, or even remotely, explains their views accurately and honestly. A language devoid of its moral underpinnings too often, Mamet suggests, fills the stage. This is why for much of the play spaces open up which prove unbridgeable. Necessity rules. Irony is constantly reborn from the frustrated desires of those who obey compulsions they would wish to resist. Further, the language becomes part of the larger fictions the men create in order to confer some legitimacy, some importance, some meaning to their world that, shorn of such fictions, would reveal the gaps, the emptiness, the void that in fact defines their world of attenuated options. Police cars pass by, menacing the would-be robbers, though in all likelihood these cops could care less about these inept men. The men look to Fletcher Post for leadership within this scaled down mob-like family, only to regard him as a cheat at poker (it's only fitting that Fletcher never appears in the play, his mugging landing him instead in the hospital). They construct a set of fictions to mask their own incompletions. Teach, Don, and Bob inhabit that relatively small space between the real and the imaginary. So, on a metatheatrical level, the men in *American Buffalo* enact their own fictions, become their own writers, are consummate performers of leading roles that, in real life, they might never get to play. Christopher Bigsby is surely right when he suggests, "At the heart of all of Mamet's plays are storytellers whose stories shape their world into something more than random experience, decay and inconsequence. That is why even his most morally reprehensible characters command respect. They are in the same business as he is. They create drama and by so doing give themselves a role."[17]

"The Battle Hymn of the Republic" epigraph Mamet evokes in the published version of the drama is not without its ironic historical and cultural resonances. The original reads, "Mine eyes have seen the glory of the coming of the Lord; / He is trampling out the vintage where the grapes of wrath are stored." Near the beginning of the American Civil War, in 1861, Julia Ward Howe composed the hymn after she visited a Union Army camp on the Potomac River near the nation's capital. She heard the men singing a tribute to the abolitionist John Brown, who had been hanged in 1859 for his participation in an attempted slave rebellion at Harper's Ferry. The wife of a notable Boston abolitionist, Howe was impressed by the soldiers singing "John Brown's Body" and by its inspiring beat, and wrote "The Battle Hymn" to the same tune the next morning. The hymn appeared in the *Atlantic Monthly* in 1862, and quickly became the rallying anthem of the Union troops. Her words later bolstered the morale of American troops during the Second World War – and were sung at Winston Churchill's funeral; two decades later, civil-rights activists sang the defiant anthem during protests – and at Robert F. Kennedy's funeral. One week after the September 11 attacks, at a service at the National Cathedral in Washington, DC, the congregation joined one current and five past Presidents in singing the hymn, which was meant to brace Americans during times of conflict. Mamet's reconfiguration of the second line, however, foretells of the degradation of a nationally sanctioned Divine presence, which now motors around back alleys: "Mine eyes have seen the glory of the coming of the Lord. / He is peeling down the alley in a black and yellow Ford" (n.p.). The first line speaks of a patriotic nation, filled with glory and God's warnings about the dangers of slavery, but, in the second, such Divine presence travels, not down the nation's grand boulevards, but down its narrow and often dangerous back streets in a Ford whose paint job hints at death and cowardice.

Julia Ward Howe's mid nineteenth-century "The Battle Hymn of the Republic" foretold of a nation's emerging potency and supposed virtue; by the time we reach Mamet's mid twentieth-century version of the tune in *American Buffalo*, the nation, and the solidities on which the ideals of the country were founded, are in terminal decay. No wonder, in a play that asks its audience to reflect on both the country's past and its future, the American bison did not stand a chance. Hunted to near extinction, the once powerful and ubiquitous American buffalo now finds itself reduced to an image on a coin, which itself is as rare today as the animal. Interestingly enough, most published versions of the play display a photograph of the buffalo-head nickel on the front cover. Sculptor James Earle Fraser, who himself grew up in South Dakota and witnessed the slaughter of the buffalo, designed the images for the coin and regarded its circulation as a way to pay tribute to the Native American Indian. Fraser lamented the annihilation of the Native American and the animal on which the Plains Indians so depended. For Fraser, as for Mamet, history hurts. Fraser's models for the coin's image? Black Diamond was a 1,500 pound bison who roamed not the Great Plains but a cage in a New York City zoo. A few years after the coin was released, in 1913, Black Diamond, despite pleas to save him, was sold to a meat-packing company. Further, while many lay-people (like me) refer to the coin as a buffalo-head nickel, numismatists prefer to call it the Indian Head nickel. If one examines the flip side of the coin, one sees a rugged and noble Indian chief. Fraser actually used three different Indian chiefs to pose for his sketches, one of whom, Two Moons, a Cheyenne, was a warrior at the Battle of Little Big Horn, where George Armstrong Custer met his fate. By combining two key images for the coin – the Native American Indian on one side, the American buffalo on the other – Fraser felt that he fulfilled his goal to create a "truly American" coin, one that embodied a "perfect unity of theme."[18]

Beside the forehead of the Indian on the coin is the word "Freedom," and above the buffalo, along with the stamp of "United-States-of-America," appears "E PLURIBUS UNUM." The ironies embedded in any reflection of the plight of the Native American Indian, the buffalo, and the spiritual slippage of America Mamet seems intent on dramatizing, are too notorious to require much comment. Once the play is contextualized thus, one cannot help but see the tragic intersection and banalization of myth, history, commerce, genocide, and slaughter. A century of progress, indeed! Given such cultural intersections, and their competing historical narratives, Mamet's invoking of the coin, and its inscribed platitudes, along with his choice of it for the play's title, gives *American Buffalo* additional layers of irony, satire, and loss, and that image of loss, particularly, deepens into a metaphysical anguish.[19] The telescoping of myth and history, of culture and performance, also gives the play its purchase on our consciousness.

At the end of such plays as *The Water Engine*, *Glengarry Glen Ross*, *Speed-the-Plow*, *Oleanna*, and *The Cryptogram* (1995) audiences are taken by the lack of closure, by the sheer indeterminacy of the plays' resolutions. Questions linger. Uncertainties remain. An ungovernable Darwinianism seems to drive the men and women of these plays, their shared lack of discernible purpose the only graspable reality. At first glance *American Buffalo* fits the same dismal pattern. In the closing exchanges of the play, Mamet heightens a kind of dread that Hemingway captures in "The Killers" (1927) and an implied menace that Pinter enacts in *The Dumb Waiter* (1957). When Don calls off the robbery and begins to defend Bob; when Teach whacks Bob on the head with a nearby object; when Don attacks Teach; when Bob suddenly confesses that he lied about seeing the coin dealer with the suitcase; and, when, in the climax, Teach grabs the dead-pig sticker and trashes the junk shop, Mamet pushes the limits of friendship to the very outposts of civilization, the fabric of the social contract stretched so thin that these men "all live like cavemen" (103). For these three men, it is apocalypse now. Almost.

Ultimately, however, the ending of *American Buffalo* differs from those of so many other Mamet dramas, though it is a dissimilarity of degree rather than kind. But a key difference remains. For Mamet shifts the texture of the action in the play's denouement. The last three pages of *American Buffalo* contain twenty-three short question-and-answer exchanges. Its questions are first tactical, then metaphysical. Unmasked by their own actions and inactions, shorn of the fictional and dramatic world they have constructed this evening, the men – especially Don – realize they have just experienced a cathartic, cleansing moment, and now recognize the true worth of their friendship. Faced with the alternative – aloneness, abandonment, dread, aimlessness, loss, disconnection, rejection, and so on – the three reformulate their own minimal but important society amongst themselves. Honor amongst thieves is, perhaps, restored. This is a play that begins with men assuring themselves that they are not "mad" at each other (4) and ends with men voicing similar assurances (104–5). The fragility of friendship acknowledged, however awkwardly and without full comprehension of the reasons for such awareness, Teach, Don, and Bob reconnect with each other.

Teach, moments earlier so incensed at even the thought of taking the injured Bob to the hospital ("I am not your nigger. I am not your wife – 100), quietly agrees to get his car ("I'll honk the horn," he says, when he pulls up to the front door – 105). In a tightly formulated ending, Mamet echoes the opening moments of the play. Apologies are offered and accepted, forgiveness brokered. Even though Bob admits that he has "fucked up" (106), Don comforts the boy: "That's all right," he says as the lights dim (106). And it is Don, the tragic protagonist, who gains insight. At the play's end, he plainly acknowledges that it is he, not Bob or even Teach, who has "fucked up." Mixing self-disclosure with self-awareness, Don recognizes his sins of the past. By implication, he will work within his own emotional speed limits to restore order, loyalty, and perhaps even love to their world. Mamet captures, at the play's end, the importance of what George Steiner, in *Grammars of Creation*, calls the "endlessness of beginnings."[20]

It is possible to construct a bleak reading of *American Buffalo*. After all, Teach, Don, and Bob half-believe in a structure of meaning for which they can find little or no evidence. They display the rhetoric of a civic responsibility which their own lives deny. They acknowledge the need for trust and mutual responsibility while capitalizing on that trust and betraying that responsibility. These men fear solitude but distrust the other. They manufacture their social significance while inhabiting a society that in reality sanctions their invisibility. Don, Teach, and Bob are men who fail to break the code of their society, fail to acknowledge human necessities. They therefore work the fringes. Hence the necessary emphasis on preparing for the robbery, although Teach and Don are not sure how they will break into the man's apartment or how they will crack the safe. These men talk about the importance of preparation but do nothing to prepare for the robbery. "Action talks and bullshit walks" (4), Don councils Bob, but such purposeful action is nowhere in evidence. Dimly aware of the values they deny, the social contract they abrogate, they obey other imperatives, disconnected from their inner lives, inimical to their fundamental needs.

Such a bleak reading of the play, however, distorts its true emphasis. There is in Mamet's characters' misguided debates a fractured poetry; there is a nervous energy and a passion to the lives of those whose demons he stages. There is, at the very end of the play, an intensity, a resonance, and a power which lift them above their social insignificance. The men in *American Buffalo* are often consummate performers, accomplished story tellers, masters of deceit who implicitly challenge the nature of the real and hence the elaborate structures erected upon it. They may not always agree with each other in the alienated environment they inhabit, but they do make momentary contact within the fictions they deploy with such evident relish as if these constituted the real drama. Despite their intense fighting at the end, the men back off and, in backing off, they forgive, while in forgiving they create the possibility of a sense of love (however displaced, muted, and underappreciated) reasserting itself. In *A Life in the Theatre*, two men perform on and off stage, sometimes reciting lines written by others, sometimes improvising their own existences. The men in *American Buffalo* find themselves living within that same tension between the given and the constructed, the determined and the free. That, indeed, is surely, in part, the basis of their claim on our attention, for in that respect they stand as paradigms of a private, a social, and a metaphysical condition.

NOTES

1. Richard Gottlieb, "'The Engine' That Drives Playwright David Mamet," *New York Times*, January 15, 1978, p. D4.
2. Arthur Schlesinger, Jr., "Tocqueville and American Democracy," *Michigan Quarterly Review* 25 (Summer 1986), p. 495.
3. Matthew Roudané, "Something Out of Nothing," in Leslie Kane, ed., *David Mamet in Conversation* (Ann Arbor: University of Michigan Press, 2001), pp. 46–7.
4. *Ibid.*, p. 47.
5. David Mamet, *American Buffalo* (New York: Grove, 1977), p. 35. All further page references are to this edition and will be cited parenthetically in the text.
6. To Maxwell Perkins, n.d. (probably September, 1928), in Edmund Wilson, *Letters on Literature and Politics, 1912–1972*, ed. Elena Wilson (New York: Farrar, Straus and Giroux, 1977), pp. 149–51.

7. Roudané, "Something Out of Nothing," p. 49.
8. Harry N. Rosenfield, "The Free Enterprise System," *Antioch Review* 43 (Summer 1985), p. 352.
9. Schlesinger, "Tocqueville," p. 499.
10. Mark Zweigler, "Solace of a Playwright's Ideals," in Kane, ed., *David Mamet in Conversation*, pp. 17–18.
11. Roudané, "Something Out of Nothing," p. 48.
12. *Ibid.*, p. 120.
13. Terry Gross, "Someone Named Jack," in Kane, ed., *David Mamet in Conversation*, p. 161.
14. Henry I. Schvey, "Celebrating the Capacity for Self-Knowledge," in Kane, ed., *David Mamet in Conversation*, p. 65.
15. *Ibid.*, p. 67.
16. Roudané, "Something Out of Nothing," pp. 48–9.
17. Christopher Bigsby, *Modern American Drama, 1945–2000* (Cambridge: Cambridge University Press, 2000), p. 210.
18. This is from information gleaned from several web sites found on the Internet, searched under the term "Buffalo Nickel."
19. The ironies only deepen when considering the various American slang definitions of the word "buffalo," which most often carried negative connotations: in the mid nineteenth century "a buffalo" referred to, among many other derogatory references, a heavy-set aggressive man; by the 1900s one who was buffaloed was confused or "rattled"; and, closer to Mamet's day, the term refers to one who was intimidated or bluffed. For a more complete discussion of the uses of the term, see J. E. Lighter, ed., *Random House Historical Dictionary of American Slang*, Vol. I (New York: Random House, 1994), pp. 288–9, and Frederic G. Cassidy, ed., *Dictionary of Regional English* (Cambridge, MA: Harvard University Press, 1985), pp. 428–31.
20. George Steiner, *Grammars of Creation* (New Haven: Yale University Press, 2001), p. 13.

4

ALAIN PIETTE

The 1980s

With the onset of the 1980s, David Mamet was widely considered a powerful, yet controversial voice in contemporary American theatre. The decade would further establish him as a playwright of world stature and also as an extremely prolific artist at home in several artistic genres: drama, poetry, fiction, children's literature, nonfiction, and film. As the decade developed, so he was confirmed as one of the most original and important voices not only of his generation but also in the history of American drama, ranking alongside Eugene O'Neill, Tennessee Williams, Arthur Miller, Edward Albee, and Sam Shepard. It was in the 1980s, too, that the dramatist's reputation began to spread internationally, so that, by the beginning of the next decade, his plays were among the most frequently performed in the Western world, in English or in translation. His fame even extended to Asia, where some of his plays were performed in Japan, South Korea, and China.

The 1980s were also marked by a number of controversies surrounding his dramatic work. These were particularly symptomatic of the disturbing nature of Mamet's theatre: they had already started in the 1970s with his early *succès de scandale*, *Sexual Perversity in Chicago* (1974), and *American Buffalo* (1975), and were to continue well into the 1990s, in particular with *Oleanna* (1992). Mamet's theatre indeed tends to shock a certain part of the theatregoing audience for four major reasons: its alleged machismo, misogyny, violence (physical and verbal), and the Jewish cultural heritage that he claims for himself, especially in his most recent work.

The present chapter hinges on some of these controversial aspects of Mamet's theatre in the 1980s – which, as we shall see, are all intimately connected – not so much for their sensationalist nature as for the insights they provide into the most disturbing features of the dramatist's art, hence perhaps also its most interesting ones.

The 1980s began for Mamet with *Lakeboat* – like *Duck Variations* (1972), *A Life in the Theatre* (1973), *American Buffalo*, and the later *Glengarry Glen Ross* (1983), an all-male play. It was written in 1970 but revised extensively for production by the Milwaukee Repertory in 1980. *Lakeboat* provoked feminist critics with the sexist words of one of its characters, who observed that women are "Soft things with a hole in the middle"[1] (208). In the words of Steven Price, then, "They'd had this date from the beginning. David Mamet had been on a collision course with feminist criticism since 1970, when he wrote the all-male *Lakeboat* and began to develop the scatologically colloquial dialogue for which he would become known."[2] Such one-liners, though drained of this apparent sexism, abound in Mamet's plays and films, from Don's "Action talks and bullshit walks" in *American Buffalo* (150), or Roma's "all train compartments smell vaguely of shit" in *Glengarry Glen Ross* (26), to Margaret's "Beg for your life" in *House of Games* (1987) as she is about to shoot down the man who has conned her both economically and emotionally.

Lakeboat takes place on a merchant marine freighter on the Great Lakes. As one of its crew members puts it, it is "The floating home of 45 men" (189). The play offers a vivid description of the daily routine and chores onboard this enclosed locus, which functions a little like a surrogate home in much the same way as the junkshop of *American Buffalo* or the Chinese restaurant and the office in *Glengarry Glen Ross*. Boredom and irritation prevail. Indeed, even though some of the men are married and have a family ashore, they seem to prefer the dull life aboard, as real life seems even duller outside their rugged cocoon. They while away their boredom by telling each other tall tales, much as the salesmen of *Glengarry Glen Ross* will do, although for somewhat different purposes. The plot centers around the disappearance of the ship's night cook, to whom something may or may not have happened after he left the ship in Chicago. For all its discomforts, life aboard, with its all-male brawny comradeship, still seems preferable to anything else they know ashore.

Lakeboat shocked some – perhaps more so in puritan America than in Europe – with its litanies of scatological and sexist obscenities. Like the tall tales they tell, the coarse language of the crew members is essentially meant to vent their frustrations. As one of the characters says: "This is why everyone says 'fuck' all the time . . . They say 'fuck' in direct proportion to how bored they are" (204). Like his distinctive one-liners, Mamet's obscenities form a kind of thread through the playwright's earlier works and reappear sporadically in his later ones.

The very ease with which his characters resort to this obscene language, however, paradoxically defuses its power. Sheer repetition reduces a sense of shock that initially comes from encountering in the theatre what is commonplace in movies or on the street. Who remembers today that the language of

Edward Albee's *Who's Afraid of Virginia Woolf?* (1962) was a major factor in the commotion that the play initially caused, much more so perhaps than the marital battle at its center? Mamet's obscenities contribute to a sense of verisimilitude but they are also at the heart of a quasi-hypnotic rhythm. The actors whom Mamet has directed in his productions of his own work have spoken of his beating out the rhythm of the obscenities. The irony, however, is that such obscenities are far less effective in most of the translations of the plays.

Nearly all Mamet critics today, with the notable exception of the feminists, agree that this much decried language should be read at another level than simply the semantic one. For Mamet, indeed, the devaluation of language merely reflects that of the universe in which his characters evolve. Their idiom has returned to the elemental: it is that of a society that has returned to a certain form of primitivism. In this, Mamet is strongly reminiscent of the American comedian of the 1970s, Lenny Bruce, whose own excoriating and obscene language was both a comment on his society and a kind of jazz riff. Mamet's plays are sober and economical in terms of theatrical effects. His characters exist on the margin, the freighter of *Lakeboat* or the junkshop of *American Buffalo*, where they exchange barroom truths and inanities to fill the void of their existence. As the American critic Ruby Cohn perceptively noted, David Mamet's characters are "small people in a big . . . country."[3]

All the elements above blend in an almost perfect mix in what many believe is Mamet's most accomplished achievement to date, the much acclaimed *Glengarry Glen Ross*. Although a prolific writer, Mamet usually spends time, both before and after a production, making revisions. This had been true of *Lakeboat* and *Prairie du Chien*, written in 1978 and revised in 1985 for a new run in the US and the UK. It was true too of *Glengarry Glen Ross*. After "completing" it, he was still unsure and sent it to his friend Harold Pinter. Mamet asked Pinter what the play still lacked. Pinter answered that it lacked nothing but production and gave it to Peter Hall, then artistic director of the National Theatre in London. The play had its world première on September 21, 1983, at the Cottesloe. It was met with rave reviews, seemingly confirming the growing suspicion that American dramatists tend to be more popular outside the US than in their own country, even opening their plays in Europe. After its London première, *Glengarry Glen Ross* opened in New York and was awarded the 1984 Pulitzer Prize for drama. Its 1991 screen adaptation, with Al Pacino and the late Jack Lemmon in two of the major roles, went on to enjoy much critical and commercial success.

Glengarry Glen Ross has a terse, somewhat asymmetric two-act structure. The first act is composed of three successive dialogues that take place at different moments in a Chinese restaurant. This place serves as surrogate headquarters for a number of real estate salesmen. From the juxtaposition of these three scenes, we finally gather that business is slow and that most of these salesmen are struggling to stay afloat by any means: one of them, Levene, is trying to bribe his superior Williamson to give him the best "leads" (a term of the trade, meaning the best addresses of potential clients); a third man, Moss, tries to convince their colleague Aaronov to rob the real estate office in order to steal the leads and sell them to a competitor. Only Roma, the star salesman of the company, seems to be doing reasonably well: the third scene of Act I sees him on the verge of concluding the sale of some Florida land – in fact, worthless plots of swamp with grandiloquent names that give the play its title – to a prospective client named James Lingk. We soon realize that, as American critic Clive Barnes wrote in his review of the play in 1984, the salesmen of *Glengarry Glen Ross* in fact sell "unreal real estate."[4] But the most important piece of information in the first act is the announcement that Mitch and Murray, the owners of the company, have decided to organize a sales contest between its salesmen: the winner will win a Cadillac, the runner-up a set of kitchen knives, and all the others will be instantly fired. It is not hard to understand why the salesmen are scrambling to boost their sales by any means possible: theirs is the primal struggle for survival.

What emerges from these three scenes is the portrait of a real estate company and a company of men devoid of ethical concerns, the paradigm of a culture emerging from the so-called "me decade" into a decade in which greed was seemingly sanctioned as a value. It is a ruthless universe steeped in a Damoclean atmosphere of one-upmanship, where a handful of hard-up petty salesmen who talk like gangsters, indeed *are* gangsters, are ready to resort to corruption, lying, and theft in order to conclude the sales that will prevent them from getting fired.

The second act darkens the picture. It takes place in the offices of the real estate company itself. They have been completely ransacked: there is broken glass everywhere. Baylen, a police detective, is running an inquiry on the premises. As the salesmen arrive for work, we learn that the robbery planned in Act I has taken place and that the leads on potential clients have been stolen, together with the telephones and some petty cash. Roma proudly announces that he has finally succeeded in selling some of the Florida land to Lingk, his client of Act I. But he will soon be disappointed, because Lingk shows up at the office to cancel the contract under pressure from his wife.

Then, it is Levene's turn to appear: he too triumphantly announces that he has sold some land, which would put him temporarily ahead in the sales contest. But his joy is shortlived too: his colleagues tell him that the clients to whom he sold the land, the Nyborgs, are in fact crazy and simply like talking to salesmen. They sign the contracts and the checks, but the latter invariably bounce and the sales are promptly cancelled.

In fact Levene is the man responsible for the break-in, a truth which he inadvertently reveals to Williamson who in turn proposes to betray him to the police. He is now a broken man. Only Roma seems to offer solace. But this gesture, too, is only a pretense: as Levene is walking towards the detective to be interrogated, Roma demands a share of his leads and commissions. *Glengarry Glen Ross* offers a portrait of a battle for survival, a Darwinian struggle in which the salesmen offer a dream of possibility. In a play about real estate there is, in fact, very little real in *Glengarry Glen Ross*.

This is a play as much about performance as about selling property, as much about the stories the characters tell themselves and other people as it is about the desperations which generate the need for such stories. This is a play about trust and trust betrayed, about dreams cynically manipulated and refashioned to serve something both more and less than human need. Mamet's portrait of the business world is akin to that which he offers in *American Buffalo*. In a sense, like Teach in that play, the salesmen of *Glengarry Glen Ross* seem to believe that the American enterprise asserts "The freedom . . . [. . .] Of the *Individual* . . . [. . .] To embark on Any Fucking Course that he sees fit. [. . .] In order to secure his honest chance to make a profit. [. . .] The country's *founded* on this, Don. You know this" (*American Buffalo*, 221). Mamet knows this firsthand: he had briefly worked in a real estate office, as he had also worked for one summer on a Great Lakes boat. The characters of *Glengarry Glen Ross* are deprived of any human warmth and compassion and are constantly steeped in an atmosphere of fear, greed, and ruthlessness: the higher the pressure, the lower the ethics.

In some ways, *Glengarry Glen Ross* seems like an updated and more caustic version of Arthur Miller's *Death of a Salesman*. Both plays stage salesmen as their central characters. Indeed the figure of the salesman is a familiar one from American literature. But *Glengarry Glen Ross* takes us a step further than *Death of a Salesman*. Mamet's salesmen seem apt representatives of the Reagan–Bush–Thatcher era, which in turn prefigured the brutal downsizing of companies which characterized the 1990s. Mamet's salesmen are not simply the agents of a callous capitalism: they are also its victims. In this respect, the burglary of the office simply replicates the predatory values of the culture. *Glengarry Glen Ross* is also something more than a play about the human folly of greed, the attempt to trade one's soul for material advantage.

As several of his critics have suggested, Mamet is something of a moralist. His salesmen are not merely symbolic, as Miller's Willy Loman essentially was: they are also parodic figures. Richard Brucher has said, "As American culture persists in defining life economically, dramatic responses to social problems (and earlier plays) become increasingly caustic, ironic, and parodic."[5] In a sense this is a defining quality of Mamet's plays which are not best read as realistic.

The world of Mamet's plays is a dark one, though lit with humor. He offers a bleak vision of human relationships and social values. There is a politics to his work which generates a particular aesthetic. A degraded language both reflects and shapes a degraded self and the environment in which that self operates. Obscene and sexist language is an evasion, a displacement, an attempt to deny profound vulnerabilities. It seems aggressive and is oppressive, but that oppression conceals self-doubt, anxiety, an insecurity that cannot be confronted or annihilated. These are lonely people, solitaries who cling together in their fantasies as they are unable or unwilling to do in reality. There are glimpses of that need but they have elaborated strategies to deny its hold on them. They are actors performing their lives and offering these performances to others but also to themselves. Yet there is a hint of redemption. Indeed the very sense of vulnerability and need suggests that there is a level on which they feel, if not acknowledge, a gap between themselves and the lies they tell, the deceits they produce, the trust they abuse.

The tall tales that the salesmen conjure up, and which are a mark of Mamet's theatre, are central to his work. The salesmen of *Glengarry Glen Ross* in part wield these as weapons to con unsuspecting clients to buy their worthless mosquito-riddled plots of Florida swampland. One of the play's best scenes is undoubtedly that in Act II in which Levene, mustering up all his past experience as a seasoned salesman for perhaps the last time, comes to the rescue of Roma, whose client, Lingk, has come to the office to cancel his contract. Both salesmen stage an impromptu drama for the gullible client, and one quickly senses that, for all its improvisation, this scene is in fact part of their routine. For these salesmen are, indeed, also experienced actors, and, like the older performer in *A Life in the Theatre*, they assuredly know their *schtick*. For Mamet, indeed, the professions of confidence trickster and actor are in a way similar: both are about the creation and selling of illusions. This is quintessentially Mametian. As Christopher Bigsby appositely puts it, friendship is "little more than a momentary coincidence of interests"; "contact is momentary, alliance a fact of shared situation"; "Relationship, it seems, is a trap, communication a snare and friendship a means of facilitating betrayal."[6] The stories they tell, however, are not without their seductiveness, their energy, their occasionally consoling forces. Story is deceit but story is also, like the play itself, an entertainment and an oblique approach to both. A story may reveal even as it attempts to conceal.

As a particularly significant moment in the second scene of Act I indeed implies, the story telling in which the salesmen readily indulge has yet another function. Moss is trying to convince Aaronov to rob the office for the precious leads. In the face of Aaronov's hesitations, he resorts to a typically Mametian trick of language as a last attempt to persuade his colleague: he suggests that, even if Aaronov does *not* commit the burglary, he has now become *de facto* his accomplice in the crime "Because you listened" (26). Language, in other words, has a power independent of its lexical meaning. But Aaronov in turn, of course, seeks to coerce his clients, to ensnare them with a web of words. And what else does Mamet do with respect to his audience if not essentially the same? There is at the heart of this play and others an element of the metatheatrical.

If violence is largely verbal in *Lakeboat* and *Glengarry Glen Ross*, it becomes physical, indeed sexual, in *Edmond*, one of the most critically disparaged of Mamet's plays, one largely shunned by theatres, and generally disliked by audiences for its shocking content, as its scanty production history already indicates (though a production at Britain's Royal National Theatre in 2003 proved a considerable success). The play is composed of a succession of brief tableaux in which Edmond, the eponymous protagonist, leaves his wife to look for the (mostly sexual) satisfaction he apparently cannot find at home. He cruises through the red-light district of New York City where he meets a stunning array of underworld figures, petty criminals, con artists, crooks, pimps, and prostitutes. He is swindled out of his money by them until his growing anger and frustration drive him to kill a black pimp who was intent on robbing him, and later a barmaid he had picked up and who had taken him to her apartment. He is promptly arrested and thrown into jail. In prison, he is raped by his black cellmate but, in a surprising closing scene, finally seems to have found his peace: the curtain falls on Edmond tenderly kissing his cellmate while exchanging with him vaguely philosophical considerations.

The play's reception in 1982 was almost unanimously negative, a consequence no doubt of the shocking racist and sexist language with which the most violent scenes are laden. Many of the critics attacked *Edmond* for its disturbing, detailed, almost complacent depiction of its protagonist's slow, yet relentless descent into the hell of prostitution, gambling, and violence. Critics also stigmatized its fascination with degradation and obscenity. Many found it lacking in credibility. What, after all, had driven Edmond to leave the relative security of his bourgeois home and job, as boring and stifling as they might be, to steep himself in the horrors of a dark, dangerous, and cruel world that would ultimately bring him to his doom?

A few critics, however, praised the play for its audacity, its economy of expression, even in the most obscene scenes. There is surely a sense, however, in which, though *Edmond* is certainly not one of Mamet's best plays, it is nonetheless one of his most interesting works for the stage. Indeed, the sexual quest of Edmond in this seedy underworld can be compared to the quasi-picaresque one undertaken by the character of Everyman five centuries before, as many critics have already pointed out. The misadventures of Edmond in the red-light district of New York City also have some echoes of Dante's *Inferno*, Georg Büchner's *Woyzeck*, Maxim Gorki's *The Lower Depths*, or even Albert Camus's *The Stranger*.

The play is also reminiscent of Martin Scorsese's *Mean Streets*, in 1973, or his *Taxi Driver*, in 1976, or, perhaps more evidently still, Richard Brooks's *Looking for Mr. Goodbar* in 1977, whose female protagonist, played by Diane Keaton, has a perfectly honorable job during the day but prostitutes herself at night without any apparent economic reason, until one night she is murdered by one of her customers. But it is perhaps from the realm of painting that the best analogies suggest themselves. Thematically, Mamet's universe is strongly reminiscent of that of Jerome Bosch. Thematically *and* formally, the play is also very close to the essentially urban and nocturnal canvasses of Edward Hopper (1882–1967). Indeed, as I have suggested elsewhere,[7] I believe that the creative techniques used by the two artists are in many ways similar and that they both have wrongly been dubbed realistic.

Mamet and Hopper do not offer us a faithful reproduction of reality, but rather fragments of that reality as it can be perceived, for instance, through a keyhole, or through a window whose frame, together with the walls that surround it, makes it impossible for us to see the complete picture of the subject observed and forces us therefore to imagine the rest, the invisible, the unseen. The window must thus be considered as both an opening onto that reality and an obstacle hiding it from our view. The best example of this technique in *Edmond* can be seen at the moment when the protagonist enters a peep show where a bored strip dancer, caged in a glass booth, is simultaneously offered to the lust of the paying customers and separated from them by the glass screen. Windows also abound in Hopper's work: windows of trains, houses, barrooms, opening on a barely sketched, ever elusive reality. The most famous of Hopper's works is perhaps *Nighthawks* (1942), where we see through the window of a barroom at night three nocturnal customers seated at the counter. From a thematic point of view, this work, like *Edmond*, offers us a vivid image of human loneliness in the alienating environment of a big city. And this is where form and content coalesce and merge: the outside environment of the barroom, which we guess more than we see because it is hidden by the frame of the window, like the frame of the canvass itself, urges us to imagine other semantic associations.

Our own experience of a modern city invites us to see an obvious tension between the three customers seated at the counter and the bartender who stands behind it, alone. If we are indeed in one of those tentacular cities like New York or Chicago, in an almost empty bar in the middle of the night, is it not plausible that one of these customers, or all three for that matter, might jump the counter in order to hold up the bartender? The title of the painting itself, *Nighthawks*, already suggests this wild predatory behavior.

There is a similar scene in *Edmond*. After having been robbed of his money, Edmond seeks help in a seedy hotel, but is promptly denied assistance by the night receptionist who is obviously afraid of being mugged by this suspicious-looking man who has no money. Like Hopper's paintings, then, the scenes of Mamet's plays are fragments of a postmodern universe and are presented by a deconstructionist technique that invites the theatregoer to imagine the missing pieces to form a complete picture.

There is, in other words, more to *Edmond* than appears. Despite its apparent realism, it goes beyond the simple representation of a lower-middle-class man who, somewhat unbelievably, leaves his secure cocoon to steep himself in the lust and decadence of a depraved universe that ultimately engulfs him. Edmond is, rather, a modern-day Romantic monster, a larger-than-life figure who deliberately locates himself on the margins of a society whose rules he rejects. Conventional morals become merely anecdotal. He loathes his immediate society for its excessive materialism and opts for a marginal, a-moral, indeed immoral existence, which isolates him even more from his fellow men and ends up excluding him completely from their society.

Finally, and this is certainly where the perverse power of the play resides, Mamet forces us to identify with this odious character by almost equating us with him. In the peep show scene, the dramatist shows us Edmond aroused by the stripper and a promise of sexual gratification which eventually fails to materialize because of the obstacle of the glass screen. The promised spectacle is thus a sham and an illusion, just as its stage representation is for the theatregoer who is separated from the action onstage by the theatrical convention of the invisible fourth wall, which functions like the transparent glass screen that separates Edmond from the naked dancer. The powerless witnesses of an elusive reality, which they end up loathing, the audience, like Edmond, is deprived of any means to change that reality or influence it. Mamet thus forces the theatregoer to share the experience of a depraved character, much as the dramatist, by forcing us to listen to the sales pitches of his salesmen in *Glengarry Glen Ross*, in effect makes us their accomplices. This identification process was at the center of a recent production of the play in Brussels, in which the audience was literally invited to follow Edmond in his peregrinations through the underworld. The Théâtre Varia was divided into four major acting areas, respectively representing the street, a bar, a church, and a prison cell, all located in various places around the theatre. As the scene shifted to these four areas, so did the audience, whose sense of shock increased with each new step down into Edmond's inferno. The overhead projection of a documentary film about the red-light district of Brussels brought the finishing touch to the identification process the audience was forced into. Its main implication was that for the audience, no less than for Edmond, attempts to discover order in a chaotic universe were doomed to fail.

Indeed, in view of the final scene, which shows us the protagonist passively submitting to his fate after a brutal rape, the play's conclusion is particularly devastating. Edmond's malaise was not only sexual: it was also moral, onto-logical, existential. At the end of the play, resignation triumphs: Edmond gives up his freedom and human dignity. He finds peace and serenity only within the confined universe of the prison, where any attempt at asserting his individualism is immediately crushed by the ruthless and brutal environment that has become his sole horizon and that, by extension, has also become ours. Ironically, then, Edmond has fled a figurative prison only to enter a literal one. His vain attempt to discover meaning in the urban inferno of the underworld ends with the realization of his total impotence and his uncondi-tional surrender. Mamet, like Hopper, is reaching through the real towards the ontological and the metaphysical.

The year 1985 proved a turning point for David Mamet. His theatre, which had been criticized for its violence, its obscenity, its machismo, its misogyny, and its homophobia, seemed to open up to another range of characters, such as homosexuals and women (*The Shawl* [1985] and *Speed-the-Plow* [1988]), and later, in the 1990s, also to young women, children, and lesbians (*Oleanna* [1992], *The Cryptogram* [1994], *A Boston Marriage* [1999]).

The Shawl is a brief four-act play with an apparently simple, yet curious plot. The cast consists of three characters: two men, one woman. One of the men, John, professes to be a medium and, in the first act, we see him in action. A woman, Miss A, has come to consult him. He tells her about her past and her present, obviously impressing her with his power of divination, and the audience is – briefly – invited by the playwright to be impressed too. The second act, however, quickly reveals the true nature of John's "powers." He explains to his assistant/lover Charles how the divination session of the first act was in fact meant to lure Miss A and to set her up for a much more ambitious confidence trick. John's divination powers, which he himself dubs "seeming divination" (97), are in fact simple logical deductions that he draws from his clients' behavior, attitudes, or even physical appearance, as well as from their responses to his leading questions. Also, we gather that his experience – he calls it his "technique" (100) – in this particular business plays a major part too. He knows that most of the people who come to see him are in some kind of confusion and that their problems invariably revolve around three main concerns: "*money* – illness – *love*" (99).

In the second act, then, John explains the tricks of his trade to Charles. As John himself puts it, "I *show* you the tricks from the back" (102). This is something that Mamet himself did in *A Life in the Theatre*, offering a backstage perspective. The tricks, in this case, are in the service of greed. John is indeed intent on cheating Miss A out of as much of her money as possible, but the greedier of the two is undoubtedly Charles who insists on receiving his share of the money immediately after the first séance, without waiting for the larger con.

This larger con occurs in the middle of the third act. Miss A has come to consult John for another séance, in which he is to make contact with her deceased mother. In order to help the medium, she has brought a picture of her mother, which she puts on the table face down. John, assisted by Charles, creates an atmosphere of mystery and mysticism, which is supposed to condition Miss A favorably. The séance begins and John adopts an incantatory voice, whose rhythms are harmonious, soothing, quasi-hypnotic, much like that of some televangelists. After putting his client in the right frame of mind, John then gets to the heart of the matter and pretends to get in contact with Miss A's mother. The act, however, ends on a *coup de théâtre*. Not fully convinced that John is indeed endowed with divination powers, Miss A has herself set a trap for him. The picture she has brought is not that of her mother but of another person. At the end of the act, she can only conclude that John could not possibly have "seen" her mother. Her disappointment is only equal to her despair: "If you can't *help* me," she shouts angrily, "NO one can help me . . . why did I *come* here. All of you . . . Oh *God*, is there no . . . how can you *betray* me . . . You . . . you . . . God *damn* you . . . for 'money' . . . ? God . . . [. . .] May you rot in hell, in *prison*, in . . . you *charlatan*, you *thief* . . ." (112). The act closes on a last attempt by John to convince Miss A of his sincerity: he calls on some details of his "vision" that must seem genuine to Miss A, but we know them to be based in fact on his "technique" and also on Charles's research of Miss A's past and present private life.

This could be the end of the play, but with Mamet there is always a late twist. The fourth act begins with John's dismissal of Charles. After his departure, Miss A surprisingly reappears: she has indeed come to thank him after all for making contact with her mother. The details invoked by John at the end of Act III have carried away her doubts: John "saw" Miss A's mother wrap her in a shawl – hence the play's title – when she was little, and this is what Miss A has fallen for. John's "technique" has finally prevailed over Miss A's rational objections. But there is a further reason for her return. As John had earlier remarked, "I suppose we all want 'magic'" (100). The same impulse will drive Margaret to offer herself as a willing victim of a much more elaborate con in *House of Games*, for which *The Shawl* seems to be a small-scale dramatic preparation.

The Shawl may not be a great play, but it is an interesting one, not least because the characters seem to move in a different direction. Their sex or sexual orientation seems of little relevance to the significance of the play itself, although feminists will argue that the victim of the con is once again a woman. His next and last play of the 1980s, *Speed-the-Plow*, would underline the shift in Mamet's work with the appearance of a strong female character who fights her victimization with increasing energy and talent, as would one of the protagonists of *Oleanna* in the 1990s.

Like *The Shawl*, *Speed-the-Plow* features three characters, two men and one woman. It takes place in an environment that David Mamet had become familiar with: that of the Hollywood studios and show business. The 1980s were the decade in which Mamet made his first incursion into the world of film, first as screenwriter of movies directed by others – such as the remake of *The Postman Always Rings Twice* (dir. Bob Rafelson, 1981), *The Verdict* (dir. Sidney Lumet, 1982), *The Untouchables* (dir. Brian De Palma, 1987), or *We're No Angels* (dir. Neil Jordan, 1989) – and then as screenwriter of films he would direct himself, in that decade *House of Games* and *Things Change* (co-written with Shel Silverstein in 1988).

Speed-the-Plow takes place in Bobby Gould's office or home. Gould is a Hollywood producer and as the curtain rises we see him reading at his desk. He is joined by his friend and fellow producer Charlie Fox. Both men are in their early forties. Fox has brought Gould the script of a prison film, a "Buddy" picture he would like him to produce, a standard script about male friendship and violence in a prison, reminiscent of the prison in the final scenes of *Edmond*: in Gould's own words, "Action, blood, a social theme" (131). To Gould, the film seems to be a sure winner: "*You Brought Me Gold*" (133).

Gold or not, the studio boss cannot receive the men right away and pushes their appointment back to the next day. The option, however, is due to expire by ten o'clock the following day and Fox is afraid he might be cheated out of the deal. He reminds Gould that he could have "Gone Across the Street" (132), to a rival studio, as Gould himself puts it. Their appointment with the boss being canceled, the two men discuss the book on Gould's desk, a novel entitled *The Bridge: or, Radiation and the Half-Life of Society. A Study of Decay*. In his essay about *Speed-the-Plow*, Steven Price noted that Mamet himself had published a short story in 1985 under the title of *The Bridge* and that the short story's themes closely resembled those of the novel Gould is supposed to read: the end of the world in radiation or a nuclear holocaust (Price, "Disguise," p. 55). The book, scarcely a commercial proposition, is to be given a courtesy read. The two men deride it in front of Gould's secretary, Karen, who is temporarily substituting for his regular secretary. At first, Karen seems clumsy, unsure how to make an appointment or even to fetch coffee. As she herself puts it, thus prefiguring the character of Carol in the first act of the later *Oleanna*, "I don't know what to do. (*Pause*) I don't know what I'm supposed to do. (*Pause.*)" (145). The act closes on Gould and Fox as they prepare to go out for lunch, Gould betting his colleague $500 that he will sleep with Karen whom Fox insists is not "just some, you know, a 'floozy'" (148) or "so *ambitious* she would schtup you just to go ahead" (148). For Gould, the film is no more than a "commodity" (152). Karen seems much the same, naïve, a believer in the purity of art. He asks her to read the book and bring a report to his home.

The second act takes place at night in Gould's apartment where Karen enters a passionate plea for *The Bridge*, arguing that the prison film is "just *degradation*, that's the same old . . . it's despicable, it's . . . It's degrading to the human spirit . . . it . . . [. . .] this rage . . . it's killing people, meaningless . . . the sex, the titillation, violence . . . people don't want, they don't *want*, they . . . they don't want this" (163). The clumsy, inarticulate woman of Act I has turned, by the end of Act II, into an eloquent and skillful advocate for the end-of-the-world movie. The act closes on Karen's revelation that she knows precisely why Gould has invited her to his home at night and is perfectly willing to sleep with him. From a shy, subdued young woman, she has been transformed into a mature woman who knows what she wants and how to assert her personality, much as Carol does in *Oleanna*.

In Act III, Gould abruptly announces that he is going to abandon the prison film in favor of the film about the end of the world. As often in Mamet, the done deal of the first act is undone in the second. At first, Fox is incredulous and attempts to dissuade Gould from doing it, but he quickly realizes Karen's influence and recognizes that he has lost his bet. Their partnership comes close to dissolving, but Karen is revealed as an opportunist rather than an idealist. The two men are re-united and Karen dismissed. Order is restored in a male-dominated world at the expense of the only female character in the play.

Yet, *Speed-the-Plow* confirms the new direction that Mamet's theatre had taken in the second half of the 1980s. Although a victim, Karen is far from a submissive woman. By the end of the play she appears in command of her own career and life. Whereas the few women in the early plays (Deborah and Joan in *Sexual Perversity in Chicago*, Grace and Ruthie in *American Buffalo*, the sailors' wives in *Lakeboat*, Levene's daughter and James Lingk's wife in *Glengarry Glen Ross*, the woman in the subway and the prostitutes in *Edmond*, Miss A in *The Shawl*, etc.) were mostly distractions, disturbances, or annoyances, Karen, in *Speed-the-Plow*, is the first strong female character to appear in a Mamet play, a fact underlined by the casting of the pop singer Madonna in the role of Karen when the play opened on Broadway on May 3, 1988. The casting of the sulfurous "material girl" in that role, although ultimately backfiring because of what some took to be her limited acting range, was more than simply an attempt to capitalize on a pop star: it drew on her own image. More importantly, however, for the first time in Mamet's work, a woman had taken charge and sucessfully fought her victimization. Others would follow in the 1990s, the most prominent being Margaret in *House of Games* and Carol in *Oleanna*.

Beneath the alienation of his characters and the disjunctions of American society that he stages, Mamet is drawn to a sense of community – social, moral, religious. He seems to presuppose a time when the genders met across something more than an unbridgeable divide. Like some of his fellow dramatists, he seems to evidence a sense of nostalgia for a past that is partly mythic, seemingly unrecoverable, and which in truth may never have existed. Nonetheless, the plays owe their existence to the fact that there is, seemingly, still a sense of need, still a vestigial awareness of incompletion that makes the theatre – by its nature inherently communal – a fit place to explore a spiritual malaise which is undeniable but not, finally, absolute.

NOTES

1. All quotations from the plays are from the three volumes of collected works published by Methuen Drama, details of which are given in the list of works cited below.
2. Steven Price, "Disguise in Love – Gender and Desire in *House of Games* and *Speed-the-Plow*," in Christopher C. Hudgins and Leslie Kane, eds., *Gender and Genre – Essays on David Mamet* (New York: Palgrave, 2001), p. 41.
3. Ruby Cohn, "David Mamet," in *New American Dramatists, 1960–1990*, 2nd edition (New York: St. Martin's Press, 1991), p. 161.
4. Clive Barnes, "Mamet's *Glengarry*: A Play to See and Cherish," *New York Post*, March 26, 1984.
5. Richard Brucher, "Pernicious Nostalgia in *Glengarry Glen Ross*," in Leslie Kane, ed., *David Mamet's Glengarry Glen Ross – Text and Performance* (New York: Garland Publishing, 1996), p. 213.
6. Christopher W. Bigsby, *David Mamet* (London: Methuen, 1985), pp. 73, 79, 118.
7. Alain Piette, "In the Loneliness of Cities: the Hopperian Accents of David Mamet's *Edmond*," *Studies in the Humanities* 24.1 and 2 (June and December 1997), pp. 43–51.

WORKS CITED

Mamet, David. *Plays: 1 (Duck Variations, Sexual Perversity in Chicago, Squirrels, American Buffalo, The Water Engine, Mr. Happiness)* (London: Methuen Drama, 1994).
  Plays: 2 (Reunion, Dark Pony, A Life in the Theatre, The Woods, Lakeboat, Edmond) (London: Methuen Drama, 1996).
  Plays: 3 (Glengarry Glen Ross, Prairie du Chien, The Shawl, Speed-the-Plow) (London: Methuen Drama, 1996).

5

BENEDICT NIGHTINGALE

Glengarry Glen Ross

David Mamet spent part of 1969 in a Chicago real-estate office he has described as "a fly-by-night operation" trying to sell "worthless land to elderly people who couldn't afford it." He would first apologize for telephoning them at home, then tell them that his company's "international president" was in town en route to New York. This gentleman wanted to meet some of the people who had requested a brochure describing "beautiful home-sites in scenic/historic Arizona/Florida" and so might be interested in investing in them: "Your views on the property would be used to help guide our development and they would, of course, be kept completely confidential."

Mamet has also said that he was not very good at the job, because he could not help identifying with those he was phoning, but he clearly handed on a fair number of "leads" to salesmen who went to the homes of "prospects" for a "sit," explaining that the president had been unexpectedly called away to Dallas, Houston, or Paris. Those men were actually selling uncharted sand or swamp but could, he has said, have sold cancer: "They were amazing. They were a force of nature . . . they were people who had spent their whole lives never working for a salary, dependent for their living on their wits, their ability to charm. They sold themselves."

Not for the first or last time, he went on to draw on his memories for a play. Indeed, all that he set out to do in *Glengarry Glen Ross*, he has said, "was to write about my experiences in a real-estate office." That sounds disingenuous, since his own comments on both the play's content and its language make it clear that he wrote and meant to write something richer and more resonant than a documentary. Yet it helps explain one of the play's strengths, which is the feeling of authenticity it unerringly transmits. Here is Arthur Miller's Willy Loman at work in the 1980s: just as vulnerable but even more driven, even more compromised and distorted by the pressures of commerce and the harshness of American society.

Nearly thirty-five years separate the first performances of Miller's *Death of a Salesman*, which opened on Broadway in February 1949, and Mamet's

Glengarry Glen Ross, which had its première at London's National Theatre in September 1983; and the main similarities between the two plays are evident enough. Both dramatists see that archetypal American figure, the drummer or salesman, not only as the representative of a capitalist system which is ruinous to personal decency and to relationships but also as its victim.

Those who thrive in the market place are morally, emotionally, spiritually damaged; those who do not continue to thrive speedily become disposable. Naturally those classified as rejects protest, sometimes invoking the very values they have willfully or (in the case of Miller's Loman) unknowingly subverted, but they soon discover they are subject to the same laws of obsolescence that are applied to mechanical objects. They have as much worth as the once-flashy, now barely functioning fridge in the Loman household. They are disintegrating old bones in the dog-eat-dog society they have helped to perpetuate. Their very survival is at risk – and, indeed, Miller's Loman ends up committing suicide and at least one of Mamet's real-estate salesmen ends up broken and headed for prison.

Perhaps they are also ultimately selling the same thing. Nowhere in *Death of a Salesman* does Miller tell us whether we would find stockings or some other goods if we looked into Loman's sample-case. In *Glengarry Glen Ross* we know that Mamet's four salesmen, Roma, Levene, Moss, and Aaranow, are busy beguiling gullible Chicagoans into investing large sums in undeveloped Florida land which has been given an exotic Scottish name but is probably fit only for ants or alligators. But, as we have already seen, Mamet has reprised the wonderfully suggestive answer that Miller gave when he was asked what Loman was selling: "himself."

However, there are also differences between Loman and (Aaranow, as we will see, is untypical) Roma, Levene, and Moss; and they are not only the obvious ones. It hardly needs pointing out that Mamet's trio are socially more marginal, their aggressiveness greater, their scruples non-existent, that these men are observed with greater detachment than an anti-hero for whom Miller and others have claimed tragic status. They are never seen in their domestic environment, and so have even less chance to engage our sympathies. After all, Mamet was responding to the economic and social ruthlessness of Reaganism (in an interview in 1984 he explicitly compared the President's values with those of the world he had recently depicted in *Glengarry Glen Ross*), and Miller to a society he believed had been corrupted, if not yet irredeemably, by market thinking and consumerist ethics.

No, the aim of Miller's salesman is not simply to sell. The paradox is that, more than anything material, Loman craves respect, gratitude, cameraderie, love. He envies the old drummer whose funeral was packed with "hundreds of salesmen and buyers." It is difficult to speculate about the home lives of Mamet's salesmen, since only a few words from Levene suggest that any of them have any personal relationships at all, but at work they seek only to keep their jobs and make money, largely at each other's expense. Cameraderie, though sometimes superficially evident, is a sham and, often, a ruse. In Miller's 1949 the American dream was deeply compromised but still had its moral and perhaps even its spiritual aspects. By Mamet's 1983 it had become heartless and soulless, a Darwinian mix of unscrupulous competitiveness and greed. Willy Loman had been reborn as a small-time Ivan Boesky.

Admittedly, Mamet is an extreme and, as we will see, provocative voice. Some may object that a writer who, in effect, condemns Wall Street on the basis of some Times Square hustlers may not score top marks for either tact or universality. But whoever thinks it is drama's duty to be diplomatic, moderate, or unchallenging? The least that can be claimed for *Glengarry Glen Ross*, as some critics pointed out at its Broadway opening in 1984, is that it gave social edge to an American drama then so preoccupied with private matters that it barely acknowledged the existence of a world beyond the back porch. And the general view in both Britain and America was well summarized by Michael Billington's "a chillingly funny indictment of a world in which you are what you sell" and Robert Brustein's "an assault on the American way of making a living at the same time savage and compassionate, powerful and implicit, radical and stoical."

Some of those adjectives may surprise a reader of the play. "Funny" would seem to reflect the difference between Bill Bryden's cool, ironic production at the National and Gregory Mosher's Broadway version, which was more effective at evoking the anguished hysteria on show. "Compassionate" and "stoical" we will consider later. But on both sides of the Atlantic the play was regarded as exceptionally hard-hitting. I myself saw it in London and reviewed it on Broadway and each time felt it was as scathing a picture of unscrupulous dealing as the American theatre could ever have produced.

What gives *Glengarry Glen Ross* bite is not just that its salesmen are battling by mostly foul means to offload worthless property. It is that Murray and Mitch, company directors who remain safely offstage yet are frighteningly omnipresent, have introduced a system which means that those salesmen are not merely in competition but effectively at war with each other. The man who sells the most land will win a Cadillac. The runner-up receives a set of steak-knives. The other two will be fired. At the beginning of the play, it appears that Roma is just one sale away from winning. Moss is running second, followed at no great distance by Levene, followed by Aaranow, seemingly the least aggressive, dishonest, and therefore productive of the sales force.

The first act consists of three short scenes, each set in a booth in the same Chinese restaurant. These demonstrate how a successful salesman, namely Roma, softens up a possible buyer and how the less successful Levene and Moss behave when they feel insecure, threatened, and resentful. The second of these scenes also sets the main plot in motion. Moss wants to persuade Aaranow to raid the office, steal the "leads" (the names and addresses of the most valuable "prospects"), and give them to him to sell to a rival estate agent called Jerry Graff.

The burglary occurs in the interval, leaving the play's second act to deal with its aftermath. The office is in chaos – according to the stage directions, "ransacked, a broken plate glass window boarded up, glass all over the place" – and the leads are missing, along with phones and other equipment presumably taken to suggest to the police that this was not an inside job. But the detective on the case, Baylen, is not convinced. He interviews the staff in a side office and he gets his man. Moss persuaded Levene to carry out the burglary. Indeed, Levene ends up admitting to the office-manager, Williamson, that he stole and sold the leads. This is probably the play's least convincing encounter, since it depends on an experienced salesman, adept at every variety of slippery behavior, not merely failing to cover up a small verbal slip but giving way to uncharacteristic weakness, naïveté and trust. On the other hand, the incident provides yet more evidence of Levene's insecurity and decline.

Insofar as there is a subplot, it involves Richard Roma, who has spent the final part of the first act talking to, or rather at, a solitary fellow-diner called James Lingk. During the interval, he has been to Lingk's home and persuaded him and his wife to sign a contract for Florida land. For him, this is a reason for rejoicing, since it means that he has now won the office contest and the Cadillac. But then Lingk appears at the real-estate office, desperate to renege on an agreement to which his wife now fiercely objects. And just as it looks as if Roma's wiles will win back his buyer, an inept Williamson makes an interpolation which, to Roma's fury, ensures that the sale is lost – as, for now, is the Cadillac.

The play ends with Levene about to be arrested and Roma returning to the place where he discovered Lingk and presumably hopes to find other prospects. The play's last line, "I'll be at the restaurant," has struck some critics as a rather downbeat close to so hyperactive a play, but it is, of course, entirely apt. A crime and its solution change nothing. This sleazy operation will continue as before. Salesmen will have their triumphs and their failures; ordinary people will be duped and fleeced. It will take more than the odd arrest, suggests Mamet, to clean up something inherently corrupt, namely American business – and, since the business of America is business, America itself.

This is not the play's only subject. Perhaps it is not even what makes it most worth seeing and studying. As we will see, one of *Glengarry Glen Ross's* great strengths is its uniquely detailed account of the language of manipulation. It also has plenty to tell us about the experience of becoming and being that creature that, for good economic as well as social reasons, inspires such dread in America: the loser. But it is certainly worth re-emphasizing that Mamet's portrayal of his microcosmic real-estate office reflects, indeed embodies, his views about the macrocosm outside.

Again and again he has made those views explicit. Talking of *American Buffalo*, which appeared in 1975, he said; "The play is about the American ethics of business. About how we excuse all sorts of great and small compromises called business. I felt angry about business when I wrote it." The result then was a play about crooks who regarded burglary as "business" and in some respects were less unscrupulous than the more legitimate operators of *Glengarry Glen Ross*.

True, the main characters in both plays seem to have nothing but contempt for prey they are careful mentally to dehumanize. "I want to go in there and gut this motherfucker" says Teach, the thief in *American Buffalo*, as he prepares to break into the house of a coin-collector. Similarly, the "prospects" whom the salesmen of *Glengarry Glen Ross* try to trick into buying worthless land, especially "Polaks," Indians, and others who provoke their racism, are "fuckers," "cocksuckers," people whose "broads all look like they just got fucked with a dead cat." Yet the professional crooks of *American Buffalo* seem first to have to convince themselves that crime is no "shame" and that their victims deserve to be plundered – which is not a mental or moral step that the business professionals of *Glengarry Glen Ross* seem to feel the need to take.

So who are the crooks and who are the businessmen? Is there any fundamental distinction between the two? Or between trade and theft in capitalist USA? Speaking of *American Buffalo*, Mamet said that "there's really no difference between the lumpen proletariat and the stockbrokers or corporate lawyers who are the lackeys of business. Part of the American myth is that a difference exists, that at a certain point vicious behaviour becomes laudable." But *Glengarry Glen Ross* reemphasizes Mamet's belief that, not only is this not so, but the corruption and viciousness have been entrenched in American society almost from the start.

Both Levene and Roma are nostalgic for what the former calls "the old ways" of closing a deal: wily and devious but also risky and daring. Both have a particular contempt for Williamson, whom they see as a "secretary" or "white bread." He sits in the office distributing leads while they are out in the real world: in Levene's words, walking up to the doors of people they do not know and "selling something they don't even want." Roma goes even further. His myth of himself is of a frontiersman, boldly venturing where others fear to tread.

That is most evident when Williamson inadvertently contradicts a lying Roma by telling the frightened Lingk that the cheque he wrote out at the salesman's bidding has already been cashed. When Lingk runs out in panic, Roma turns on Williamson, calling him "a fairy," a "fucking child" and worse. "Whoever told you you could work with men?" he asks. Towards the end of play, talking to Levene, he makes his view still clearer: "It's not a world of men . . . It's a world of clock watchers, bureaucrats, office holders . . . there's no adventure to it . . . we are the members of a dying breed."

Through Roma, and to a lesser extent Levene, Mamet is surely invoking, questioning, and slyly attacking pioneer myths that he himself has explicitly disowned. Unlike his contemporary, Sam Shepard, who seems to hanker for an "old West" that has become corrupted with the passing of time and the invasion of the impure, Mamet believes that the old West was corrupt from the start:

> In America we're still suffering from loving a frontier ethic – that is to say, take the land from the Indians and give it to the railroad. Take the money from the blacks and give it to the rich. The ethic was always something for nothing. It never really existed when the American frontier was open . . . it never was anything more transcendent than something for nothing . . . the idea of go West and make your fortune, there's gold lying in the ground, was an idea promulgated by storekeepers in the gold rush and the railroads in the westward expansion as a way of enslaving the common man and woman . . . playing on their greed.

It is an ethic that gives Roma and Levene a gratifyingly macho rationale for playing on the greed of, and economically enslaving, the common men and women of modern Chicago. It also gives a spurious historic precedent for the jungle law which prevails in the real-estate office itself. Mamet has declared that "three cheers for me, to hell with you" is the operative axiom of American business. He has gone still further, saying that in a culture founded on the idea of strive-and-succeed, "your extremity is my opportunity . . . it's very divisive . . . Economic life in America is a lottery. Everyone's got an equal chance but only one guy is going to get to the top. 'The more I have the less you have.' So one can only succeed at the cost of the failure of another."

That, he added in the same 1986 interview, was the subject of "a lot of my plays," including *Glengarry Glen Ross*. And could there be a better way of dramatizing this than by showing the extremes of fear and rivalry engendered by a Cadillac-or-bust contest which, as Levene points out to Williamson in the play's opening encounter, soon becomes inherently unequal? The office manager's job is to give the "premium leads" to those salesmen who are already proving their worth by moving ahead in the competition. Anyone who falls behind has little or no chance of re-establishing himself since he is now given leads that the failing Levene sums up as "toilet paper." No wonder Levene begins the play badmouthing Roma, who is his protégé and the closest to a friend and admirer he has in the office. No wonder that, when a helpful-seeming Roma suggests to him they should become partners, it is evident that Roma intends to take most of the profits they make. No wonder it is an office where bribery and blackmail surprise nobody. For Mamet, quoting Robert Service to the effect that "there isn't a law of God or man that goes north of ten thousand bucks," the lure of money encourages cruelty while the tradition of something-for-nothing and "the myth of the happy capitalist" have promoted dishonesty.

He has also said, this time invoking Thorstein Veblen's *Theory of the Leisure Class*: "Sharp practice inevitably shades over into fraud. Once someone has no vested interest in behaving in an ethical manner, and the only bounds on his behaviour are supposedly his innate sense of fair play, then fair play becomes an outdated concept." And as *Glengarry Glen Ross* makes clear, this is not purely an individual decision. "The code of an institution ratifies us in acting amorally," Mamet has said, "as any guilt which might arise out of our acts would be borne not by ourselves but shared out through through the institution . . . if they are done in the name of some larger group, a state, a company, a team, those vile acts are somehow magically transformed and become praiseworthy." That is so much the case, he has said in relation to *Glengarry Glen Ross*, that "if you don't exploit the possible opportunities, not only are you being silly, you're being negligent."

Take that endemic attitude, very evident when Roma berates Williamson for telling a "truth" that is actually a miscalculated professional lie, add pressures – exerted by Murray and Mitch from their eyrie outside the office – which will inexorably lead to men being consigned to the trashcan at a time and (it seems) an age when re-employment will be tough to find, and it would be surprising if the salesmen were anything but conscientiously dishonest and deceitful.

So the play is not simply an exposé of ugly business practices that, fairly or unfairly, are intended to be exemplary. It also implicates an America that, as Mamet has said, is "a very violent society full of a lot of hate: you can't put a band-aid on a suppurating wound." But the play relieves the salesmen of some of their responsibility for egregious conduct. It re-emphasizes that, much as they exploit and abuse others, they are exploited and abused themselves. Aaranow, whom Mamet has described as the play's "raisonneur," seems to sense this; and not just because he is the least successful of the salesmen:

> Throughout the whole play he's saying, "I don't understand what's going on." "I'm no good," "I can't fit in here," "I'm incapable of either grasping those things I should or doing those things I've grasped." Or his closing lines, "Oh God, I hate this job.". It's a kind of monody throughout the play. Aaranow has some degree of conscience, of awareness; he's troubled. Corruption troubles him. The question he's troubled by is whether his inability to succeed in the society in which he's placed is a defect – that is, is he manly or sharp enough? – or if it's in effect a positive attribute, which is to say his conscience prohibits him.

Aaranow does not refuse to sell land he must know to be worthless nor does he fail to show interest when Levene implies he might get a job with a rival estate agent who is himself corrupt enough to agree to buy stolen leads. But when Moss suggests that Murray and Mitch are ripping off the salesmen, he defends them by pointing out that they have overheads to pay. When the office he refused to burgle is trashed, he worries about whether it is insured. And though he receives what he calls a "Gestapo" grilling from Baylen, he does not expose Moss. He has scruples, a sense of fair play, and a certain camaraderie.

Several critics commented on the powerful effect when James Grant, who played Aaranow at the National, used the word Moss carefully avoids: "robbery." His sudden candour, wrote Irving Wardle in *The Times*, "came like a blow in the face." The three other salesmen seem virtually incapable of such candor, let alone the other moral qualities Aaranow uncomfortably displays. Yet Mamet does not demonize them as villains any more than he sentimentalizes them as victims. In 1985, when an interviewer asked if he was "dumping" on the salesmen of *Glengarry*, his reply was robust: "I don't write plays to dump on people. I write plays about people whom I love and am fascinated by." And he went on to put the case even for the wintry Williamson, who, he said, was simply "doing the job of a sales manager," which was to "inspire, frighten, tempt, cajole and do any other thing he can do to increase sales." Mamet even defended the deceit and vindictiveness

Williamson displays to Levene towards the play's end: he is indulging in "the very human propensity" to assert himself over people who have spent the play abusing him.

Nor does Mamet's understated compassion end there. He shows, quietly and unsentimentally, that Levene has a good personal reason for panic. It is clear that he is already on the economic edge. In the opening scene he claims to have left his wallet in his hotel, so cannot pay his share of the restaurant bill, let alone come up with the $100 bribe Williamson demands for giving him better leads. Two words, "the gas," suggest that he cannot afford to fill up his car. Yet he has someone he cares for and uses as the basis for his plea for help both here and after the burglary: "my daughter," he says, with the written text italicizing the noun each time and on the first occasion demanding a "long pause" before the phrase. There are many pauses and silences in *Glengarry Glen Ross* for the actors to fill with emotion or mental calculation or both, and in this case one senses the vulnerability and pain of a divorced man (why else is a hotel his home?) who has lived precariously yet still takes pride in having put "my kid through school."

Mamet clearly also has mixed feelings about his salesmen when they are operating professionally. He may officially deplore nefarious behavior, but there is surely also a side of him that takes delight in the inventive energy of people – "a force of nature" – who must live off their wits or perish. He has said in interviews that he has personally sought out marginal, even criminal people, and relished their company. *House of Games*, a fine film about conmen, derives from just such experiences. Whatever his feelings about the abuse of frontier myths, Mamet cannot altogether resist a gifted buccaneer, which is what Roma is and Levene vestigially remains.

"The salesmen were primarily performers," he has said of the Chicago office where he worked: "They went into people's living rooms and performed their play about the investment properties." We see or hear several examples of this in *Glengarry Glen Ross*. Roma prepares Lingk for his sales pitch. In words that might almost be used by a Method actor ("I locked on them, all on them, nothing on me, all my thoughts are on them") Levene brings vividly to life a scene in which he sold no fewer than eight properties to a couple who, unfortunately for him, are notorious for signing contracts they cannot fulfil. And, most strikingly of all, the two men improvise a scene meant to dazzle, distract, impress, and win over the anxious Lingk. Levene plays a senior American Express executive called D. Ray Morton, eager to expand his holdings in Florida; Roma has become his family's friend as well as a trusted advisor; and they both are about to hurry off to the airport. It is bravura stuff, and might have succeeded in its aim, were not Lingk so frightened of his wife and had Williamson not been so incautious.

They are conmen, a class of person Mamet secretly admires. They are actors, for whose imagination and pluck he has a well-attested admiration. Perhaps one could also say that they are, in effect, dramatists. They marshal words and scenarios supposed to grip, please, and persuade and, like Mamet himself, they are dependent on their creative artistry for their living.

Glengarry Glen Ross offers us plenty of opportunities to anatomize that artistry, or attempted artistry, starting with Levene's first-scene attempt to persuade Williamson to give him better leads. His argument is that he is a fine salesman who is the victim of "bad luck," and should be helped through his losing "streak" because he has done excellent work in the past. He has, he says, made enormous profits for Murray and Mitch, once effectively paying for the latter's car and buying the former a trip to Bermuda: "Those guys lived on the business I brought in." But there is a major flaw in his argument. Levene is invoking triumphs in the 1970s, even in the 1960s, and this is a world where history, loyalty, and friendship count for nothing. You must succeed today, not yesterday. "Not lately it isn't" is Williamson's stony response to Levene's claim that his ability is greater than Moss's.

Levene runs down Roma ("he's throwing the leads away") as well as Moss ("he's an order taker") in a sales pitch for himself that becomes more angry and desperate as it continues. He tries to play on Williamson's guilt-feelings, his humanity, and, though he says he does not want pity or charity, his pity and charity. But subsequent events indicate that Williamson does not himself feel secure enough in his job to succumb to emotions that he anyway does not appear to possess. Cool though he remains, the office manager gives some sign of resenting the frantic, fractured hostility that, as if to prove himself a failure and a loser, Levene now seems unable to resist displaying ("you're saying I'm fucked"). In the end only a bribe will work – and, as we have seen, Levene cannot come up with enough money to offer an effective one.

The second scene suggests that Moss is, indeed, far the better salesman. He too fails in his aim, which is to manipulate Aaranow into carrying out the burglary of the office, but his skill is evident. He plays both on the sense of justice that, alone among the salesmen, Aaranow retains and on his unease and unhappiness in the job. The pressure created by Mitch and Murray is "too great." A competition weighted in favor of already successful salesmen is "not right." Moss even agrees with Aaranow when he adds that "it's not right to the customers." What he wants is to create the kind of consensus between them that Mamet had in mind when, in a 1997 interview, he recalled his own experience in that real-estate office.

It was, he said, vital to "keep talking, get them in the habit of saying yes, and then you've got them in the habit of accepting what you're giving them." In other words, Moss is successfully using professional weaponry against a fellow-professional. Having done that, he can move on to the next phase, which is to talk up the firm's rival, Jerry Graff, who is "clean," self-employed, and "doing very well." The first of those claims is untrue and the third questionable, but Moss has the assurance and force of personality to carry Aaranow with him.

Now Moss is ready to excite Aaranow's indignation. The two of them are slaves of people who, instead of building up their sales force, offer them meaningless prizes, treat them like children, axe them, "fuck them up the ass." "You're absolutely right," says Moss, bolstering their consensus by falsely implying that these criticisms were initiated by Aaranow, and moves a crucial step further. Someone should "strike back," that is to say steal the leads. And Aaranow has been sufficiently won over to ask an uncharacteristic question: "how much could we get for them?"

So Moss can warily move on, which he does with several lies. He pretends that he has not talked to Graff about the idea, though he has; he thinks each of some 5,000 leads might be worth $3, though it is soon apparent that the real offer is $1.50; he goes along with the comically false distinction that he and Aaranow are just "speaking" about the robbery as an "idea," not "actually talking" about it. Now that his fellow-salesman is thoroughly disorientated and somewhat compromised, Moss can replace his original lies with tempting new ones. They will "split half and half" what he implies is a total of $5,000 but appears in fact to be $7,500, with Aaranow due to receive only $2,500. And when Aaranow asks if Graff will give him a job, Moss subtly muddies his answer: "He would take you on. Yes."

By now Aaranow is not just compromised but incriminated. Moss is able to ask him to perform the break-in and, if he refuses, suggest that he will anyway be "an accessory, before the fact." "In or out," asks Moss; "You tell me, you're out you take the consequences." "Why?" asks his victim. "Because you listened" comes the brusque, brutal answer. The politics of the conversation have taken a final twist. Manipulation has become domination, and, though we later discover that Aaranow has opted for "out," we can see that the reasons he does not later inform on Moss, whom he must suspect of having done the burglary alone, go beyond residual camaraderie. A powerful, plausible threat has helped to silence him.

If that scene shows why Moss is ahead of Levene in the Cadillac stakes, the next explains why Roma is at the front. He can pick out a stranger and, then and there, prepare him for a "sit" and a sale. Much of what is virtually a monologue directed at Lingk seems irrelevant, and some of it even obscure, but that is the point. He, Roma, is apparently relaxing at the end of a long day and sharing casual thoughts about life in general with a friendly face. Not until the very end, by which time his quarry has been readied for the kill, does he move into salesman mode – and then in a way ("'Florida bullshit.' And maybe that's true") which offhandedly suggests that he is not especially interested in making a sale. He preempts future objections by flatteringly implying that Lingk will look skeptically at any attempt by him to do so.

But the whole monologue is actually purposeful. Roma seems to sense what Lingk's later behavior confirms. He is passive, repressed, and fundamentally scared of his wife. At any rate, Roma appeals to a side of him that is not wholly intimidated by conventional morality and maybe would like to assert itself and even take risks. "When you die you're going to regret the thing you don't do," says Roma. People cheat on their wives, have sex with little girls, and live with it. Flatteringly, he implies that the man whose macho self he hopes to discover and exploit is, like him, a world-weary stud: "The great fucks that you may have had. What do you remember about them?"

Like Moss with Aaranow, Roma is creating a shared sense of values, experience, sophistication, identity. Though the wimpish Lingk is all but silent, he is being cajoled into "the habit of saying yes." And now Roma must appeal to his conventional, conscientious, perhaps even guilty self. Having been lured into a fantasy of betraying his wife, Lingk is asked to think of disasters which include her death in a plane crash. Probably such fears are needless, adds Roma, but they may be realized, so it is reasonable to act boldly to increase one's sense of security. That way, disaster will find one not only prepared but strong and fearless. In other words, Roma is reconciling the opposite aspects of Lingk's personality by maneuvering him towards the paradoxical belief that to take risks is to achieve security: for instance, by investing sight unseen in Florida land.

It is a stunning feat, the more so for being so heavily camouflaged. Roma's spiel at the Lingk home was plainly effective, too, for only after he has left does Mrs. Lingk have second thoughts about the contract she and her husband have signed and send him to renege on the deal. And even then Roma is able to entice Lingk back into his clutches by simultaneously acknowledging the good husband and appealing to the suppressed man: "You have certain things you do jointly, you have a bond there . . . and there are other things. Those things are yours. You needn't feel ashamed. You needn't feel that you're being untrue . . . or that she would abandon you if she knew, this is your life." It is not surprising that Lingk effectively defies his wife by preparing to go for a drink with the salesman or that, told by Williamson that his check has been cashed, he actually apologizes to Roma ("I know I've let you down") when he rushes off in search of his money.

What strikes one is not just Roma's psychological insight. It is also his ability to exploit words that captivate, enchant, confuse, tantalize, nudge, convince, prompt action. Again, one sees the similarities between the drummer, who must persuade or perish, and the dramatist, whose own professional survival depends on the wit and skill with which he wins belief for fictional situations and (so to speak) passes off chimerae in Florida or Arizona as plausible realities. Mamet's accomplishment in *Glengarry* is to use a bravura way with words in order to sell us a vision of a man whose bravura way with words enables him to sell his own vision and, like Mamet, himself.

Actually, "bravura" understates the case, for the language in *Glengarry Glen Ross*, though often brusque and brutal, has a texture seldom found in American or English drama nowadays. Indeed, the play provides as good an example as any of a gift for dialogue that seems ultra-naturalistic, has been described by its author as "a poetic restatement of my idea about how people talk," and, by way of compromise, could be summed up as a form of naturalism so energetically and imaginatively colloquial it intensifies into a kind of poetry.

Always you feel Mamet is trying to replicate the minutiae of speech, with its unfinished sentences, its twists, its redundancies, its emphases, its muddles. Thus, Levene, exhilarated by an improbable sale says, "And, and, and, and I *did* it. And I put a kid through *school*. She . . . and Cold *calling* fella. Door to door. But you don't know. You don't know. You never heard of a *streak*." The speech reflects the vindictive triumph of the moment but also reflects Levene's impulsive, erratic character and chaotic state of being. This *soi-disant* winner, it suggests, is a loser on the brink of breakdown.

And, though the salesmen share an argot, they use language differently. The bullying Moss is blunter, more punchy, Aaranow more tentative, Roma more mesmerizingly canny and intricate. The very verbal mannerisms tell you why these men are placed as they are in the Cadillac contest. And at times the language of any of them, but especially of Roma and Levene, may become what is indeed a kind of brazen poetry: a gaudy, swaggering idiom which leaves you feeling that Mamet is the bard of streetwise barbarism, the laureate of the four-letter word – yet somehow still convinces you he is recording everyday speech in urban Illinois.

Nor is the poetry so hypnotic, or the ear for character so true, that the play's larger moral thrust gets even momentarily lost. Not only does the glitter of the language expose the trickery, help us analyze the allure, see through the wiles, and warn us of the dangerous wizardry of people – salesmen, politicians, dramatists – who covet our minds and menace our security, the language tells us that things could be different. Mamet has described America as "spiritually bankrupt." His interviews confirm what his plays implicitly and sometimes almost explicitly show – that he means this almost literally: "The spirit has to be replenished. There has to be time for reflection, introspection and a certain amount of awe and wonder." But what chance of reflection when people are as trapped and driven as the men of *Glengarry*? What chance of awe and wonder in a world where material wants and needs define and diminish virtually every human contact? Come to that, what chance of love when relationships with both colleagues and clients are ultimately hostile relationships?

The paradox is that in their very destructiveness these men's potential for constructiveness is evident. They use their creativity to con and ruin but, as Aaranow seems dimly to recognize when he ends the play with "oh god, I hate this job," there are better uses for creativity. A different society might have allowed Roma's mental and verbal agility, as well as his yearning for adventure and what C. W. E. Bigsby has aptly called "misplaced utopianism," to evolve in some new direction. Coming from some other socially aware dramatists – Wesker, say – this might seem a sentimental suggestion. But that is not an accusation easily directed at *Glengarry*, a play virtually unequalled in the quantitative and qualitative evidence it provides for moral dismay and grim social reflection. In any case, it is a matter of hint, inference, vestigial wishfulness. So Mamet is not the stoic that Brustein postulated in his review. He may espouse no political creed, demand no particular change. His observation may seem dispassionate. But he does not quite accept that the world of *Glengarry Glen Ross* is fixed and unalterable. He sees the loss. He laments the waste. He knows things could and should be otherwise.

6

HEATHER BRAUN

The 1990s

David Mamet's theatrical ventures throughout the 1990s reveal some surprising shifts in tone, theme, and dramatic form. Experimenting with various literary genres and historical venues, he defies stereotypes that confine him to the aggressively masculine world of such previous plays as *American Buffalo* and *Glengarry Glen Ross*. The impressive number of essays, novels, screenplays, and films that Mamet has produced and directed since 1990 might, at first, suggest a movement away from writing expressly for the stage.[1] It is during these years, however, that he crafts some of his most enigmatic and politically engaging plays to date. These were years of transition for Mamet as a playwright: he continued to revise such earlier tropes as the confidence man, precarious states of language and power, the art of teaching, homecomings and goings, and the picaresque. Yet throughout the 1990s and into this century, Mamet expanded his scope to include such controversial topics as sexual harassment, child abuse, lesbian estrangement, and ethnic identity. In his most recent plays, he is more willing than ever to provoke and unsettle, refusing to provide the comforting closure of transparent morals and simple resolutions.

Mamet's four major plays since 1990 are *Oleanna* (1992), *The Cryptogram* (1995), *The Old Neighborhood* (1998), and *Boston Marriage* (1999). Each explores how language can be used as a weapon that is far more dangerous than the guns and knives appearing throughout his films and earlier plays. Like much of Mamet's earlier work, these four plays use minimalist, staccato dialogue to show how everyday language can become "a potential door for chaos."[2] Similarly, verbal attacks often turn physical, sometimes instantly, when words fail to resolve confusion and potential disputes. In those moments when language begins to conceal more than it reveals, Mamet's characters frequently resort to violence, forcefully and often futilely trying to recapture the seeming control that their words alone cannot master.

The decade was heralded by a series of short plays and monologues: *Goldberg Street* (1989). *Five Television Plays* followed in 1990 and consisted primarily of brief episodes written for 1980s shows like *Hill Street Blues*. Then came *Oleanna* in 1992. It was first performed at the Hasty Pudding Theatre in Cambridge, Massachusetts. Here, as in London a year later, under the direction of Harold Pinter, it provoked intensely divided responses from impassioned viewers. About a year after its debut in the United States, the film version of *Oleanna*, directed by Mamet, sparked even further heated controversy over its portrayal of three separate encounters between a male professor and his female student: what begins as harmless "talking" soon catapults into charges of sexual harassment and verbal rape.

Oleanna consists of only two characters: John, a middle-aged college professor (originally played by William H. Macy), and Carol, a twenty-year-old undergraduate (originally played by Rebecca Pidgeon, Mamet's second wife) inquiring about her grade. All three acts are set in John's office. In Act I, the longest of the three acts, Carol is portrayed as hesitant and naïve in both demeanor and speech; as the play progresses, however, her seeming vulnerability turns alarmingly vindictive, a transformation from a timorous schoolgirl to a fast-talking, rabid feminist that seems more suspect than it does surprising.

The play appeared in the United States nearly one year after the Anita Hill and Clarence Thomas Senate hearings (see p. 124). Such an intense historical moment undoubtedly influenced the play's immediate reception: it became a focal point for discussion of sexual harassment and specifically the various types of power that are wielded, inverted, and withheld in the name of higher education. Appearing at a time when "sexual harassment" had become a particularly loaded term, *Oleanna* helped fuel ensuing debates about political correctness and the framing of harassment policies in academic settings. In a 1994 interview with Geoffrey Norman and John Rezek, however, Mamet claimed to have written *Oleanna* nearly a year before the Hill–Thomas hearings began; however, he later admitted to having been motivated by the hearings to return to the play and complete its final act.[3]

Many critiques of the play consider Mamet's depiction of Carol to be further evidence of his misogynistic habit of reducing female characters to submissive stereotypes or offstage threats to the ever-important business of male bonding. Such limited critiques, however, fail to account for the female characters who get even with the men who attempt to control and deceive them.[4] By emphasizing gender, these feminist-centered critiques also threaten to detract from other factors such as age, social status, and economic class that intensify the misreadings between John and Carol. Hence it is difficult to determine with certainty that Mamet sympathizes solely with either of these characters; at various points in the play, he appears to be speaking through both.

During Carol's first visit to John's office in Act I, the narrative is laid out and its two characters sketched briefly on the basis of intellectual, social, and economic status. John is planted firmly in the academic discourse: ironically, it is his experience of teaching the failings of the educational system that helps promote his success in it. He has just been (unofficially) awarded tenure and is about to purchase a new home "to go along with the tenure." Carol, however, is repeatedly denied entry into the world of Academy-speak, a world of privilege that John seems to believe belongs to him because of his achievements in his field. Unfortunately, the individual words and phrases he uses when he speaks to Carol make sense only within this specialized field of education to which, we soon see, she is repeatedly denied access.

John's personal demeanor complements his self-described duties as a professor. Hearing only one side of John's phone conversations, Carol becomes even more distanced from a discourse that has become virtually incoherent. The longer John speaks, the more confused and frustrated Carol becomes. John is quick to assure her, however, that her response is appropriate and even to be expected:

> JOHN: . . . that's my job, don't you know.
> CAROL: What is?
> JOHN: To provoke you.
> CAROL: No.
> JOHN: . . . Oh. Yes, though.
> CAROL: To provoke me?
> JOHN: That's right.
> CAROL: To make me mad?
> JOHN: That's right. To force you . . .
> CAROL: . . . to make me mad is your job?
> JOHN: To force you to . . . listen . . .[5]

Whether he means to or not, John continues to provoke Carol with pretentious language, dizzying progressions of thought and an abrupt, patronizing tone. The brief exchange above contains the language of provocation, anger, and "force," each of which is intricately connected, at least for John, to the art of listening. Ironically, though, John is far more proficient at demanding this skill from others than in practicing it himself.

Throughout Act I, John controls not only the progression of the conversation but the specific language that is used. One way he maintains control is to draw attention to Carol's inadequate use of language in her term paper; in doing so, he emphasizes his own ability to speak fluently a privileged language that is frequently lost on its primary audience: the students who are required to read John's book. Similarly, this first act highlights John's reluctance to give up power and his willingness to sustain the illusion that he knows beforehand what Carol will say and feel. John seems most uncomfortable at moments when he is forced to depart from his pre-rehearsed script. At the end of Act I, for example, he learns that a surprise party is being held for him as they speak. John mumbles sadly that surprises can often be "a form of aggression" (44), leaving Carol once again with no chance to respond to his cryptic statement: the act abruptly ends here. Yet even before John tells us that he dislikes surprises, we already know that he backs away from situations that interrupt his precarious control over a self-contained world of rote responses. By trying to avoid such surprises, John can maintain control over his own behavior and the authority he believes he has over others. This theory may hold for the first act of the play, but it shatters the moment we learn of Carol's surprise: her accusations to the tenure committee of sexual harassment and her request for John's tenure to be revoked.

At the beginning of Act II, John summons Carol to his office, apparently to answer aloud his own questions. During this second meeting, John continues to demonstrate a model of learning in which open discussion is nearly impossible. He avoids Carol's direct questions, and his long speeches manage only to reaffirm the imbalance of power between them. At one point during his monologue, John explains: "I find comfort . . . in exchange for what? Teaching. Which I love. What was the price of this security? To obtain *tenure*" (44). Without letting Carol respond, John reclaims authority by widening the distance between the knowledge-giving professor and knowledge-receiving student. Carol finally interrupts him with the assertive question: "What do you want from me?" Not surprisingly, John once again ignores the hint; rather than turning back to the charges against him, John continues to relate his feelings: "I was hurt. When I received the report. Of the tenure committee. I was shocked. And I was hurt" (45). Deaf to Carol's appeal that the charges are not about his feelings, John repeats his woes; Carol quickly drops out of the conversation, as though she had never even spoken.

In the film version of *Oleanna*, Mamet highlights the miscommunication between John and Carol and its destructive effects with visual devices that the script alone cannot offer. Mamet makes it clear that John (again played by Macy) is in control throughout Act I by highlighting certain physical gestures that will dictate the pattern of speech to follow. While it is unclear who has the upper hand in his personal life, John's professional demeanor suggests a power of speech that he is not afraid to use and an eagerness to express his opinion without necessarily defending it from behind his protective desk. As Carol furiously takes notes, John delivers effusive and pedantic monologues;

he answers his own questions and jots down personal reminders to himself. In the film's first scene, John primarily keeps his back to Carol, who continues to face him directly with confused and imploring eyes. John continues to talk as he grabs his jacket and leaves the office, all the while seeming to expect Carol to follow him.

It is not until Act II of the play and film that a transfer of power occurs: in the film, this transfer is explained visually when Carol begins to move more freely around John's suite of rooms, frequently raising her voice in exasperation and forcing John to look her in the eyes. There are also a series of doorway scenes in the film that are not referred to explicitly in Mamet's script. One character opens a door and another immediately closes it; power is being claimed and denied with the threat of closure as well as with the ability to prevent it. Carol opens the door to leave: "I came here to, the court officials told me not to come" (60). John hears this remark, asks what she means by "court officials," and then continues to push on with his meandering speech. Carol clearly knows something John does not, yet he leaves her no chance to reveal this information. Instead, with the door now closed, John tells her that he understands her pain, that he can help her if she would just let him.

In Act III, when all these words finally fail to convince, physical response seems the only option that remains. In a moment when words become most frustratingly insufficient, the phone rings. As John answers his wife's call once again, Carol grabs her coat, opens the door and suddenly stops. Carol's final remark as she holds the doorknob most radically breaks the divide between personal and professional: ". . . and don't call your wife 'baby'" (79). It is this which provokes the ensuing assault. It is only after the assault, when John lowers the chair from above his head and mutters "Oh my God," that these two characters finally seem to hear one another. "Yes. That's right," Carol twice observes, thereby ending the play.

Since 1992, critics have returned to *Oleanna* to consider how this play continues to confront the dilemma of finding and using words, particularly within specialized modes of discourse. Implicit and linguistic modes of authority are continually manipulated by both John and Carol: the ability to read situations accurately, for example, seems to decrease dramatically as formal education increases. In this way, acts of reading and misreading connect intricately to notions of social and political power, to who has it and how it can shift suddenly from one sentence to the next. In his updated edition of *Modern American Dramatists, 1945–2000*, Christopher Bigsby argues that *Oleanna* is "a reminder of the power of interpretation, of the fact that language defines the nature of the real."[6] One way that this play depicts this power is through the breakdown of verbal power into physical abuse, the one often disappearing easily into the other without warning.[7] Physical abuse, in much of Mamet's work, frequently occurs when misreadings accumulate and words begin to lose their force.

Other critics have tried to explain the connection between verbal and physical abuse by looking at specific "code words" of child abuse that arguably appear throughout *Oleanna*. Such focused discussions refute harsher readings of Carol as vindictive by referring to moments when she tells John "I'm bad" and "I have never told anyone this" (38), instances that may suggest yet another layer to Carol's misreadings of John's supposed gestures of sympathy. Nevertheless, by the third act of the play, these misunderstandings hold the most power as both John and Carol beckon mutely to the air, standing on two stages, speaking two markedly different languages.

Mamet's reluctance to attach a moral resolution to this play may further heighten the strong responses to issues such as political correctness and sexual harassment as audiences argued which of *Oleanna*'s two characters was ultimately to blame. Mamet claims, for example, that both characters believed they were correct and that the strength of their righteousness is what ultimately brings about their destruction.[8] Such assertions, however, failed even to tone down angry responses from playgoers who, like the characters of Mamet's plays, also resorted to verbal and physical violence against actors and each other after numerous performances.

While the branding of Mamet's male-dominated plays as misogynistic was established long before *Oleanna*, the play became an irresistible target for critics eager to prove that Mamet showed greater empathy for John, the unsuspecting victim, than for Carol, his naïve and vindictive attacker. Furthermore, Mamet's frequent allusions to Aristotle's claims about tragedy suggest that Mamet, too, was eager to produce fear and pity with devices such as character reversal and swift progression of action. In defense against these criticisms, Mamet insists that the play depicts a "fair fight" and that gender alone does not clearly distinguish the victim from the oppressor. In a 1994 interview in the *New York Times*, Mamet explains: "The play is not a candygram. It's not a melodrama [that] awakens feelings of pity for the person with whom we identify, and fear of the person with whom we don't. It's tragedy."[9] Perhaps if the play had appeared two years earlier, the events depicted might have seemed far-fetched, unlikely to escalate to such violent extremes as depicted in the play's final scene.

While *Oleanna* may be one of Mamet's most controversial plays of the 1990s, it is far from his only play to explore the dangerous imbalances not only between men and women but also between business associates, same-sex lovers, and even family members who possess radically different notions of success, commitment, and love. Mamet's next play,

The Cryptogram, presents an atypical household in which a quickly disintegrating family comes to terms with the truth of the past and its relevance
to their individual futures. Set in Chicago in the 1950s, this play depicts
three characters quite different from the pseudo-macho males of Mamet's
earlier dramas: Donny (a middle-aged mother, played originally by Lindsay
Duncan), Del (her gay friend, played by Eddie Izzard), and John (Donny's
ten-year-old son, played alternately by Danny Worthers and Richard
Claxton).

   The Cryptogram first appeared at London's Ambassador Theatre in June
of 1994, debuting in America seven months later at the C. Walsh Theatre in
Boston. Perhaps more than any of Mamet's previous plays, *The Cryptogram*
explores the slippery linguistic code spoken by adults in the presence of
children. As Donny and Del struggle to soothe and escape their own troubled
consciences, John is forced to comfort himself, retrieve his own blankets,
and accept answers that he knows are lies. John's repeated pleas for help
are rarely heard, granted only in an attempt to hurry him off to bed. Yet
it is evident throughout the play that John remains skeptical of Donny and
Del's efforts to appease him with empty promises and altered accounts of the
truth.

   Under Mamet's direction of the 1995 Boston production, the actors were
told to remain expressionless and to exaggerate already lengthy pauses in
the script. The play's repetitive and often bland three-way dialogue creates a
more pronounced distance between characters, many of whom can no longer
decode even their own sentences. Donny rarely speaks *to* her son; instead,
she muses aloud on topics a ten-year-old could not possibly comprehend. In
Act III, for instance, John tries yet again to talk to his mother by asking her
about her secret wishes. Instead of responding to John's insistent question –
"Do you ever wish that you could die?" – Donny explains to him that:
"Things occur. In our lives. And the meaning of them . . . the *meaning* of
them . . . is not clear . . .":

> JOHN: . . . the meaning of them . . .
> DONNY: That's correct. At the time. But we assume they have a meaning.
>   We must. And we don't know what it is.
> JOHN: Do you ever wish you could die? (*Pause.*) Would you tell me?[10]

Rather than interrupt his mother's monologue, John attempts to find something in it that the two of them can share. Sadly, her response to her son
remains consistent: she acknowledges his question merely by repeating it to
him.

   The line between verbal and physical violence is challenged to varying
degrees in both *Oleanna* and *The Cryptogram*. In *Oleanna*, this fragile divide

collapses in the final scene as John begins to detect his own powerlessness. In *The Cryptogram*, such violence is merely suggested in the final scene. First, Del wants to give John a knife because he believes it is symbolic of John's father's bravery in war. When Del does give the knife to John, however, it is to quiet him and to let him open a box. Rather than help him with the box or hold him because he is cold, Del and Donny remain preoccupied with a coded dialogue that John cannot understand. When Del hands the knife to John, Donny says nothing. Apparently, there is nothing left to say. The knife implies an eerie entrance into a wordless world of actions, one that John is forced to inhabit when he is shut out from coded adult-speak.

Like the knife, other tangible objects take on increasing value as words become unbearably elusive: a photograph and an old stadium blanket from the attic underline Mamet's insistent claim that change cannot be avoided, no matter what we may do to try to keep things the same. When John asks for a blanket, Donny responds with the troubling retort, "*Each* of us . . . Is alone." That John is cold seems no surprise to us since Donny remains absorbed in her own needs throughout, calling upon her son for parenting advice: "What can I *do* about it, John?" and in other moments asking him, "Can't you see I need comfort? Are you blind?" (90). Each time her questions are met with silence or the expected "I don't know," the audience may wonder why Donny cannot see her own failures and simply provide what John asks for.

The blanket, an object that might symbolize both maternal warmth and an unnamed moment in the past, remains buried in a box and tied with twine that John cannot break without the help of his father's old knife. This knife becomes an especially cryptic symbol towards the end of the play. On the one hand, it has a practical use: "to cut things" (65) and to extricate prized objects from their hiding places. On the other hand, it is also an instrument of violence that is connected inextricably to the past. Del believed this knife to be a token of war; when he learns that John's father, Richard, was a pilot and had purchased the knife on the streets of London, the knife is stripped of its symbolic meaning and becomes, once again, merely an object with a specific and practical function.

In his recent book of essays, *Jafsie and John Henry*, Mamet devotes an entire chapter to "Knives," informing us that he likes a knife "to have a story – that, after all, is the joy of collecting, to understand the story. The joy of use is to add to it."[11] Del gives John use of the knife without a story, an object reduced to its original function in the moment that Del hands it over to John. This gesture also reminds us of the deception that John learns by watching adults who fail to see him. *The Cryptogram* leaves us to ponder this final image of John holding the knife, trying to tell these two adults that he hears voices and cannot fall asleep. The play ends with this unanswered plea.

Recent criticism of *The Cryptogram* challenges the assumption that Mamet's later plays experiment with theatrical worlds no longer inhabited and controlled solely by men. Linda Doorf argues, for example, that *The Cryptogram* is preoccupied with myths about male identity that helped to construct Mamet's earlier plays. *The Cryptogram* works under the guise of a domestic or "family play" in which the absent father becomes the center of the play through the use of such symbolic objects as the knife, the photograph, and the blanket. While neither the boy nor the gay male come to embody myths of the emotionally distant male represented in earlier plays such as *American Buffalo* and *Glengarry Glen Ross*, *The Cryptogram* comes to express the futility of complete comprehension and the impossibility of escape from the "crippling fictions of male mythology" and the cryptic language they come to exemplify.[12]

Even in his earlier works, Mamet insists upon the often-indistinguishable line that separates needlessly confusing and pointedly provocative drama. Mamet's later plays, like many of his early ones, contain hardly any stage directions. Anything that fails to answer the driving question "What does the protagonist want?" is immediately deleted. Mamet's requirements for challenging and engaging drama include "cutting, building to a climax, leaving out exposition, and always progressing toward the single goal of the protagonist."[13] Mamet has remarked on several occasions that the best writing draws upon Hemingway's example of concision: "I always knew that a . . . good writer was one who threw out what most people kept . . . But then it occurred to me that a good writer is also one who keeps what most other people throw out."[14] As a result, this unconventional weeding out process often creates language that seems haphazardly obscure. Mamet rejects criticisms of his plays as "unclear" by suggesting instead that they are "provocative."[15]

He is quick to point out the benefits of provocation in drama. Echoing and amending Aristotle's call for tragedy that shows us something "surprising and inevitable," Mamet creates moments of potential tragedy that are also upsetting, disturbing, and inconclusive. Mamet's concern with provoking his audience rather than comforting them with easy resolutions is evident in the non-linear structure of his plays. Most begin *in medias res* and use pointed dialogue to indicate what has already happened before we arrived on the scene: the audience is immediately drawn in, asked to fill in the blanks in action that has occurred previously, and wonder at what actions will follow. This way, Mamet explains, their beliefs are not merely reaffirmed; they can continue to think about these uncertain scenarios long after they leave the theatre.

Mamet's next play was ostensibly more transparent than *The Cryptogram*. By decreasing even further the complexity of dialogue and narrative structure, Mamet gains more freedom and space in which to develop emerging themes of ethnic and geographic heritage. The notion of potential community and its varying degrees of dislocation are explored in considerable depth in *The Old Neighborhood* (1998), a trilogy of plays that suggests potential barriers that individuals must face when they return to the place where they came to know community. *The Old Neighborhood* consists of three plays held together somewhat loosely by the middle-aged character, Bobby Gould. In these three episodes, each only about thirty minutes in length, Bobby attempts to reconnect with his ethnic past and personal identity by returning to his old Jewish neighborhood of Chicago's South Shore. As Bobby talks less and less from one part to the next, his hopes of taking action or making a definitive decision also begin to dwindle rapidly. In the frequently insipid yet strangely poignant dialogue between Bobby and his old friend Joey, we begin to see how the wistful memories of a particular location can bring to the surface a cultural memory that has long since disappeared. Like many of Mamet's later plays, *The Old Neighborhood* calls attention to individual accounts of a more comprehensive, less visible ethnic identity implicit within these narratives.

Mamet's renewed interest in Judaism, informed further by his own childhood memories, is introduced explicitly at the beginning of the first part, *The Disappearance of the Jews*. This first play has been called the "pearl" of the entire trilogy for its subtle rendering of boyhood memories, as two old friends try to separate their idealized accounts of the past from the disenchanted reality that such ideals inevitably produce. Here, Bobby refers to his recent separation from his gentile wife. Characters reach out only to find connections to a past that never existed: "Because everything is so far from us today. And we have no connection."[16] As second-generation Chicago Jews, Bobby and Joey struggle continually to retain cultural identity as they become more and more assimilated into a world beyond the old neighborhood. Bobby's failure to connect with the individuals and distinct memories of his childhood becomes increasingly apparent as we move into the play's second and third acts.

The second play is entitled *Jolly*, Bobby's nickname for his sister, Julia, a neurotic and bitter woman who has clearly retained all the anger that she felt growing up. Jolly's perpetual, self-appeasing reliving of her painful childhood is sustained to an even greater extent by the repetitive, often vacuous exchanges between brother and sister. Jolly explains cynically to Bobby (or Buub, as Jolly calls him) that their hypocritical father is "learning – you're going to love this: He's learning to live 'facing the past'":

> BOB: Facing his past.
> JOLLY: Facing his past.
> BOB: Well, of course. Of course. That's how they *all* live. Facing the past.
> Facing the past. Looking at the past. *Fuck* him. AND fuck "counseling," is
> the thing I'm saying. (51)

The word "past" appears six times in this short exchange, reminding us of Bobby's own efforts to return to his past even as he supports his sister, repeating her opinions back to her and staying quiet as she continues to repeat herself. This repetition is especially effective since Jolly is incapable of perceiving her present situation without referring to pain caused by her insensitive, selfish parents. Jolly's inability to exist in a present uncontaminated by the pain of the past is emphasized further in her marriage to Carl. Jolly marries Carl to show her parents that a good man could, in fact, love her. Similarly, her relationship with Bobby is built heavily on his having seen what "they" did to her all those years. This isolation of an unnamed yet overpowering "they" will return in the opening and close of the final part of *The Old Neighborhood*.

In the third play, *Deeny*, Bobby meets up with his old high-school girl-friend. As Deeny talks incessantly and somewhat incoherently, Bobby hardly speaks. Incidentally, the speech attributions switch from "Bobby" in the first play to plain old "Bob" in the final two. This minor change seems also to reflect the marked shift in tone from the nostalgic recreation of the first act to the dawning detachment and disenchantment of the later acts. Throughout this final part, Deeny is half-present, musing over such disparate themes as a garden she will probably never cultivate, those "stupid *molecules*" that scientists are trying to make smaller, and, even more vaguely, the lingering pangs of regret. It often feels as though Deeny were giving a series of isolated monologues with occasional and brief references to Bobby's presence in the room. It is this unspecified distance between Deeny and Bobby, however, that gives a lasting effect to what may seem mere chatter; it emphasizes a longing to connect with something or someone, a desire left unfulfilled, ending as abruptly as it does despondently.

Throughout the third part, Deeny is unable to sustain her interest in practical matters of the present for long before lapsing into such pseudo-philosophical matters as the difference between longing and acquiring, love and mere convenience. In the opening lines of this final play, Deeny muses on having a garden of her own. She could watch her garden grow while drinking coffee and smoking cigarettes, two activities that, according to Deeny, help to "paralyze" and to "cut down" one's ability to "use the world" (91). She wants to create, to "force" or "bring out" the life of her imaginary garden, but she cannot move beyond the thoughts and words of desire to produce such life (92).

Near the end of the third play, Deeny lapses into more disjointed ruminations that emphasize the aloofness she feels in her present life. She has difficulty even talking about her work, her home, arguing that it is only significant to her. Such assumptions further complicate her longing for connection and affirmation, though she is far less likely to request Bobby's support than Jolly is in the previous act. The impossibility of community that Deeny perceives is especially evident when she abruptly asks Bobby, in the midst of this detachment, "How's *your* life?" to which he replies, "As you see" (96). Deeny's unforeseen reflection on those "tribes that *mutilate themselves*" also highlights the space between individuals who share no "ceremony," no "sorrow of years" that might "force" them to "surrender" themselves to a larger community, the tone of regret, "the old thing" that becomes a final transition back to the opening lines of what "they" have said about the frost. She again agrees with what "they" have said, though Deeny stipulates that she agrees "[d]espite the fact that they say it" (99).

Deeny and Bobby continue drifting "back and forth," wistful of the things they "could not have" and "the things [they'd] given up." Bobby occasionally answers a question with a dull or cryptic fragment. Deeny talks of "stupid *molecules*" that keep getting even smaller, helping to reaffirm the futility of one's search for finality. While she recognizes that she may never have anything but an imaginary garden, she sees it as "waiting, waiting, just beyond" (94). Deeny's depiction of growing up and growing old is both potentially hopeful and barren: the "we" of her musings are in a constant state of waiting for and "turning" away, perhaps from living itself. What was cherished in earlier years becomes worn and tiresome; passions are muted and grow cold from neglect. In the end, there is little left to say. Instead, Deeny and Bobby go back to their opening dialogue, reiterating what "they say" about the impending frost as they exchange goodbyes. The "cold comfort" that something will ultimately replace the love and memories lost over time lingers after the play has ended. In these final lines of abstractions and farewells, the imagined community of *The Old Neighborhood* dissolves, leaving two characters strangely united through a shared commitment to move forward, both aware that they can no longer go back.

Despite Deeny's integral contribution to the tone of this play, various critics have called *Deeny*, the play and the character, the "disaster" of the piece, primarily because she is such a difficult character to master. Such criticism may also suggest, however, just how significant Deeny is to expressing the larger crux of the play. Numerous actresses, such as Rebecca Pidgeon, have gone so far as to play her dispassionately, thereby neglecting the potential richness of her role in Bobby's homecoming. Such interpretations of Deeny's character, as well as reviews of *The Old Neighborhood* in general, focus largely on the superficial problems of plot posed by the unconventional organization and structure of the play. As we recall from so much of Mamet's earlier work, his plays require effort, encouraging us to draw conclusions about characters long after the play has ended. When we get to *The Old Neighborhood*, there are no confidence men, no crafty thieves or duplicitous masters of deceit to reckon with. The markedly unsentimental and, arguably, unsympathetic character of Deeny may offer one way of patching together the ostensibly disparate parts of this play. It is, after all, Deeny who seems to offer the most resolute response to Bobby's quest for a community of his past. By firmly rejecting the existence of such a community, Deeny tries to warn Bobby that he cannot go back, that nothing will ever be as he has left it or attempted to recreate it.

The Old Neighborhood can be seen as one potential link between Mamet's early work and his plays since 1990. Here, Mamet at first appears to introduce a sentimental component that is rarely seen in his earlier plays; it soon becomes evident, however, that this play is about the disappointments of nostalgia and the various ways in which it often fails to connect explicitly with notions of the real. Bobby attempts to go back, to bridge the gaps between his memories and his present situation. During this final exchange with Deeny, Bobby may begin to see that his memories of the past cannot save him from facing his fears in the present. His memories have separated from him, moved on as he has, and many are no longer recognizable. It is clear that throughout his conversations with Joey, Jolly, and Deeny, Bobby is worried about his own situation at home. Returning to *The Old Neighborhood* seems only to have convinced him of his lack of any solid roots in his present or his past.

Some of Mamet's most memorable characters have been revised considerably since 1990: his female leads, for example, are no longer portrayed as impenetrable threats to the securing of male identity; rather, they are often just as clever and aware of how to manipulate power as their unsuspecting male opponents. In the second half of the decade, Mamet introduces a variety of engaging female foils for his devious leading men, such as Margaret Ford, the female psychiatrist turned con artist in his film directorial debut, *House of Games* (1987). In *The Spanish Prisoner* (1997), Rebecca Pidgeon's unlikely "girl next door" character reveals that she has been setting the rules all along. Despite the controversy surrounding Mamet's portrayal of such highly strung, infuriatingly rigid female figures as Carol in *Oleanna*, these characters more often than not succeed at what they set out to accomplish: namely, to make sure that those in authority do not use their power to fix decisively the non-threatening position of those beneath them.

Boston Marriage (1999), Mamet's most recent play, departs from shifty con artists and subtly controlling heroines. The play, produced by the American Repertory Theatre and directed by David Mamet, debuted in June of 1999 at the Hasty Pudding Theatre in Cambridge, Massachusetts. According to the original program, *Boston Marriage* refers to a proto-feminist euphemism for "a long-term monogamous relationship between two otherwise unmarried women," the term first appearing soon after Henry James's portrayal of "New Women" in *The Bostonians* (1886). *Boston Marriage* takes us back to nineteenth-century Victorian England to follow the interaction and increasing isolation of three women: Anna and Claire, Mamet's sharp-tongued lesbian lovers, and Anna's maid, Catherine. Catherine endures Anna's merciless abuse and the apathy of both women, who continue their pretentious chatter despite her attempts to be audible and to correct them. Apparent to Catherine, though not to her supposed superiors, this ridicule reaffirms power contained within their higher social position: neither Anne nor Claire allows Catherine to forget her place beneath them.

When Catherine first comes onstage, neither Anna nor Claire acknowledges her. When Anna calls for tea, she casually calls Catherine by the name of "Bridey" and then ignores the maid when she attempts to correct her four different times. On the fifth attempt, Anna turns to Catherine and asks:

> ANNA: Not *Mary?* (Pause) Not "Mary," I said? Or "Peggy"? (Pause) Cringing Irish Terror, is it? What do you want? Home Rule, and all small children to raise geese? O . . . Ireland, each and all descended from kings who strode five miles of lighted streets in Liffey whilst the English dwelt in Caves. Is that the general tone, of your Irish divertimento? (Pause) Eh?
> MAID: I'm Scottish, miss. (Pause)[17]

This dialogue between the maid and Anna provides some comic relief from Anna's melodramatic monologues and the biting banter between the estranged lovers. At a certain point in the play, however, the maid's protests become intermingled with the whinings of Anna and Claire. This intermingling of loud voices becomes especially evident in the stage performance of the play. It is not until the end of the play, however, that we begin to wonder where authority truly lies within this triangle of voices.

While Mamet's characters may repeatedly ridicule one another, they rarely subscribe to purely patronizing tones. By steering his characters away from extreme or static personalities, he redeems them from being reduced to roughened, seemingly dull exteriors. The all-female cast of *Boston Marriage*, for example, recalls and contrasts sharply with the traditionally unsentimental male cast of such earlier plays as *Speed the Plow* and *Glengarry Glen Ross*. In these plays, female characters are rarely present on stage, yet it is nevertheless clear that these women do wield power over their men. As offstage characters, they repeatedly interfere with the masculine enterprise of deceptive language, business demeanor, and personal profit and are frequently portrayed as threats to masculinity itself, particularly in Mamet's pre-1990 plays.

Mamet's *Boston Marriage*, much like his adaptation of Terence Rattigan's *The Winslow Boy* (1999), explores a particular historical moment from an undeniably skeptical distance. In each of these works, Mamet keeps an eye on a not-so-distant past that continues to shape present and future attitudes and actions, even as he alludes to the contemporary social and political concerns shaping our understanding of this past. Half turning away from the masculine, street-clipped jousting of his earlier work, he begins to consider how a particular moment in history has "used language to mask its true intents."[18] As a result, his depictions of particular historical moments, of the appearances and voices of characters living in a specific sociopolitical timeframe, often feel excessive or even artificial.

Various critics refer to this artificiality when they assess Mamet's attempts to work with nineteenth-century settings. John Heilpern, for example, compares the flaws of *Boston Marriage* to those of *The Winslow Boy*, concluding from the juxtaposition that a true "sense of period isn't among Mr. Mamet's strengths." Heilpern goes on to describe how *Boston Marriage* in particular, which he sweepingly terms a "flying flea circus," does little to expand Mamet's previous female roles other than to show that women can be just as vulgar and cunning as men. "It's scarcely news," Heilpern concludes, especially when expressed through such "inconsequential" epigrams and a disappointingly "witless" Wildean touch.[19]

Boston Marriage is one of the first plays in which Mamet departs from his most characteristic writing style, termed "Mametspeak" by various critics of Mamet's earlier plays. Mametspeak – its tendency towards fractured dialogue and polysyllabic pretension – is still audible in this play. It is most noticeable in the play's occasional obscenities and its proclivity for long-winded detours and harangues. This familiar mix of clipped diction and clever one-liners sometimes clashes with the pretentious tone of these "kept" women. They are undoubtedly educated women, waxing eloquent to the point of absurdity on several occasions. The play's attention is directed primarily towards the pointed exchange between its three sharp-witted characters. Throughout *Boston Marriage*, we continue to hear the abrupt, back-and-forth banter of Mamet's earlier plays; its often anachronistic diction – a mix of antiquarian as well as colloquial word choices – makes it difficult to follow or believe the "stilted," murky exchanges among these almost "campy" Victorian women.

The disjointed and implausible quality of dialogue throughout *Boston Marriage* is most apparent in the private exchanges between Anna and Claire, particularly those in which the two heroines finish each other's sentences. In Act II, Scene i, Anna and Claire discuss a plan to remedy the earlier dilemma in Act I in which we discover that the necklace Anna's lover has given her belongs, in fact, to the mother of Claire's new would-be lover. In her proposal of "the Perfect Plan" to remedy this awkward dilemma, Anna suggests that she pose as a "Famous Clairvoyant," one of many flimsy attempts to explain how she has acquired another woman's necklace:

> ANNA: And he brought her mother's Jewel . . .
> CLAIRE: Say on . . .
> ANNA: In order to divine by it. (Pause) Whdja Think?
> CLAIRE: It is the least credible explanation of Human Behavior I have ever heard.
> ANNA: Of course. But you miss the point.
> CLAIRE: The point being . . .
> ANNA: That it is not to be *believed* . . .
> CLAIRE: Mmm?
> ANNA: Our tale is offered, but as a fig leaf of propriety. Not to "explain," but to clothe with the, the . . .
> CLAIRE: Mantle of decency.[20]

The above passage illustrates the various ways in which Anna and Claire create their own versions of the truth, suggesting just how far they might go to "clothe" reality with their own preferred versions. In this short exchange, we hear the familiar, fragmented aspects of Mametian dialogue, its give-and-take of agency and its quick and witty rebuttals. Anna and Claire, like many of Mamet's male characters, also recall the world of con tricks and cunning power plays typical of Mamet's former works, even if they are less than successful at pulling off their hypothetical scams.

In many of the exchanges of *Boston Marriage*, these women compete desperately to be heard, to correct false information, to be witty, or to wound with the most cutting response of all. Yet they rarely look at one another as they speak. More often, Anna and Claire look off into the darkened theatre as they deliver their lines, seeming neither to expect nor to desire a direct response to their musings. The result is often the feeling of three women occupying the same small space onstage but rarely acknowledging one another's presence. One memorable exception is the moment near the end of the play when Anna and Claire come together at the front of the stage. After both admit to being deliberately deceptive in order to keep the other around, they kiss. This is one of the few moments in the play that refers directly to the sexual as well as romantic relationship between Anna and Claire. And yet it is coldly, matter-of-factly executed in this final moment in which both women appear together before the curtain falls.

The 2002 New York Shakespeare Festival performance of *Boston Marriage* at The Public Theater, directed by Karen Kohlhaas and starring Kate Burton, Martha Plimpton, and Arden Myrin, received some less favorable reviews than the 1999 Cambridge première starring Rebecca Pidgeon and Felicity Huffman. Though the reviews diverge dramatically as to Mamet's flaws and potential successes, a number of reviewers concede that, despite its all-female cast, Mamet has yet to create truly plausible or sympathetic female characters. In this particular performance, Claire inflates her lines to such a degree that their ironic lightness often becomes lost beneath their over-pronouncement. Michael Feingold, in his review in the *Village Voice*, summarizes the performance as "archness posturing in a void, as if the 1890s were not a different time but a different planet, and women not an alternative gender to men but a different species altogether."[21] At certain moments in this production, Anna's melodramatic long-windedness becomes both distracting and exhausting. While she touches on some potentially engaging topics – the motivations of motherhood and the sadness of living retrospectively, for example – these topics quickly become lost in a series of pretentious allusions to the Bible, a mythical India, and chemical explanations for the Irish Famine.

David Kauffman echoes Feingold's assertion about the disconnectedness between Mamet's female characters and the Victorian world they supposedly inhabit. According to Kauffman, if *Boston Marriage* was, in fact, written to correct critiques that Mamet "previously avoided tackling female characters, it has produced the opposite effect."[22] The chameleon-like set – its frequent lighting fades from Pepto-Bismol pink to muted peach – further underscores the remote relations between and among these three women. Similarly, the Freudian-style psychiatric patient couch at center stage allows Anna and Claire to remain physically separated. Anna and Claire take turns sitting on the couch and then standing, pacing, and looking away from each other. Each of the three characters of *Boston Marriage* is at once alone and terrified of being left alone. Yet each attempts to hide or conquer her fears in very different ways. Anna becomes a mistress to a man who can afford to keep her and Claire living comfortably. Claire seeks companionship in the idealized form of a young girl who seems unaware of her intentions. Finally, Catherine talks of homesickness and desperation even as she finds solace in the arms of a fellow servant.

Reviews of The Public Theater production of *Boston Marriage* criticized its use of ostentatious or vulgar language that adds little to plot or character development. One reviewer called the shift between high Victorian prose and crude "dirty" banter "a game which engages the audience with its hard-to-follow cleverness, and tells you nothing interesting or intimate about its characters."[23] Certain lines, however, prove more memorable than others for their daring and clever diction. Anna, for example, slyly tells Claire, "Let me get my auger," as she implores Claire to let her watch the latest seduction of a young girl. Anna's cutting remark seems doubly appropriate against the backdrop of a nineteenth-century "Boston marriage."

Mamet's sparse style of playwriting is abandoned in certain moments throughout the play in exchange for lengthy harangues that feel more like pointless soliloquies. Anna, in particular, falls frequently into swooning sermons that have no apparent bearing on the present conflict between her and Claire. In such moments, the audience may secretly long for an interpreter to step onto the stage and explain to us the reason for these circuitous speeches. John Heilpern refers, for example, to the frustrating "tedium" of listening to these women "speaking in tongues or the dramatist's elaborately arch, blatheringly convoluted 'Boston-speak,'"[24] while David Kauffman suggests, perhaps facetiously, that the "contemporary theatergoer may feel greater need for an antiquarian dictionary than a program, in order to follow the story."[25]

Boston Marriage replaces the proverbial male exchange of plays like *Glengarry Glen Ross* and Act I of *The Old Neighborhood* with a very different kind of female banter in which desire and affection often become indistinguishable from jealousy and deception. By transforming the familiar clipped Mametspeak into a prim and proper Victorian verbosity, *Boston Marriage* mixes high society with the supposed crudity of lower-class diction, calling attention to social positions even as it exposes them as precariously arbitrary. The slips of the tongue and moments of near-illiteracy characteristic of Mamet's earlier work propel the plot forward, allowing it to unravel beyond the characters' ability to stop it. In *The Cryptogram*, Del allegedly lends his apartment to Donny's husband; he thus becomes an accessory to Richard's adultery and thereby betrays his friend, Donny. Similarly, Anna agrees to let Claire seduce another woman in her home if Claire agrees to let her watch the exchange. Big lies are heaped on top of smaller ones; high-class, self-righteous characters reveal self-hatred in their harsh criticism of others.

Like many of Mamet's earlier plays, *Boston Marriage* uses halting dialogue to present imbalances of power unmediated by language alone. This dialogue frequently "lurches between anachronism and Gilded Age archaism."[26] By avoiding the temptation to preach to his audience, Mamet lessens the likelihood of easy resolution of tension-filled moments that teeter at the edges of tragedy. While Mamet's affection for tragedy is visible throughout his career, his later plays begin to ask what it is about the tragic form that makes it both compelling and memorable. Throughout his career, Mamet continues to work in multiple theatrical forms, enter unexplored territories, and confront larger social and political issues. According to Mamet, a *tragedy* that relies heavily on individual choice will be far more riveting than a *drama* built solely upon circumstance that is beyond the scope of the narrative.[27]

Criticism of Mamet's work often mirrors the extremes represented in his plays. The harsher critiques call it non-dramatic, deliberately underwritten, and provocative without a purpose. One forthright critic attacks the pointless statements and shock-value sound bites of Mamet's *The Old Neighborhood*: "The dramatist of earlier, superior plays, such as *American Buffalo* and *Glengarry Glen Ross*, has long since settled for dramatically less. Mr. Mamet now prefers merely to provoke."[28] Others refer to Mamet's characteristically stark dialogue, minimal screen direction, and lack of character psychology.

Despite such negative criticisms, Mamet nevertheless succeeds at following his own advice to "get into the scene late, get out of the scene early" since playwriting is always a "working back and forth between the moment and the whole . . . the fluidity of the dialogue and the necessity of a strict construction."[29] In *True and False*, Mamet compares the sparseness of playwriting with the pointedness of joke telling: "In a well-written and correctly performed play, for example, everything tends toward a punchline . . . If we learn to think solely in terms of the objective, all concerns of *belief, feeling, emotion, characterization, substitution* become irrelevant. It is not that we 'forget' them, but that something else becomes more important than they."[30] Mamet's straightforward advice to serious actors becomes visible in his own plays, many of which he argues "are better read than performed"[31] since the dialogue tends to favor spontaneity and impulsive actions rather than premeditated, checked emotion.

Mamet's interlacing of individual lines of dialogue within a tight, larger structure is evident in his almost obsessive use of repetition. In *Staging Masculinity: Male Identity in Contemporary American Drama*, Carla J. McDonough discusses the reduced options for Mamet's male characters who can claim "a powerful masculine identity for themselves only within the moment of speech, and that space disappears the moment they are silent."[32] Mamet's obsessive use of expletives in plays like *Glengarry Glen Ross*, for example, supports the notion that words often delay characters from making decisions and acting upon them. Skillful talkers win the game and make the sale while mute and bumbling stragglers stay behind to recreate real or imagined moments of past victory.

In each of the four major plays of the 1990s and beyond, Mamet provides a sense of things moving forward, of progressive change seen through dialogue that can seem to go nowhere, leaving characters more confused about one another's ideas than when they began. Christopher Bigsby's synopsis of Mamet's earlier plays seems to unite his latest four aptly: in each, "[a]ction is character; action is also a language whose rhythms, tonalities, intensities, and silences generate and reveal crucial anxieties."[33] These later plays reinforce Mamet's enduring interest in the potency and failings of language, with the many different ways in which words can come to replace the need for overt action. In these plays Mamet continues to revise and expand his dramatic scope to incorporate such marginal characters as female con artists, neglected children, and estranged lesbian lovers into previously male-centered scripts. If the growth and experimentation of the 1990s is any indication of future maturity, Mamet's forthcoming projects are liable not merely to provoke us but to keep us guessing about his next move.

NOTES

Thanks to June Schlueter of Lafayette College for making this project possible.

1. Mamet has written and directed nearly twice as many films as plays since 1990, including *Glengarry Glen Ross* (1992), *Hoffa* (1992), *Oleanna* (1994), *American Buffalo* (1996), *The Spanish Prisoner* (1997), *Ronin* (1998), *The Winslow Boy* (1999), *State and Maine* (2000), *Dr. Jeckyll and Mr. Hyde* and *Lakeboat* (both forthcoming).
2. Jonathan Kalb, "Crypto-Mamet," *Village Voice*, February 28, 1995.
3. Leslie Kane, ed., *David Mamet in Conversation* (Ann Arbor: University of Michigan Press, 2001), p. 124.
4. In *House of Games* (1987), Margaret Ford (played by Lindsay Crouse, Mamet's first wife), a successful psychiatrist turned con-woman, is an apt example of Mamet's recent portrayals of female characters who cleverly wield power over unsuspecting men.
5. David Mamet, *Oleanna* (New York: Vintage, 1992), p. 41; subsequent references will appear parenthetically in the text.
6. C. W. E. Bigsby, ed., *Modern American Dramatists, 1945–2000* (Cambridge: Cambridge University Press, 2001), p. 233.
7. Richard Badenhausen, "The Modern Academy Raging in the Dark: Misreading Mamet's Political Incorrectness in *Oleanna*," *College Literature* 25.3 (Fall 1998), pp. 1–19.
8. Kane, ed., *David Mamet in Conversation*, p. 125.
9. Bruce Weber, "Thoughts from a Man's Man," *New York Times*, November 17, 1994.
10. David Mamet, *The Cryptogram* (New York: Vintage, 1995), p. 79. Subsequent references will appear parenthetically in the text.

11. David Mamet, *Jafsie and John Henry* (New York: Free Press, 1999), p. 55.
12. Linda Doorf, "Reinscribing the 'Fairy': The Knife and the Mystification of Male Mythology in *The Cryptogram*," in Christopher C. Hudgins and Leslie Kane, eds., *Gender, and Genre* (New York: Palgrave, 2001), pp. 175–90.
13. David Mamet, *The Paris Review: Playwrights at Work*, ed. George Plimpton (New York: Modern Library, 2000), p. 374.
14. Kane, ed., *David Mamet in Conversation*, pp. 151–2.
15. *Ibid.*, p. 125.
16. David Mamet, *The Old Neighborhood* (New York: Vintage, 1998), p. 33. Subsequent references will appear parenthetically in the text.
17. David Mamet, *Boston Marriage* (New York: Vintage, 2000), pp. 9–10.
18. Donald Lyons, "A Play on Language," *New York Post*, June 14, 1999.
19. John Heilpern, "Mamet's Latest Grand Scam: Sayeth It Ain't Soeth!" *New York Observer*, December 2, 2002.
20. Mamet, *Boston Marriage*, p. 74.
21. Michael Feingold, *Village Voice*, November 27 – December 3, 2002, p. 66.
22. David Kaufmann, "Mamet Goes Wildeing," *Nation*, December 30, 2002, p. 37.
23. Susannah Clapp, Review, *London Observer*, March 25, 2001.
24. Heilpern, "Mamet's Latest Grand Scam: Sayeth It Ain't Soeth!"
25. Kaufmann, "Mamet Goes Wildeing," p. 37.
26. Desmond Ryan, "A Comedy of Manners from a Man of the Streets," *Philadelphia Inquirer*, November 26, 2002.
27. Kane, ed., *David Mamet in Conversation*, pp. 118–19.
28. John Heilpern, *How Good is David Mamet, Anyway: Writings on Theatre and Why it Matters* (New York: Routledge, 2000), p. 226.
29. Kane, ed., *David Mamet in Conversation*, pp. 151–2.
30. David Mamet, *True and False: Heresy and Common Sense for the Actor* (New York: Pantheon, 1997), p. 82.
31. *Ibid.*, p. 64.
32. See Carla J. McDonough's *Staging Masculinity: Male Identity in Contemporary American Drama* (Jefferson, NC: McFarland, 1997), p. 99.
33. Christopher Bigsby, *David Mamet* (London: Methuen, 1985), pp. 13–14.

7

BRENDA MURPHY

Oleanna: language and power

Both elusive and allusive, the title *Oleanna* is a good introduction to the play's linguistic strategies. It was so bewildering to the first audiences and critics that David Mamet added the epigraph from a folk song he had sung at camp to the published version:

> Oh, to be in *Oleanna*,
> That's where I would rather be.
> Than be bound in Norway
> And drag the chains of slavery.

Oleanna was a nineteenth-century utopian community founded by the Norwegian violinist Ole Bull and his wife Anna: thus "Oleanna." This agricultural community failed because the land it had bought was rocky and infertile, and the settlers had to return to Norway. The application to the failed utopian dream of academia becomes evident as the play unfolds, as does the application of Mamet's second epigraph, from Samuel Butler's *The Way of All Flesh*, which suggests that children who have never known "a genial mental atmosphere" do not recognize its absence, and are easily prevented from finding it out, "or at any rate from attributing it to any other cause than their own sinfulness." *Oleanna* points out some of the most basic failures of American education and the long-term effects of the damage it does to young people. To say that *Oleanna* is about education, however, would be like saying that *Glengarry Glen Ross* is about the real-estate business. Mamet uses the education system as a vehicle for his perennial subject, what he calls "human interactions,"[1] in this case the ironic desire for both power and understanding in human relationships.

At the time of its première in 1992, and for several years afterward, the meaning of *Oleanna* was greatly influenced by a contemporaneous cultural event, the Senate Hearings on Clarence Thomas's appointment to the Supreme Court, in which the issue of sexual harassment took center stage. The play was widely thought to be "about" sexual harassment and the newly articulated cultural concept of "political correctness," and was even said to be based on the hearings, although Mamet has said that it was begun some time before they started. It was widely treated as a problem play about the ascendancy of political correctness in academia, the majority of critics agreeing with Harry Elam, Jr., that "Mamet decidedly loads the conflict in favor of his male protagonist, John, the professor."[2] One of the most quoted lines in the early critical pieces was Daniel Mufson's observation that "*Oleanna*'s working title could have been *The Bitch Set him Up*."[3]

Mamet has repeatedly resisted this interpretation of the play, first of all stating that it is not "a play about sexual harassment" and that "the issue was, to a large extent, a flag of convenience for a play that's structured as a tragedy . . . about power" (Kane, *Conversation*, p. 125). Secondly, he insists, "I don't take, personally, the side of the one [character] rather than the other. I think they're absolutely both wrong, and they're absolutely both right" (144). He told an interviewer that "if a play has any life past its being a *succès scandale*," it is because "it's provocative in a way larger than the issues" (144). Perhaps because of its early critics' preoccupation with sexual harassment and political correctness, *Oleanna*'s implications for the larger culture have only begun to be explored.

Although Mamet resists the idea that the play is primarily about education, there is no doubt that it is intended to contribute to a growing body of dramatic works that expose the power dynamics of the student–teacher relationship and the abuses to which it is prone. Several critics have noted *Oleanna*'s relationship to Ionesco's *The Lesson*, the seminal dramatization of the dangers inherent in educational power dynamics for the twentieth century.[4] Critics have seen Mamet as commenting, through John, on particular educational theorists or philosophers as varied as Friedrich Nietzsche, Thorstein Veblen, and Paolo Freire.[5] As Richard Badenhausen has noted, the play "offers an ominous commentary on education in America and more particularly functions as a dire warning both to and about those doing the educating."[6] As he points out, Carol proves to be quite a good student, for the real education she gets from John is in the art of "deception, dishonesty, and skepticism" that pervades academia, and she masters many of John's tricks, "including a penchant for intellectual bullying; an ability to use language ambiguously so as to get her way; and an outlook on the world informed by a deep-seated cynicism about human relations" (14).

Another interesting line of interpretation has been developed in the context of the late twentieth-century "culture wars." Marc Silverstein contends that, through Mamet's humanism, *Oleanna* "inscribes a 'cultural imaginary' that lends itself to articulation in terms of neoconservative social ideology."[7] Thomas Porter has read the play as a battle between the "postmodern ideologue" Carol and the fraudulently self-proclaimed "liberal humanist" John, contending, as does David Sauer, that the play itself is postmodern.[8] After the first wave of reviews in both New York and London, most critics have attended to Mamet's insistence that the play is primarily about power. The most influential critical approach has been Christine MacLeod's suggestion that "the narrow critical preoccupation with sexual harassment, political correctness and beleaguered masculinity in *Oleanna* has obscured what is in fact a far wider and more challenging dramatic engagement with issues of power, hierarchy and the control of language."[9] Shifting the interpretive ground from gender to language, she suggests that "gender *becomes* a crucial factor as and when Carol discovers that she can use the rhetorical strategies of sexual politics to change her position in the hierarchy. It is a matter of tactics, of deploying to best advantage the best available weapons" (MacLeod, "Politics," p. 207).

Mamet often introduces a key concept that underlies the meaning of a work early in the context of the action. In *House of Games*, it is the concept of the "tell," the key to the film as well as the con game. In *Glengarry Glen Ross*, it is the maxim "Always Be Closing," an epigraph in the play that he opens out to a long scene in the film. In *Oleanna*, the key concept is the "term of art," which Mamet foregrounds in the opening scene. As the play opens, John, an assistant professor in his forties, is talking on the telephone to his wife. The subject of the conversation is ostensibly a problem with an easement that has arisen in their negotiations for the house they are buying, although it is really a ruse to get John to come to the new house for a surprise party celebrating the announcement of his tenure decision. As he tries to calm his wife's apparent anxiety, he says, "What did she *say*; *is* it a 'term of art,' are we *bound* by it?" A few seconds later he repeats the phrase: "'a term of art.' Because: that's right."[10]

The student, Carol, having overheard the whole conversation about the house while waiting for John to speak to her, opens her conversation with "What is a 'term of art?'" (2). John, who does not really know the definition, tells her, "it seems to mean a *term*, which has come, through its use, to mean something *more specific* than the words would, to someone *not acquainted* with them . . . indicate. That, I believe, is what a 'term of art,' would mean" (3, Mamet's ellipsis). In a most fundamental sense, *Oleanna* is about the use and abuse of terms of art, specialized language or jargon which serves as the ticket of admission into restricted linguistic communities that confer power, money, and/or privilege upon their members. The linguistic communities in the play are those of real estate, academia, the feminist movement, and the law.

In Act I, Carol is seeking admission into academia, a community from which she knows she is excluded because she does not understand the language. As she tries haltingly to explain to John, "It's *difficult* for me . . . The *language*, the 'things' that you say" (6). Her reason for trying to understand the language is clear: "I *have* to pass this course" (9). She tries to do this by taking possession of the language she does not understand: "I sit in class I . . . (*She holds up her notebook*.) I take notes" (6, Mamet's ellipsis). She hopes that admission to the club, a passing grade, will come from following the rules that she hears John articulating: "I did what you told me. I did, I did everything that, I read your *book*, you told me to buy your book and read it. Everything you *say* I . . . everything I'm told" (9). Her demand of John that he "*teach*" her is a demand that he give her the key to understanding his incomprehensible book, "to be *helped* . . . To *do* something. To *know* something. To get, what do they say? 'To get on in the world'" (12). She is not, as she frankly tells him later in the scene, interested in what John thinks or says; she just takes notes "To make sure I remember it" (34).

What Carol fails to understand are the rather lame catch-phrases that pass for John's ideas about education: "Virtual warehousing of the young" (11); "The Curse of Modern Education" (12); "hazing," defined as "ritualized annoyance" (28). John's book seems to be little more than an expression of his own anger at the educational system in language that is acceptable to the academic community. Carol's statement in her paper, "I think that the ideas contained in this work express the author's feelings in a way that he intended" (8), ridiculed by John, is actually an accurate description of John's book, and his academic discourse generally. But because Carol cannot use the language of John's linguistic community effectively, he makes fun of her efforts, asking, "What can that mean?" (8). Within the rules of this linguistic community, Carol rather accurately gauges the effect of her inability to understand or use academic discourse: "that meant I'm stupid" (14); "you think I'm nothing" (13). What she wants from John, her teacher, is that he open up the mystery of the words she does not understand so she can get on in this world. Instead she is frustrated and mystified by "concepts" and "precepts" (14) that she thinks everyone in academia understands except for her. She thinks it is her situation in life that has excluded her from this linguistic community, which she describes, in terms that will be acceptable to John, as her "problems" and her "social" and "economic" background (8), factors that he nonetheless ignores in dealing with her as a student.

While Carol tries to convey her needs and desires to John, he is engaged in a parallel struggle to negotiate a new specialized discourse, that of real-estate law, which is making him feel as frustrated and unsure of himself as she is. The question of the "easement," which he is afraid will jeopardize first "the yard for the boy" (2) and then the entire agreement for the house (39), may be a term of art. He may be dealing with a reality that is constructed by a specialized discourse that he does not fully understand, a frightening prospect when his material well-being and that of his family are at stake. Like Carol looking to her teacher to demystify academic discourse, John looks to his lawyer Jerry and the realtor, initiates of this linguistic community, to put him at ease by giving him the knowledge he needs. Like Carol, he seeks refuge in possessing language, the notes on the transaction he thought his wife took, but is disappointed by their apparent inadequacy (1). At the end of the mildly disturbing phone call that opens the play, he displaces his desire to "take the mysticism out of it" (3) onto Carol, brusquely demanding "you have some 'thing.' Which must be broached" (3).

In the course of the first act, successively more urgent phone calls from his wife and Jerry make John more and more frustrated and unsure of himself. His insecurity is displaced through his increasingly hostile remarks about the education system and, by association, the tenure process that is his ultimate source of anxiety. He tells Carol that, as a student, he saw exploitation in the education process, that he hated school, teachers, and everyone in authority because he was sure he was going to fail, and that the tests "which you encounter, in school, in college, in life, were designed, in the most part, for idiots. *By* idiots" (23). Reverting to the real source of anxiety that has been awakened by the real-estate problem, he brings up the Tenure Committee, which is administering the current test for his full membership in the club of academia, and for whom he professes contempt: "they had people voting on me I wouldn't employ to wax my car" (23). He confesses to Carol his fundamental fear that he will be found out, that the committee will discover his "Dark secret," his essential "badness," and the corresponding impulse to preempt them by failing, "to puke my *badness* on the table, to show them" (23). Finally conflating his own sense of inadequacy with his feelings about academia, his "theory" of education is revealed to be just what Carol had said it was: "I. Know. That. Feeling. Am I entitled to my job, and my nice *home*, and my *wife*, and my *family*, and so on. This is what I'm saying: that theory of education which, that *theory*" (24).

It is at this point that John finally takes action against his feelings of inadequacy and frustration by refusing to answer the telephone and proffering to Carol the "deal" that subverts the rules of academia, that says he is in control, which is also the action that precipitates his downfall in terms of the play's tragic action. In response to Carol's questions about her grade, John says they will start the class over and that Carol's grade will be an "A" if she will meet with him on a tutorial basis: "What's important is that I awake your interest, if I can, and that I answer your questions" (26). When Carol protests that they cannot start over, John asserts control over the academic process through control of the words:

> JOHN. I say we can. (*Pause*) I say we can.
> CAROL. But I don't believe it.
> JOHN. Yes, I know that. But it's true. What is The Class but you and me?
> (*Pause*)
> CAROL. There are rules.
> JOHN. Well. We'll break them.
> CAROL. How can we?
> JOHN. We won't tell anybody.
> CAROL. Is that all right?
> JOHN. I say that it's fine.
> CAROL. Why would you do this for me?
> JOHN. I like you. Is that so difficult for you to . . .
> CAROL. Um . . .
> JOHN. There's no one here but you and me. (26–27, Mamet's ellipsis)

Ironically, this language, John's assertion of control over the teacher–student relationship, and, through it, over academia, is what leads to his downfall.

Mamet has described *Oleanna* as a "tragedy about power" (Kane, *Conversation*, p. 125), and, like any Mamet play, it is ultimately about "human interactions." The tragedy results from the fundamental failure of John and Carol to meet as human beings at any point in the three conversations that make up the three acts of the play. As Lenke Németh's analysis of the "adjacency pairs" in their dialogue has shown, neither has any interest in what the other character is trying to communicate. Each of them develops his or her topic independently, and the most frequent connection between them is contradiction.[11] In Act I, they essentially carry on parallel monologues. Their miscommunication is further fueled by the extreme self-absorption of both characters and by the fact that each is talking both to relieve anger and frustration and to get what they want, a passing grade for her and tenure, a house, and security for him.

In Acts II and III, the tragedy takes what Mamet calls its "shocking and inevitable" course (Kane, *Conversation*, p. 145), as each character becomes more entrenched in a potentially empowering position. John, attempting to manipulate the academic discourse that is his accustomed source of power, steadily loses ground to Carol as she becomes empowered by the language of her new linguistic community, her presumably feminist student "Group." John begins Act II by trying to assert his power over Carol through the language that has worked in the past in order to get her to withdraw her complaint against him. Describing his attitude towards teaching, he uses words like "heterodoxy," "gratuitously," "posit orthodoxy," "detriment" (43), words that could presumably be intimidating to Carol, who previously expressed difficulty with concepts such as "hazing," "index," and "predilection." As he had in the first act, John tries to appeal to Carol's humanity by building her sympathy for his predicament with the Tenure Committee; by cultivating a shared anger at the educational establishment; by suggesting that she has injured him, shocking and hurting him; and finally, by turning her own complaint back on her, insisting that he does not understand what she is telling him.

His strategies prove ineffective, as Carol takes control of the dialogue. Instead of confessing her ignorance of the meaning of academic words, she demands that non-specialized terms be substituted, such as "model" for "paradigm" (45). And this time it is Carol who refuses to engage with the human distress before her and, like John in the first act, demands "What do you want of me?" (45). When John hedges and obfuscates, talking about "the spirit of *investigation*," and saying "I suppose, how I can make amends . . . It's pointless, really" (46), Carol baldly states that he has asked her there to bribe her, to convince her, to force her to retract (46). When John demurs from her formulations, she counters with "I have my notes" (47). Thus her note-taking, which John took as a sign of submission, or "obeisance," in Act I, is transformed into a sign of power.

As John reads Carol's statement to the Tenure Committee, prepared with the help of her Group, it becomes clear that the terminology of this linguistic community constitutes an interpretive framework that is powerful enough to construct a meaning for his actions entirely at odds with his understanding of them. Actions which to him seemed innocent have become sexist, elitist, and pornographic. His saying he "liked" Carol has become harassment of her. Carol denies his right to determine the meaning of his actions: "you think you can deny that these things happened; or, if they *did*, if they *did*, that they meant what you *said* they meant" (48). Her applying her "own words" to these events transforms their meaning and gives her control over them and him. Having found her source of power within the institution, Carol declares her independence from John, no longer needing him to provide her with the key to linguistic power: "I don't think that I need your help. I don't think I need anything you have" (49). She denies his power to demand her attention or to make a claim on her empathy: "I don't *care* what you feel. Do you see? DO YOU SEE? You can't *do* that anymore. You. Do. Not. Have. The. Power." (50). Insisting on employing her linguistic community's words and not his, she constitutes his thoughtless comment about the Tenure Committee's being "good men and true" as "a demeaning remark. It is a sexist remark, and to overlook it is to countenance continuation of that method of thought" (51).

Having established her own power, she goes on to name John's actions: "You love the Power. To *deviate*. To *invent*, to transgress . . . to *transgress* whatever norms have been established for us" (52, Mamet's ellipsis), while at the same time he profits from the system. Carol names John "vile" and "exploitative." It becomes clear that, in assuming her anger arises from the same resentment of authority as his does, John has completely misunderstood Carol. Carol does not object to authority or to the institutions that wield power, she simply wants access to them. Her objection to John is that he tries to deny that *he* is wielding power and is making *her* feel bad for doing so.

After his failure to seize control through academic mystification, John tries to keep the discourse within the terms of the vague humanism he is comfortable with, trying to create a commonality of feeling with Carol by using terms such as "hurt," "angry," "upset." When this fails, he tries to appeal to a broader common humanity through the linguistic ploy of starting with the formula, "Good day," and moving towards the principle that "I don't think we can proceed until we accept that each of us is human" (54). When Carol's reversion to the stuttering articulation of Act I indicates that John is making inroads on her position and he becomes somewhat patronizing about her Group, Mamet once again intervenes with a phone call, now raising a real question that might make him lose his house. John makes an unknowing but fatal self-revelation by telling his wife not to worry because he is "dealing with the complaint" (55), demonstrating to Carol that his purpose in asking her there, to get her to recant, has not changed. After the phone call, Carol draws back into the security of the "'conventional' process," the forms of institutional authority with which she is comfortable. As she is about to slip away, John seals his doom by using the one form of power he is still sure of and physically restraining her. Carol's resistance, through language, appeals to institutional authority and, by its formulation, constitutes John's action as an assault: "LET ME GO. LET ME GO. WOULD SOMEBODY *HELP* ME? WOULD SOMEBODY *HELP* ME PLEASE . . .?" (57, Mamet's ellipsis).

As Act III opens, Carol has clearly won the linguistic power struggle between them. It is her definition of reality that operates, and she is in power. Again it is she who asks John what he wants, and he requests that she hear him out, saying that it will put him in her debt. Her linguistic control is indicated by John's accession to her insistence that he not call the charges against him "accusations" but "facts": "They have been *proved*. They are facts . . . those are not 'accusations'" (62). She shows no insecurity at not understanding the word "indictment," but insists, "you will have to explain that word to me" (63). When John uses the word "alleged," she says "I cannot allow that" (63). She insists on an authority derived from John's "superiors" in defining him as "negligent," "guilty," "found wanting," and "in error." Brushing aside his appeal to her humanity, "they're going to discharge me" (64), she says flatly that he is responsible for his position, and that she will not recant. Assuming complete control over the language of their communication, she tells him to use the word "happen" instead of "transpire": "*say* it. For Christ's sake. Who the *hell* do you think that you are?" (66).

Foreshadowing the ending of the play, she names as rape the exploitation of his "paternal prerogative" through sexist remarks to his students (67). Carol now assumes the role of teacher, telling him, "I came to explain something to you. You Are Not God. You ask me why I came? I came here to instruct you" (67). Her lesson is that John has come to hate her because she has power over him and that free discussion is impossible in this situation. Ironically, however, it turns out that what Carol finally wants is not revenge or power, but "understanding." She has come to see understanding, not as the key to unlock the doors that are shut against the degreeless, but in the way that John sees it, as human communication. Of course, both of these characters being who they are, it is always a matter of others understanding *them*. Once again, John makes a damaging and inevitable error. Instead of trying to meet Carol's admittedly uneven gesture at some form of human connection, the thing he has been asking for throughout the play, John fails to see beyond his own self-interest.

> CAROL. . . . I don't want revenge. I WANT UNDERSTANDING.
> JOHN. . . . *do* you?
> CAROL. I do. (Pause)
> JOHN. What's the use. It's over.
> CAROL. Is it? What is?
> JOHN. My job.
> CAROL. Oh. Your job. That's what you want to talk about.
>
> (71, second ellipsis is Mamet's)

This moment having passed, Carol's next move is to solidify the power of her Group within the University. Introducing her list of books to be banned, she asserts her right to control the University's very essence, knowledge. Because John has admitted earlier that "any atmosphere of free discussion is impossible" (69) within the power structure of the University, his appeal to the sacredness of academic freedom rings hollow. The absolute relativism of Carol's position is an ironic reflection on John's earlier egalitarian gesture of abandoning grades and rules: "someone chooses the books. If you can choose them, others can. What are you, 'God?' . . . You have an agenda, we have an agenda" (74). Although he does not reject the idea until he sees that they want to ban his own book, this challenge does provoke him to take action. His final position is essentially the appeal to authority that he has been resisting throughout the play: "I am a teacher. Eh? It's my *name* on the door, and *I* teach the class" (76). He thinks he has reached some kind of firm moral ground in evoking a responsibility to himself and to the profession, and by being willing to lose his job, in effect for the University, for taking a stand against Carol who is "wrong" and "dangerous" (76).

Mamet is not through with him yet, however. John had not reckoned on "rape" as a term of art. His forcible restraint of Carol, by her account his "pressing" his body into hers, is, "under the statute," battery and attempted rape (78). He may say that his action was "devoid of sexual content," a fact the audience has also seen, but it is Carol's construction of reality that rules: "I SAY IT WAS NOT . . . IT'S NOT FOR YOU TO SAY" (70). Carol has found an even more powerful linguistic community that supports her view of their relations, that of the law, which can now define and punish him as a rapist. As John feels his tenuous control of his life slip away, Carol adds the last insult when she intrudes into his intimate life, and attempts to legislate for his most private linguistic community, his family: "don't call your wife, 'baby'" (79). John immediately loses any pretense to principle, reverting to a language that expresses his raw misogynistic hatred: "You vicious little bitch . . . You little *cunt*" (79). As at the end of Act II, John resorts to physical violence when his linguistic powers fail him, beating Carol, and raising a chair over her. As Thomas Porter has noted, Mamet has long prepared us for the shock of this ending. In 1986, he wrote, in "True Stories of Bitches," that the ultimate response a man feels in an argument with his wife is "of course, physical violence": "People can say what they will, we men think, but if I get pushed just one little step further, why I might, I might just ____ (FILL IN THE BLANK) because she seems to have forgotten that I'M STRONGER THAN HER."[12] In *Oleanna*, John crosses that line into physical violence after he drops out of civilized discourse into verbal abuse.

The meaning of John's action, and Carol's response, the repeated line, "Yes, that's right," has been the subject of a good deal of critical disagreement. As was noted earlier, most of the early reviewers saw Mamet as endorsing John's position. A typical response to the ending is Harry Elam, Jr.'s suggestion that "[John's] brutality re-establishes the authority of the old patriarchal system against the insurgency of Political Correctness. Through his physical assault on Carol, John symbolically reclaims his power and privilege" (Elam, "'Only,'" p. 161). Deborah Tannen summed up the consensus of feminist reviewers when she wrote, "right now, we don't need a play that helps anyone feel good about a man beating a woman."[13] Mamet has insisted that, although many spectators thought the play was slanted towards John's position, "a lot of people thought the opposite" (Kane, *Conversation*, p. 164). The reviews, however, suggest that most audiences for the early productions, and for the 1994 film directed by Mamet, approved and even cheered the beating.

Mamet has made it clear that he does not intend the ending as a triumph for John, or even a justified action, but a tragic defeat: "It's structured as tragedy. The professor is the main character. He undergoes absolute reversal of situation, absolute recognition at the last moment of the play. He realizes that perhaps he is the cause of the plague on Thebes" (Kane, *Conversation*, p. 119). Mamet has strengthened this implication in subsequent versions of the ending. The earliest ending, revived by Harold Pinter in 1993 for the London production, had John in defeat, reading a McCarthyist confession, a motif that Mamet later used as an unrealized visual threat in the film through the poster that Carol puts up, but did not actually stage, probably because it casts John too strongly in the role of victim. The ending that Mamet settled on for the New York production, and both versions of the published text, is John's reversion to verbal abuse and physical violence. The moment of recognition is indicated in John's lowering the chair he holds over Carol, moving to his desk and arranging the papers on it before finally looking over at her and saying, "well." The two look at each other as Carol says "Yes. That's right." She then looks away and lowers her head as she repeats "yes. That's right" to herself (80). In the film, William H. Macy's response to his own violence conveys the tragic recognition that Mamet has suggested, as a look of bewilderment and then utter grief crosses his face.

What has appeared most ambiguous is Carol's response to John's abuse. Most critics agree with Richard Badenhausen's conclusion that it is a "chilling acknowledgment" of John's misogynistic rhetoric (Badenhausen, "Modern," p. 16). Others agree with Thomas Porter that it is "an ambiguous comment on the play's final moment" because "it is not immediately clear what Carol is affirming" (Porter, "Postmodernism," p. 27). Is she indicating that John's actions show that her charges against him were right or that her punishment was deserved for provoking him? Thomas Goggans has suggested a reading that gives Carol's experience equal weight with John's and helps to explain the disturbing impact of the ending. He suggests that Carol "finds herself in a situation which replicates through her interpretive screen some sort of previous abuse."[14] As he has noted, in Act I, "Carol constantly traffics in the code words of incest and child sexual abuse, speaking and responding in ways that are recognizable to anyone familiar with the representation of sexual abuse" (Goggans, "Laying Blame," p. 435). Goggans has shown that the dialogue in Act I is "a pastiche of phrases and clichés associated with the secrecy and psychological manipulation of incestuous abuse" (436). In other words, it may constitute another specialized language, to which Carol, unfortunately, has access and John does not. If we understand Carol's tantalizingly unrevealed secret, which makes her think of herself as having been "bad" all of her life, as incestual sexual abuse, her disturbance by John's proposal to "break the rules" and not tell anybody because he "likes" her, and his attempt to persuade her that "it's fine" because "there's no one here but you and me" take on a heightened significance, as do her shouting "NO!" and pulling away when he puts his arm around her shoulder, and her mishearing of John's remark, "Look. I'm not your father":

CAROL. What?
JOHN. I'm
CAROL. Did you say you were my father?
JOHN. . . . no . . .
CAROL. Why did you say that . . . ?
JOHN. I . . .
CAROL. . . . why . . .? [Mamet's ellipses]   (10)

Goggans suggests that Carol's reading of sexual implications in John's actions may be a "misinterpretation fated by her personal history and merely mis-channeled by the self interested Group which pursues, in John, a legitimate perpetrator of hierarchic abuse but the wrong representative of Carol's literal 'patriarchal' abuse" (440). Mamet, of course, resists any attempt to provide "backstory" for his characters, insisting that the play is in the words, but such a reading of the dialogue holds up, and Mamet's direction of the film lends it further support.

While Goggans has provided a revealing subtext for the play, I would suggest a different reading of the ending. He suggests that Carol has profited from John's misfortune "in overcoming the self-loathing and uncertainty of Act One" by joining forces with the Group and making John "stand for something," which is literally patriarchal abuse. I would suggest that the beaten Carol, lowering her head and repeating "yes. That's right" to John's "You little *cunt*" is an image of defeat, not of triumph. The ending indicates that Carol's empowerment through the feminist language of her Group has been an illusion, just as has John's empowerment through the language of academia. He is reduced to spewing abuse and beating up a woman because he is stronger than she, and she is reduced to accepting him at his hateful and demeaning word, despite the fact that the linguistic code of the law now empowers her to put him in jail.

Mamet has insisted in every interview about *Oleanna* that each of the characters, "the man and the woman, is saying something absolutely true at every moment and absolutely constructive at most moments in the play, and yet at the end of the play they're tearing each other's throats out" (Kane, *Conversation*, p. 164). Both have been damaged by adults who demeaned them when they were young; both are hopelessly self-absorbed and full of rage; both are seeking understanding *and* power; both are victims *and* aggressors; both are destroyed, although they achieve some form of power over each other. The difference is that Mamet has made John the protagonist. He is the more conscious and the freer to act of the two, and thus the more guilty. Carol speaks with the relentlessness of tragedy when she says: "What has *led* you to this place? Not your sex. Not your race. Not your class. YOUR OWN ACTIONS" (64). And he will be punished. Nobody wins, although, with Mamet directing, John does achieve a level of enlightenment. The tragic irony, of course, is that it comes too late.

NOTES

1. Leslie Kane, ed., *David Mamet in Conversation* (Ann Arbor: University of Michigan Press, 2001), p. 135. Subsequent references will appear parenthetically in the text.
2. Harry Elam, Jr., "'Only in America': Contemporary American Theater and the Power of Performance," in Marc Maufort and Jean-Pierre van Noppen, eds., *Voices of Power: Co-Operation and Conflict in English Language and Literatures* (Liège: Belgian Association of Anglicists in Higher Education, 1997), p. 160. Subsequent references will appear parenthetically in the text.
3. Daniel Mufson, "Sexual Perversity in Viragos," *Theater* 24.1 (1993), p. 111.
4. See Verna Foster, "Sex, Power, and Pedagogy in Mamet's *Oleanna* and Ionesco's *The Lesson*," *American Drama* 5.1 (Fall 1995), pp. 36–50; Craig Stewart Walker, "Three Tutorial Plays: *The Lesson*, *The Prince of Naples* and *Oleanna*," *Modern Drama* 40.1 (Spring 1997), pp. 149–62; Miriam Hardin, "Lessons from *The Lesson*: Four Post-Ionescan Education Plays," *CEA Magazine* 12 (1999), pp. 30–46.
5. See Walker, "Three Tutorial Plays"; Hardin, "Lessons"; Robert Skloot, "*Oleanna*, or the Play of Pedagogy," in Christopher G. Hudgins and Leslie Kane, eds., *Gender and Genre: Essays on David Mamet* (New York: Palgrave, 2001), pp. 95–107.
6. Richard Badenhausen, "The Modern Academy Raging in the Dark: Misreading Mamet's Political Incorrectness in *Oleanna*," *College Literature* 25.3 (Fall 1998), pp. 1–19, p. 2. Subsequent references will appear parenthetically in the text.
7. Marc Silverstein, "'We're Just Human': *Oleanna* and Cultural Crisis," *South Atlantic Review* 60.2 (May 1995), p. 105.

8. Thomas Porter, "Postmodernism and Violence in Mamet's *Oleanna*," *Modern Drama* 43.1 (Spring 2000), pp. 13–31, p. 28 (subsequent references will appear parenthetically cited in the text), and David Kennedy Sauer, "*Oleanna* and *The Children's Hour*: Misreading Sexuality on the Post Modern Realistic Stage," *Modern Drama* 43 (Fall 2000), p. 436.
9. Christine MacLeod, "The Politics of Gender, Language and Hierarchy in Mamet's 'Oleanna,'" *Journal of American Studies* 29.2 (1995), pp. 199–213, p. 202. Subsequent references will appear parenthetically in the text.
10. David Mamet, *Oleanna* (New York: Vintage, 1993), p. 2. Subsequent references will appear parenthetically in the text.
11. Lenke Németh, "Miscommunication and Its Implication in David Mamet's *Oleanna*," *B. A. S.: British and American Studies* (1997), pp. 174–5.
12. David Mamet, *Writing in Restaurants* (New York: Viking, 1986), p. 44.
13. "He Said . . . She Said . . . Who did What?" *New York Times*, November 15, 1992, Sec. 2, p. 6.
14. Thomas Goggans, "Laying Blame: Gender and Subtext in David Mamet's *Oleanna*," *Modern Drama* 40.4 (Winter 1997), pp. 433–41, p. 436. Subsequent references will appear parenthetically in the text.

FURTHER READING

Bechtel, Roger. "P. C. Power Play: Language and Representation in David Mamet's *Oleanna*," *Theatre Studies* 41 (1996): 29–48.
Rich, Frank. "Mamet's New Play Detonates the Fury of Sexual Harassment," *New York Times*, October 26, 1992, Sec. C, p. 11.
Ryan, Steven. "*Oleanna*: David Mamet's Power Play," *Modern Drama* 39.3 (1996): 392–403.
Showalter, Elaine. "Acts of Violence: David Mamet and the Language of Men," *Times Literary Supplement*, November 6, 1992, pp. 16–17.

8

DON B. WILMETH

Mamet and the actor

David Mamet has frequently admitted that he was an ineffective actor, even a terrible one.[1] As recently as May 2002, when asked how he could direct something he could not do himself, in this case magician Ricky Jay's 2002 magic show, *On the Stem*, Mamet responded, "It's not much different from acting. I certainly cannot act, which anybody who has ever seen me attempt it can tell you."[2] Furthermore, in 1996 he also confessed in *Make-Believe Town* that he "was a terrible acting student."[3] Rather than give up the theatre, however, he became first a stage director and then a playwright. Actually, before he tried acting professionally as an adult (he had been a child actor in Chicago and performed at the Hull-House Theatre in the early 1960s) and while a student at Goddard College during the late sixties he wrote several drafts of early plays, including *Sexual Perversity in Chicago*. Few failed actors have substituted one career track for another – or in Mamet's case, two others – with such stunning success. Ironically, Mamet has often stated that he began writing plays not so that he would become a recognized writer but in order to provide young actors with illustrations for points he was making in his teaching and because his first theatre company, the St. Nicholas, could not afford to pay royalties.[4]

In truth, Mamet's experience as a student in formal acting training was severely limited. In a program of study away from Goddard, Mamet spent his junior year (1967–8) at the Neighborhood Playhouse in New York City studying with the late Sanford Meisner. However, Mamet was not one of those invited back for a second year.[5] In his own publications Mamet never directly credits Meisner with his own acting philosophy, yet there are some clear similarities, which will become evident in this chapter. However, the exposure he missed in a second year with Meisner might have altered some of Mamet's subsequent ideas about what is appropriate in the way of actor training and technique. As C. C. Courtney, a current instructor at the Neighborhood Playhouse, explains, "Meisner spent much of the second year of his two-year course on exercises using scenes from non-realistic plays and, though not most of the time, he often chose nonrealistic plays for the final productions, stating over and over that one of the actor's greatest challenges is to be believable in unbelievable circumstances."[6]

Though Mamet is prone to quote Stanislavsky frequently, he undeniably eschews much of Stanislavsky's teachings, the basis of much of Meisner's system, at least as he understands them and as Meisner's program's first year tended to imply. This habit might have been less prevalent if he had understood more completely Meisner's belief (and, indeed, the essence of much of Stanislavsky's late commentary on acting) that "In no sense is the Stanislavsky trained actor limited to naturalism."[7]

Mamet nonetheless gleaned some of his most important lessons from his Meisner experience, several of which would later be adapted and integrated into his most complete statement on acting in his book *True and False* (1997). One of Mamet's earliest academic critics, Dennis Carroll, succinctly summarizes Meisner's first-year focus: "Emphasis was placed on intent and motive, on the practical matter of playing objectives beat by beat, according to an analysis of the through line and superobjective of the play. Meisner trained his students to focus on others on stage, to respond honestly to 'the moment' as created anew through stage contact each night between actors."[8] Though Mamet would certainly modify these ideas, he nonetheless never lost sight of the practicable aspect of the Meisner technique, among other facets of Meisner's teaching.

To date, the most outspoken critique of Mamet's book *True and False* and his apparent anti-Stanislavsky stance has come from Bella Merlin in a 2000 essay in *New Theatre Quarterly*.[9] Merlin, a champion of Stanislavky's Physical Actions (which she correctly sees as similar to Mamet's emphasis on finding the action in a scene, discussed later in this chapter), seems angry towards Mamet as she accuses him of being antagonistic towards Stanislavsky in his extended essay. Drawing absolutes from any one Mamet essay, however, is a mistake. Merlin would have done well also to look at the more practical application of Mamet's philosophy of acting in the aptly titled *A Practical Handbook for the Actor*, written by his disciples (see below), and to have read his essay "Stanislavsky and the Bearer Bonds" in *Some Freaks*, in which he notes that so-called "schools" or approaches to acting change, as was true also of Stanislavsky – "All his [Stanislavsky's] work was to the one end: to bring to the stage the life of the Soul. As his vision of that life changed, he discarded the old and moved on."[10] When Mamet in *True and False* calls the Stanislavsky "Method" (note he says Method, the term for the Americanized version of the System as developed primarily by Lee Strasberg) and "the schools derived from it" nonsense, I believe he is reiterating the belief that workable approaches change and that "schools of acting" like The Actors

Studio have become outmoded "cults," not changing adequately with the times.[11] Perhaps, as Merlin has suggested, Mamet has failed to comprehend completely Stanislavsky's third book on acting, *Creating a Role*, though in truth, due in some measure to a poor English translation, few who have not read the book in its original language truly understand the Russian master.

Although Mamet's *True and False* appears to be anti-Stanislavsky (he concludes that his ideas are not valid in practical terms), Mamet truly seems to be more anti-Method or anti-emotional in his approach than anti-Stanislavsky, whom he frequently extolls in various contexts, though often with reservations. There is a great deal that seems both sensible and practical (some might say simplistic) in Mamet's pronouncements as compared to those in Stanislavsky's three major published books on acting (*An Actor Prepares*, *Building a Character*, and *Creating a Role*), though often masked by his tendency for overstatement or generalization (for example, he seems to believe the old bromide that teachers elect "institutional support over a life of self-reliance."[12]

Despite Mamet's apparent rejection of Stanislavsky and his own training in general (as will be explained, he denies the value of all formal actor training and higher education in general),[13] some of his own basic tenets nevertheless reflect aspects of the Meisner approach, such as focusing on others rather than yourself; demanding truthful, moment to moment responses to other actors; and even a down-playing of Stanislavsky's "emotional memory." Although Mamet is quite clear as to how he believes an actor should deal with emotion on stage, Meisner, though not really denying the importance of emotion, did believe that there were many ways an actor could achieve a needed emotion in a scene or even a moment, perhaps not all that dramatically different from Mamet's beliefs.

Whatever might have been the root cause of Mamet's ultimate rejection of formal training for the actor, it is undeniable that in essence his acting philosophy evidences scorn for the authority of acting teachers and the belief that most are charlatans. Furthermore, he declares that most approaches to actor training are confusing and unhelpful (and rarely understood by students), and being a student forces one to think like a child. However, all discussion of Mamet's ideas on acting should be prefaced with several warnings. First, Mamet is, by his own admission, contradictory and inconsistent. As a rhetorical device, his statements are often dogmatic, opinionated, hyperbolic, or absolute, leaning towards delphic pronouncements, a characteristic he seems to find in others, including on occasion Stanislavsky. He takes great pleasure in causing debate or even arousing anger from the reader or listener. In person or on the page Mamet is an intimidating presence who wants to be in charge.[14] Whatever his personal objective might be, certainly he seems to strive to be thought-provoking for those who accept or reject his ideas and challenges the reader even when that reader might be in complete agreement with him.

A final preliminary observation is that Mamet's comments on actor training and education, apparently conditioned by his own unsalutary experiences with both, are misleading given his own history. Mamet has been teaching acting off and on since 1970 when he took a position at Vermont's small Marlboro College as an acting instructor. The following year he became an artist-in-residence at his alma mater where, along with his students William H. Macy and Steven Schachter, his first theatre company was founded (St. Nicholas), followed in 1985 with the formation of the Atlantic Theater Company with Macy. His involvement with this latter company, still in existence (its 1999–2000 season was devoted to Mamet's plays), included several years of intensive acting instruction both in the summers at his summer home in Vermont and at New York University; ultimately the Atlantic Theater Company Acting School of Practical Aesthetics was created, today still using his name (and Macy's) prominently in its promotional material. In addition, at one time or another Mamet has taught acting at Yale, Harvard, New York University, and the University of Chicago, as well as shorter master classes elsewhere.

Mamet now admits that he has no new ideas on acting (and confesses that most of his ideas came early in his career), suggests with some hesitation that there are other ideas as valid as his own, and has essentially stopped teaching acting. His incessant condemnation of all actor training and education thus emerges as one of his many overstatements and an obvious inconsistency in his own behavior. Given his own teaching and ongoing support of the Atlantic Theater Company Acting School, perhaps what he really means is that in his opinion only his approach and those that teach that approach are acceptable. He did state prior to writing *True and False* that there are no "correct" schools of artistic thought but that there are incorrect or useless schools, those "that do not serve the purpose of communion between the artist and the audience" (*Some Freaks*, p. 71).

All discussion by Mamet on actors and acting, not surprisingly, begins with his observations on training and the ill-advised notion of pursuing formal training. Alternatively, a would-be actor should go directly into a career in the theatre and bypass college; even graduate school or conservatory training is too late for the actor. "Part of the requirement of a life in the theatre is to stay out of school," he proclaims (*True and False*, p. 18). The best teacher is the audience. Doing the play for the audience "is what acting is," he states; "The Rest is just practice" (p. 4). He believes that the only viable training is to be on the stage, even if that means creating your own theatre (which, in fact, has been true of members of the Atlantic Theater Company, who have made their own opportunities while frequently surviving on non-theatre jobs). Mamet's belief in "doing" it rather than being trained to do it is not a new idea. Indeed, others have made similar observations. For example, Simon Callow in his important book *Being An Actor* (1984) writes, in reference to his first job in a repertory company, "I learnt almost as much again on my feet, in six months there . . . as I had in three years at the Drama Centre [the London drama school]. I *couldn't* have learnt what I learnt there in a drama school. It's only *doing* it that teaches." Unlike Mamet, Callow, who similarly believes that work of this sort leads to boldness on the part of the actor, does warn that simply learning to act in such a situation also "can lead to nasty habits, facility, generalization, cheap effects, and . . . losing touch with why one puts on plays at all."[15] Such common traps, also possible products of poor training, are not addressed by Mamet.

Mamet in reality is not against all formal training. However, the only specific instructional experience that he clearly endorses is external and, he avows, practical – that is, vocal (especially diction) and physical (including yoga and martial arts) training, since this work will give the actor the self-respect needed and the tools that will allow the actor to "do the job." In *True and False* he states often that the major job of the actor is to communicate the play to the audience: "To do so the actor needs a strong voice, superb diction, a supple, well-proportioned body, and a rudimentary understanding of the play" (p. 9). Mamet stresses his point about forsaking other kinds of education – a somewhat spurious point – by stating that the founders of most great theatres were dropouts (similarly, he categorically claims "Nobody with a happy childhood ever went into show business," p. 87). In a later context Mamet suggests that actors do better when they enter the field at a young age, when their expectations and needs are not particularly great, and when the actor should be out there getting their "teeth kicked in and learning something and meeting some people and working hard."[16] Regardless, the bottom line seems to be that Mamet decries the coddling and permissiveness that he claims is encouraged by most acting teachers, who can only be pleased by students "being abject and subservient to their authority" (*True and False*, p. 47).[17] Furthermore, Mamet believes that a talented young actor is superior to most teachers in inspiration, vigor, and inventiveness, even if not in experience. That experience comes from working in the theatre, not going to school.

Mamet's most complete explication of his acting philosophy, as already noted above, is to be found in his 1997 book, *True and False: Heresy and Common Sense for the Actor*, although echoes of this extended essay can be found in earlier writings and lectures, such as a lecture ("Decay: Some

Thoughts for Actors") delivered to William H. Macy's acting class at Lincoln Center in 1985 and his Spencer Lecture at Harvard the following year (both texts are in the Harvard Theatre Collection).[18] He has clarified since the book's publication that he does not mean it to be an "instructional" manual but rather "a book about how to think; it's a book about how to think about acting," meant primarily for young actors.[19]

Fully to comprehend Mamet's ideas on acting, however, it is recommended that as a companion volume to *True and False* a student also read *A Practical Handbook for the Actor* (1986), which includes explanations and examples not found in Mamet's book. This handbook was written by a group of Mamet and Macy students and is based on their acting classes during 1983 and 1984 in Vermont, at New York University, and at the Goodman Theatre in Chicago. Melissa Bruder and the five other authors attempt to provide a blue-print for the "craft" of acting (the word "art" rarely appears here or in Mamet's book). Mamet's introduction to this handbook points forward to the more expanded statements in *True and False*. He notes, for example, that the actor "must follow the dictates of your common sense," and he emphasizes his belief in a simple stoic philosophy (he frequently cites the stoic philosopher Epictetus in his works): "be what you wish to seem."[20]

Throughout Mamet's numerous comments on acting, two words frequently stand out in describing effective acting – simplicity and clarity. His ultimate rejection of Stanislavsky (and especially the Method) is fundamentally because he finds these systems too complex and confusing, asking the actors to carry too much baggage with them on stage: "You can't act all that stuff . . . when one shows up on stage, that all goes out the window. One can only take on stage, 'What do I want from the other person?' That's it – period; that's all one can take on stage."[21] It is difficult if not impossible to summarize or even paraphrase adequately Mamet's already distilled and codified explanation of or guide to acting in *True and False*. In general, his platform is anti-intellectual: "The skill of acting is finally a physical skill; it is not a mental exercise" (p. 19), or "one can no more base a performance on an idea than one can base a love affair on an idea" (p. 30); anti-emotional: "nothing in the world is less interesting than an actor on the stage involved in his or her own emotions" (p. 11); and anti-impersonation: "There *is* no character. There are only lines upon a page" (p. 9), and "The work of characterization has or has not been done by the author. It's not your job, and it's not your look-out" (p. 114).

Throughout *True and False* Mamet uses a technique not uncommon to his plays – repetition and restatement. For instance, he repeatedly says the following, in essence the heart of his arguments: "I don't know what talent is, and, frankly, I don't care. I do not think it is the actor's job to be interesting.

I think that is the job of the script. I think it is the actor's job to be truthful and brave – both qualities which can be developed and exercised through the will" (p. 98). In addition, rather than talent, "hard work and perseverance *will* be rewarded" (p. 99); "When the actual courage of the actor is coupled with the lines of the playwright, the illusion of character is created" (p. 21); "Acting is a physical art. It is close to the study of dance or of singing. It is not like the study of mechanical drawing or literature to which the academics would reduce it" (p. 80). If Mamet has an acting motto it is "invent nothing, deny nothing," which to him is the meaning of demystifying character for the actor and is stated in numerous contexts in his treatise.

At the heart of Mamet's acting ideas is his belief that "emotion is a by-product, and a trivial by-product, of the performance of the action" (p. 13). "Action" is defined in the *Practical Handbook* as "The physical pursuance of a specific goal" (p. 87). Consequently, in a typical overstatement, Mamet rejects "emotional memory," "sense memory," and all similar tenets in Stanislavsky and the American Method as "hogwash" (*True and False*, p. 12); he accuses Stanislavsky's theoretical contributions of having been those of a dilettante and concludes that they "rarely, if ever, show demonstrable results" (p. 15). In the final analysis Mamet believes "Any method of acting . . . which is based upon the presence or absence of emotion sooner or later goes bad" (p. 116). In numerous interviews Mamet has repeated the following: "Acting has absolutely nothing to do with emotion or feeling emotional . . . People don't go to the theater to hear the emotion [here he is referring to a violin concert]; they go to hear the concerto. The emotions should take place in the *audience*. It just doesn't have to be dealt with from the actor's viewpoint."[22]

Certainly Mamet believes strongly in truth on stage (he eschews the word "believable") but fundamentally rejects the Method's way of achieving it. His formula is simple, as noted previously: "It is the writer's job to make the play interesting. It is the *actor*'s job to make the performance truthful." It is the "courage" of the actor that makes a performance truthful. One problem for actors in accepting all of Mamet's tenets is that it is difficult to apply his approach to all playwrights. Perhaps if all understood the actor as well as Mamet the playwright and wrote as well, it would be easier to accept more fully Mamet's acting principles. Although Mamet's playwriting has become ever more complex, with greater subtext in some of his late plays and films, actor Joe Mantegna, a seasoned Mamet collaborator, has suggested that "David's a master of not giving you a lot of back story. In other words, what you see is what you get. You invent for yourself who these people are. That's his real talent there. He doesn't waste hours of explanation."[23] Alas, the simple fact is that not all writers provide plays of artistry and skill comparable to those by Mamet, thus actors cannot always depend on the words and appropriate actions alone to make for a truthful performance. It seems a bit cavalier to state, as Mamet does, that one rehearses only "to learn to perform the play" – that is, rehearsals are never needed to "explore the meaning of the play," since a play "*has* no meaning beyond its performance" (*True and False*, p. 52).

Nevertheless, Mamet's key idea of using preparation time to "find the simple actions" associated with the dialogue or lines is a sensible one, not totally out of line with his early training with Meisner or with Stanislavsky's "Method of Physical Action." To quote Mamet again, the job of the actor is to "learn the lines, find a simple objective like that indicated by the author, speak the lines clearly in an attempt to achieve that objective" (p. 57). Script analysis in the traditional sense is useless for the actor (other than to understand the mechanics of a scene). Similarly, "It is not necessary to believe anything in order to act" (p. 57), since one cannot control what is believed. What is vital is for the actor to focus on an action – an "attempt to achieve a goal" (specific suggestions and examples for finding an action are enumerated in *A Practical Handbook* while Mamet is vague and general in his explanations in his treatise).

As Mamet explains it, "Each character in the play wants something. It is the actor's job to reduce that something to its lowest common denominator and then act upon it" (*True and False*, p. 74). Acting on these objectives does not "require preparation" but rather "commitment." Furthermore, the actor should look at scenes rather than the complete play, carving "the big tasks up into small tasks" and performing those, for "there *is* no arc of the character," rather you will move from one scene to the next, each with its own task – "the total of them is the play" (pp. 75–6). What seems to truly irk Mamet are actors who attempt to embellish what is provided by the playwright with their "good intentions and insights and epiphanies" (p. 80). His solution is clearly stated: "If you play each scene, the play will be served. If you try to drag your knowledge of the play through each scene, you are ruining whatever the worth is of the playwright's design, and you are destroying your chances to succeed scene by scene" (p. 76).

Similarly destructive to Mamet are actors who attempt to manipulate the emotions of others or who "*narrate* their own supposed emotional state" (p. 77). The addition of an emotion to a situation "which does not organically create it is a lie" (p. 78). Mamet, who intensely dislikes the concept of Great Actors (he uses Laurence Olivier as his prime example of an actor who forces the audience to pay more attention to his technique than to the story), believes rather that the "greatest performances are seldom noticed" and "seem to be a natural and inevitable outgrowth of the actor" (p. 79). To counter the temptation to impose emotion or other embellishments on an action, Mamet compares the actor's process to telling a joke, with everything spoken related to the punchline. "In a well-written play, and in a correctly performed play, everything tends toward a punchline. That punchline, for the actor, is the *objective*," and if the actor learns to think solely in terms of the objective (which Mamet says should be fun; something that you want to do), "all concerns of *belief, feeling, emotion, characterization, substitution,* become irrelevant" (p. 82). Following this formula will prevent "portrayal" by the actor rather than action.

Finally in this process, Mamet suggests the use of the "as if" device as a way to jog one's memory or serve as a reminder "to help you clarify to yourself the action in the scene" (p. 91). In *A Practical Handbook* this is explained as the third step in analyzing a scene, after determining what the character is literally doing and identifying the essential action therein. Step 3 becomes "What is that action like to me? *It's as if . . .*" (19). The handbook, unlike Mamet's treatise, provides a number of specific examples for each step in this analysis of a scene and its action.

Mamet states bluntly in one of the final chapters in *True and False* that "acting has nothing whatever to do with concentration" (p. 94), which on the surface seems in conflict with virtually all schools of thought about acting. What Mamet provides, however, is the alternative that acting "has to do with the ability to *imagine*" and that concentration, as he defines it, cannot be forced or controlled any more than emotion or belief. A semantic difference, perhaps, for what he really seems to be urging, as did Meisner, is the avoidance of "self-absorption." He even states "The more a person's concentration [he uses the word] is outward, the more naturally interesting the person becomes"; that is, the actor should direct him or herself towards the actions of the play – "to *do* them is more interesting than to *concentrate* on them" (p. 95).

Mamet's treatise does not stop with theoretical beliefs but includes towards the end some very practical considerations – which are stated somewhat differently in *A Practical Handbook* in a chapter entitled "Keeping the Theatre Clean" (pp. 76–83). Briefly, Mamet advises the actor that "In the theatre, as in other endeavors, correctness in the small is the key to correctness in the large. Show up fifteen minutes early. Know your lines cold. Choose a good, fun, physical objective. Bring to rehearsal and to performance those things you will need and leave the rest behind" (*True and False*, p. 101). Furthermore, he specifically urges the actor to leave personal concerns on the street and to leave a performance behind in the theatre. The actor's job includes being generous to others ("Yearning to correct or amend something in someone else will make you petty" – 102) and cultivating a love of skill, the habit of mutuality, and the habit of truth in yourself. As he states often, "That is not a *character* onstage. It is *you* onstage" (p. 104).

Mamet believes that his approach to the art and craft of acting is applicable to all forms of drama, regardless of period or genre. Perhaps he is correct. Regardless, some of his own efforts, primarily as director, with plays or adaptations not his own have been less than successful, although these have been few during his career, perhaps because of their failure. For example, an early attempt at directing at the Circle Rep (his first Off-Broadway outing) of *Twelfth Night* was severely criticized, one critic suggesting that his approach to dialogue can lead to affectedless monotone from the actors. On the other hand, his adaptations of Chekhov (*The Cherry Orchard*, *Uncle Vanya*, and *Three Sisters*) have been somewhat more successful ventures, in large measure because Mamet uses a verbal idiom not unlike that in his original plays, stripping away excess and thus creating an idiom in sync with actors who excel in Mamet's plays.

Indeed, somewhat separate from his theories of acting is the subject of the actors of Mamet's work. Undeniably, there are those actors who for various reasons seem ideal for Mamet's verbal style and, on the screen, his visual counterpart. Mamet has been extraordinarily faithful to his theatrical friends over the years – and especially actors – though arguably this has worked to his benefit as much as theirs. In 1994 on National Public Radio (*Fresh Air*) Mamet stated: "one of the nice things about working with the same people over and over is that it's great to be trusted. It's great to be able to give an actor a script and know that he or she will trust that the line's going to work and read the line as it's written."[24] Actor Joe Mantegna, in a 1990 interview, echoes this belief and adds: "You spend less time acquainting yourself to each other than you do the work . . . You can get down to business" (quoted in Kane, *David Mamet: A Casebook*, p. 267).

To some extent, then, Mamet has developed, for both stage work and films, a kind of unofficial stock company – actors with extensive theatre experience (even if known primarily for their screen work) and invariably identified with a kind of American stage or cinematic realism. Some talent has worked in Mamet projects both on stage and in films. Not too surprisingly, since until fairly recently (with *Oleanna* and *Boston Marriage*) Mamet has written primarily male roles, most actors associated with him are men, with the notable exceptions of his first and his current wife. Among those actors who have appeared in Mamet's plays, in some cases for decades, and often directed by Mamet or his long-time collaborator (and his "hero") Gregory Mosher, include William H. Macy, Mike Nussbaum (a Chicago-based actor Mamet got to know while working backstage), the late J. T. Walsh, J. J. Johnston (an acquaintance since both played animals in a children's play, before Mamet became a writer),Joe Mantegna, Robert Duvall, Felicity Huffman, Mary McCann, Treat Williams, Christopher Walken, Ron Silver, Robert Prosky, Ed Begley, Jr., William Petersen, Patti LuPone, and his former wife Lindsay Crouse and his current one Rebecca Pidgeon. Actors seen prominently in his films include Andy Garcia, Ricky Jay, Alec Baldwin, Dustin Hoffman, Jack Lemmon, Jessica Lange, Charles Durning, Robert DeNiro, Jack Nicholson, Kevin Spacey, and John Mahoney.

Mamet has a special and unique relationship with Ricky Jay, a sleight-of-hand artist and frequent consultant to Mamet on card sharks, crooks, con men, and various lowlifes; Mamet has also directed Jay's two one-person staged "magic" shows, seen Off-Broadway in 1994 and 2002. Of those who have been in both Mamet stage productions and films directed by Mamet, two stand out as quintessential Mamet actors: Joe Mantegna (Roma on stage in *Glengarry Glen Ross* and, on the screen, major roles in the films *House of Games* and *Things Change*, among others) and William H. Macy (most recently seen on stage and screen in *Oleanna*). Joe Mantegna, born in 1948, is Mamet's contemporary and shares a similar background. A native of Chicago, Mantegna was trained at the Goodman Theatre and began his career there in 1969, appearing first in a Mamet play (*A Life in the Theatre*) in 1977. In 1999 he directed a film version of Mamet's 1970 play *Lakeboat* (released in 2000). Macy, a couple of years junior to Mamet, first encountered Mamet at Goddard College when they were both studying there, co-founded the St. Nicholas Theatre Company with Mamet and fellow-student Steven Schachter. Macy's association with Mamet, including a period in Chicago, continues to the present – as actor, acting teacher, and director. In Mamet's 1991 film *Homicide* Mantegna and Macy played police partners, Bobby Gold and Sullivan respectively.

Central to virtually all Mamet's work is his unique, frequently discussed dialogue, with its broken sentences, inconclusions, abrupt silences, interruptions, and repetitions. The writing creates what is a unique style for the actor. The actor who is unable to adhere faithfully to the lines will invariably fail. In 1990 William H. Macy, commenting on Mamet's dialogue, noted that it was "difficult to memorize because it is simply more complex [than most playwrights' dialogue]" in part because of its staccato nature which he noted "is so finely tuned that improvising is nearly impossible. If you paraphrase it, it suddenly becomes very clunky in your mouth, as if you stumbled over the carpet."[25]

When *Glengarry Glen Ross* played in Boston, the late critic Kevin Kelly focused on the rhythm of Mamet's language that he observed "has the exhilaration of a perfectly timed minuet which, given the hoarse nature of its utterance, may seem odd; it's also completely accurate."[26] Numerous actors have commented on the tricky nature of Mamet's language, as well as its musicality, and the importance of delivering Mamet's lines exactly as they are written. As James Ryan warns, "in the mouth of the wrong actor Mamet's hyperrealistic dialogue can sound stagey and melodramatic."[27]

In the same Ryan essay cited above, which uses the film version of *Glengarry Glen Ross* as its centerpiece, Al Pacino (who plays Ricky Roma) is quoted as saying, "It comes down to accepting Mamet's world," and, apparently not knowing that Mamet is a good amateur jazz pianist, adds that the dialogue "feels like it has sort of a jazz feeling with occasional riffs throughout. There's a kind of sound within that has an evocation, that is communicated and received." Frequently critics have commented similarly on Mamet's dialogue as "counterpoint" that creates an interplay more like jazz than speech. Jack Lemmon (Shelley Levine in the film), also resorting to a musical analogy, reinforces the idea that Mamet's language is difficult to master but that once that is accomplished it effortlessly brings a character to life, an idea very much in agreement with Mamet's theory of acting. Lemmon stated in the Ryan article: "His [Mamet's] ear is incredible at catching the rhythms and the speech of Mr. Man in the Street. Really great writers have very distinct rhythms." Lemmon illustrates by indicating that even the most seemingly insignificant word or phrase or hesitation (the "ahs, the ehs and the dots") are essential. If the actor drops or adds a note, an ah or eh, it will not work.[28]

John Lahr, one of Mamet's most astute critics, ably summarizes what seems truly unique about Mamet's dialogue for actors, when he recognizes that the plays are rooted in reality but are truly fables, unique because of their "distinctive music – a terse, streamlined orchestration of thought, language, and character which draws viewers in and makes them work for meaning."[29] Later, in the same profile, Lahr demonstrates how Mamet's rhythm, in *American Buffalo*, gave the words and pauses emotional impact, and cites Mosher, the director, who suggests that Mamet's dialogue is a string of iambs. Mantegna, who, though he did not appear in *American Buffalo*, was involved with the initial reading as Teach, told Lahr that he saw Mamet tapping out the iambs with a pen (p. 41).

It is not surprising that Mamet has used many of the same actors on stage and in his films, for he sees little difference in the demands made on the actor in the two media. Even the visual style that he has evolved for films is similar to the verbal style in his plays – as Sidney Lumet, director of *The Verdict* (1982), posited when he described Mamet's film style as lean, spare, tough, staccato, unsentimental but hot and never unpassionate.[30] Mamet declares that "Good acting in film is . . . the same as good acting on stage.

It's intention, absolute intention. What specifically does an actor want, and what is he or she willing to do to get it?" (quoted in Bragg interview, Kane, ed., *David Mamet in Conversation*, p. 148). On his film script for *Things Change*, in the Harvard Theatre Collection, Mamet has written: "Do the beats." And frequently, his stage dialogue is heard almost unaltered as film dialogue, other than to allow the camera to remain focused on one character for longer lengths of time, as was the case in the film version of *Glengarry Glen Ross*.

Mamet loves actors and has great respect for the art (and craft) of acting. As early as 1977 he said "I think acting is the greatest thing in the world," and, paraphrasing Russian director Alexander Tairov, added, "It's the most difficult art to master, and it looks like the easiest."[31] Almost twenty years later Mamet clarified his own explanation for his failed acting career when he suggested that he did not have the personality to be an actor, and added, "I think it's [acting's] a great gift. I think acting is a skill that many people can learn a little bit of and that few people can learn a lot of and that several people are born with a great talent for" (1994 interview with Terry Gross, in Kane, ed., *David Mamet in Conversation*, p. 159). In Mamet's estimation he belonged in none of those categories. Three years later he added that "It is a gift from God to be able to act . . . it takes an extraordinary, very, very rare gift to be able to do it surpassingly" (1997 interview with Charlie Rose, in Kane, ed., *David Mamet in Conversation*, p. 187). In a 1995 *Playboy* interview he reiterated his affection for actors, classifying them as "absolutely the most interesting people I know."[32] As a playwright and storyteller who believes audiences come to the theatre, a place of magic, to celebrate, Mamet continues to admire the role of the actor in the theatrical event even though as he gets older he feels that how one accomplishes what he sees as a blue-collar job is more difficult to comprehend and explain.

NOTES

1. Some of the comments and observations in this chapter are based on a two-hour masterclass in acting observed by the author, a question-and-answer session that followed, and a private conversation with Mamet at Brown University, October 3, 2001.
2. Jesse McKinley, "A Memory of Houdini and, No Escaping It, It's a Gabfest," *New York Times*, June 16, 2002.
3. David Mamet, *Make-Believe Town* (Boston: Little, Brown and Co. 1996), p. 32.
4. See Mamet's comments on writing motivation in Leslie Kane, ed., *David Mamet in Conversation* (Ann Arbor: University of Michigan Press), pp. 60, 72, and, on royalties, p. 115.

5. Although Mamet may well have been one of the most famous of Meisner's students, he was not one of its "most famous graduates" as stated in C. C. Courtney's "The Neighborhood Playhouse," in David Krasner, ed., *Method Acting Reconsidered: Theory, Practice, Future* (New York: St. Martin's Press, 2000), p. 291. Some two-thirds of first-year students are rejected annually.

6. Quoted in *ibid.*, p. 292.

7. Sanford Meisner, "The Reality of Doing," *Drama Review* 9.1 (Fall 1964), p. 155.

8. Dennis Carroll, *David Mamet* (London: Macmillan, 1987), p. 6.

9. Bella Merlin, "Mamet's Heresy and Common Sense: What's True and False in 'True and False,'" *New Theatre Quarterly* 16 (August 2000), pp. 249–54. Her ideas are expanded in *Beyond Stanislavsky: The Psycho-Physical Approach to Actor Training* (London: Nick Hern; New York: Theatre Arts Books / Routledge, 2001).

10. David Mamet, *Some Freaks* (New York: Viking, 1989), p. 73.

11. David Mamet, *True and False: Heresy and Common Sense for the Actor* (New York: Pantheon Books, 1997), p. 110.

12. *Ibid.*, p. 6.

13. In a conversation with Mamet in October 2001, he admitted to me that there is some value in attending college after all. Perhaps this is a result of his own daughter now being in university, or perhaps he has altered this dogmatic stance, at least in private. Certainly, based on his numerous comments about education and actor training specifically, it is easy to conclude that his own experiences with both must have been unsatisfying and even counter-productive.

14. William H. Macy, a long-time friend and arguably the prototypical "Mamet" actor, suggested that Mamet disliked acting because he "wasn't in charge," which also helps to explain his directing career, where he is in charge. See Samuel G. Freedman, "The Gritty Eloquence of David Mamet," *New York Times Magazine*, April 21, 1985, p. 64.

15. Simon Callow, *Being An Actor* (London: Methuen, 1984; New York: Grove Press, 1988), p. 46.

16. Mamet in conversation with Barbara Shulgasser ("Mountebanks and Misfits"), November 20, 1997, Herbst Theatre, San Francisco. Reprinted in Kane, ed., *David Mamet in Conversation*, p. 199.

17. Given Mamet's feelings about the negative impact of authority on the actor, the following comment in John Lahr's review of *Oleanna* underscores the intimidating effect Mamet can have on most people: "Both Mr. Macy and Ms. Pigeon are a bit under wraps here, at once awed and cowed by Mamet's authority, which takes some of the acting oxygen out of the air" (in "Dogma Days," *New Yorker*, November 16, 1992, p. 124).

18. See also Stacey Okun, "Postgraduate Pioneers of the 'Mamet Method,'" *New York Times*, August 2, 1987, Sec. 2, pp. 5, 14.

19. Mamet in conversation with Charlie Rose (*A Great Longing to Belong*) on WNET-TV, New York, PBS, November 11, 1997. Reprinted in Kane, ed., *David Mamet in Conversation*, p. 187.

20. Melissa Bruder, *et al.*, *A Practical Handbook for the Actor*, with an Introduction by David Mamet (New York: Vintage Books, 1986), pp. x–xi. Mamet's introduction is also included in *Some Freaks*, pp. 31–3.

21. Mamet interviewed by Melvyn Bragg (*South Bank Show*) and aired on October 16, 1994 on London Weekend Television. Reprinted in Kane, ed., *David Mamet in Conversation*, p. 149.

22. Matthew C. Roudané, "Something Out of Nothing," *Studies in American Drama, 1945–Present* 1 (1986). Reprinted in Kane, ed., *David Mamet in Conversation*, p. 51.

23. Joe Mantegna, quoted in Leslie Kane, *David Mamet: A Casebook* (New York and London: Garland Publishing, 1992), p. 253.

24. Mamet in conversation, October 17, 1994, with Terry Gross ("Someone Named Jack"). Reprinted in Kane, ed., *David Mamet in Conversation*, p. 158.

25. Unidentified clipping, dated 1990, in the Harvard Theatre Collection Mamet file.

26. Kevin Kelly, *Boston Globe*, February 13, 1986; Kelly expanded upon this idea in the *Globe* on February 21. For another view of Mamet's language, in *Oleanna*, see David Richards, "The Jackhammer Voice of a Mamet Encounter," *New York Times*, November 8, 1992.

27. James Ryan, "Playing Mamet's Music," *Boston Sunday Globe*, September 27, 1992.

28. Similar comments were made by Ed Begley, Jr. when he played Del in *The Cryptogram* in Boston. See Renee Graham, "Talking in Mamet's Code," *Boston Globe*, January 29, 1995. Mamet's own comments on music, piano lessons, and writing appeared on July 15, 2002 in *New York Times* ("Hearing the Notes That Aren't Played").

29. John Lahr, "Fortress Mamet," in *Show and Tell: New Yorker Profiles* (Woodstock and New York: The Overlook Press, 2000), p. 28.

30. Sidney Lumet quoted in an unidentified clipping, April 16, 1987, Harvard Theatre Collection Mamet file.

31. Mamet interview with Ernest Leogrande ("A Man of Few Words Moves On to Sentences"), *New York Daily News*, February 13, 1977. Reprinted in Kane, ed., *David Mamet in Conversation*, p. 29.

32. Mamet interview with Geoffrey and John Rezek, *Playboy* magazine (April 1995). Reprinted in Kane, *David Mamet in Conversation*, p. 219.

FURTHER READING

Bruder, Melissa, Lee Michael Cohn, Madeleine Olnek, Nathaniel Pollack, Rober Previto, and Scott Zigler. *A Practical Handbook for the Actor*, with an Introduction by David Mamet (New York: Vintage Books, 1986).

Carnicke, Sharon M. *Stanislavsky in Focus* (Amsterdam: Harwood Academic Publishers, 1998).

Hodge, Alison (ed.). *Twentieth-Century Actor Training* (London / New York: Routledge, 2000).

Kane, Leslie (ed.). *David Mamet in Conversation* (Ann Arbor: University of Michigan Press, 2001).

Krasner, David (ed.). *Method Acting Reconsidered: Theory, Practice, Future* (New York: St. Martin's Press, 2000).

Luckhurst, Mary, and Chloe Veltman (eds.). *On Acting: Interviews with Actors* (London: Faber and Faber, 2001), (see "William H. Macy").

Mamet, David. "Stanislavsky and the Bearer Bonds," in *Some Freaks* (New York: Viking, 1989).

   True and False: Heresy and Common Sense for the Actor (New York: Pantheon, 1997).

Meisner, Sanford, and Dennis Longwell. *Sanford Meisner on Acting* (New York: Vintage Books, 1987).

Merlin, Bella. "Mamet's Heresy and Common Sense: What's True and False in 'True and False,'" *New Theatre Quarterly* 16 (August 2000): 249–54.

9

STEVEN PRICE

On directing Mamet

There is a moment in *Vanya on 42nd Street* that everyone remembers, though it is not quite the same moment for every spectator. It happens shortly after the quasi-documentary opening sequence of Louis Malle's film, once the stage director André Gregory and his actors have made their way to Manhattan's New Amsterdam Theatre to rehearse *Uncle Vanya*. Inside, expository conversations about the building and the production suggest that the dialogue has been, if not scripted, at least prompted, creating a curious hybrid of *cinéma vérité* and theatre that persists as two of the actors, Phoebe Brand and Larry Pine, discuss drinking habits. At some point, probably during this conversation, each spectator will suddenly realize that the play has already begun: there must have been an unnoticed shift from the conversation of the actors to the dialogue of Chekhov's characters, Marina and Dr. Astrov, and the mind momentarily goes into reverse, trying to find the moment when it happened, before picking up the thread of the play again. It is a stunning transition.

No-one is quite sure where the idea came from. It is not, of course, in the adaptation of Chekhov's play by David Mamet (drawing on a translation by Vlada Chernomordik) that Gregory used for this production; Gregory, credited with the idea by Malle, denies it came from him; Pine thinks it originated with one of his suggestions.[1] Whatever prompted it, this seamless transition was assisted by the ensemble approach to theatre and the "uninflected" style of acting affirmed by Mamet himself: as Wallace Shawn (Vanya) puts it, "[t]he goal of the whole project was to reach a point where you didn't think about it, where the lines popped out of your mouth as the most natural thing to say in the circumstances."[2] After the prologue, Gregory appears only between the acts, as a benign host and spectator; we do not see him guiding the actors, although in reality he had been holding workshops with them since 1989, five years before the film was made. In effect, he is erased as the performance gets underway, leaving only the text and the actors; there is not even a stage, as the theatre was dilapidated and each act was filmed in a different part of the auditorium.

The film shows the director as one member of a company, his energies expended in bringing to the stage not his personal vision, but the intentions of the playwright realized in the performances of the actors. It is close to an ideal of the theatre company, and of the role of the director, that Mamet has held from his earliest experiences of writing *Camel* and *Lakeboat* for his students to perform at Goddard and Marlboro. Co-founding the St. Nicholas Theatre Company on his return to Chicago, he helped to create an "organic theater," which "consisted of a company of actors who also directed and also wrote and also designed. Everybody did everything. There was no mystery about it . . . that was the community and the tradition that I came back to in the seventies in Chicago."[3] It is a tradition quite different from the then-influential life and theatre experiments conducted by groups such as the Open Theatre, the Living Theatre, and the Performance Group, whose politics and practices, honed in the anti-authoritarian aesthetics of the 1960s counter-culture, exhibited a "resistance to language"[4] quite alien to Mamet, who has no time for performance art and would doubtless question the judgment of those who believe that "[t]he dominant creative force in today's theatre is the director."[5] On hearing of an all-female production of *Glengarry Glen Ross* in 1995, he was "reminded of Stanislavsky's statement: Any director who does something 'interesting' with the script doesn't understand the text."[6]

The major productions of his plays have usually been staged either by long-term collaborators, such as Gregory Mosher in Chicago and New York or Bill Bryden in London, or by fellow playwrights such as Harold Pinter, all of whom, to some extent, share Mamet's "practical aesthetics" that couple "the truth of the actor struggling bravely with uncertainty, with the portrayal made by the dramatist."[7] They avoid thematic interpretations and concentrate instead on finding a relationship between the characters that will form the major action of the play, whether or not that reproduces realistically the relationships in the plot. In *American Buffalo*, for example, the characters appear to be bachelor thieves, yet most directors treat Donny as a parent trying to raise a son; Pinter found that *Oleanna*'s highly problematic confrontation between a professor and a student made good sense when played as a sexual relationship. When character and plot are treated in this way the underlying dramatic action comes to the fore; when the plays are directed more realistically, they can appear distractingly fragmented.

The partnership between Mamet and Mosher began when Mosher was appointed Artistic Director of Chicago's Goodman Theatre in 1974. Mamet's plays had already attracted attention in the city; now, as Associate Director and later as writer-in-residence, he would work with Mosher at the Goodman's small, 135-seat Stage Two, which the director describes as the "bridge" between the Goodman and Chicago's thriving avant-garde, Second City theatre scene.[8] Here Mosher directed the premières of *American Buffalo* in 1975 and *A Life in the Theatre* in 1977, *Lone Canoe*'s 1979 production in the Goodman's main 700-seat theatre being a sign of the playwright's increasing success. Its disastrous reviews provided Mamet with his first major setback, but the creative partnership at the Goodman continued with a rewritten *Lakeboat* in 1982, the première of *Edmond* (in the Goodman's Studio space) in the same year, *The Disappearance of the Jews* in 1983, and *Glengarry Glen Ross* in 1984.

These productions featured actors such as Joe Mantegna, William H. Macy, J. J. Johnston, Mike Nussbaum, Colin Stinton, and others who would later become familiar to a wider audience as members of the extended family which Mamet cast in his films. Mosher has fond memories of working with Mantegna, Nussbaum, Mamet, and stage manager Tommy Biscutto on rehearsals for *A Life in the Theatre*: "Five feet of snow in Chicago, forty below, and we're the only people out on the streets. No buses. No taxis. No subways. We were rehearsing this play that we loved and going out into the night through these snowdrifts. That, to me, is happiness."[9] The nostalgic glow contains a hint of illicit freedom, the actors seemingly outside all society but their own. It is bound up with those connections between theatre and criminality invoked by Mamet at the beginning of *True and False*, where he reminds the reader that "[a]ctors used to be buried at a crossroads with a stake through the heart,"[10] and in his repeated suggestions earlier in his career that he is destined for the jailhouse. He told John Lahr that had he not worked in the theatre, "it's very likely I would have been a criminal. It seems to me to be another profession that subsumes outsiders, or perhaps more to the point, accepts people with a not-very-well-formed ego, and rewards the ability to improvise."[11]

Certainly this contributes to the effect of Mamet's finest plays, which are all about small-time crooks rehearsing for their next scam. In *American Buffalo* Teach and Don prepare for the robbery that will never happen, debate whether to cast Bobby or Fletcher, and try to memorize their lines before using the telephone. In *Glengarry Glen Ross* all of the salesmen worry about their ability to perform to a paying audience, whether that be Mitch and Murray, Jerry Graff, or the "leads"; and Roma and Levene stage an extemporized performance for Lingk at a moment's notice, displaying the near-telepathic communication of the theatre double-act. These characters are actors, and the resale shop, the Chinese restaurant, and the real-estate office are the offstage spaces where they prepare their performances.

The rehearsals Mosher remembers so fondly were for a play about rehearsals; and it was he who had the idea of situating all of its action in a theatre.[12]

Fostering the sense of a community of free outlaws is perhaps the first requirement of a director of such plays, though it comes with the territory. Certainly Mosher had no difficulty in resolving the potential tension between the collaborative process and the authority of the writer:

> ultimately he has the final say on what they say, and I have the final say on how they say it, or on any other aspect of the production. But, it's so collegial now that it's hard to know where one of us stops and the other starts . . . And then if it's Mantegna, or Macy, or Stinton, then it's like family; we have spent literally thousands of hours together in rehearsal rooms and bars.[13]

At ease in these surroundings, neither writer nor director felt any need for elaborate set design. Mamet felt that "the trick was to be able to do it on a bare stage, with nothing but one or two actors,"[14] and Mosher had similarly minimalistic tastes. There are exceptions: the design for *Lone Canoe* was inspired by the Russian director Vakhtangov,[15] while Mosher and Michael Merritt created for the 1975 première of *American Buffalo* an abstract set born of necessity. The budget was $100, and the play was performed in the evenings in a room used during the day for other rehearsals, so the set was "stripped every day. There were all these chairs . . . and so I thought, we'll build this set out of chairs – hundreds of metal chairs – and that will be the back wall."

By contrast, a realistic set built for Mosher's New York production "hurt the play terribly."[16] Mamet's plays, particularly early in his career, were quite routinely described as realistic, and although the poetic structure and cadences of the writing have since become unmistakable, the realistic staging remains commonplace. For Mosher, however, the mise-en-scène denuded of props furthers "the function of the theatre," which in true Mametian style "is to reveal the dream life of the culture, not the conscious life of the culture."[17] His basic restaurant set for the first act of the 1984 *Glengarry* was an abstraction from the everyday, leading the audience to focus not on the surroundings but on the series of small human gestures that constitute the necessary physical action of the play. One of the actors was required to show some money; and "when he pulls out that fat wad of bills, peels one off, puts it down on the table and slides out of that booth – boy, eight hundred people were looking at those ten fingers and that little piece of green paper."[18] The attention to hands and money is a reminder of the confidence games and sleight of hand prevalent in the playwright's work. Mamet directed *Ricky Jay and His 52 Assistants*, a one-man show in which the illusionist's colleagues on stage are a pack of playing cards, and it is an interest manifested in *House of Games*, notably in a shot of Joe Mantegna manipulating a coin. The art of Ricky Jay is a good analogy to that of the director or the actor on Mamet's stage: shunning the assistance of design or machinery, attention to simple physical gesture will carry the meaning of the play, whether the aim is direction or misdirection.

This emphasis on the action, rather than the text, initially seems surprising in connection with a writer famed for his dialogue, although it does follow from Mamet's invariable insistence that the well-designed play is "a series of incidents in which and through which the protagonist struggles toward his or her goal," and that the actor should simply "learn the words by rote, as if they were a phone book, and let them come out of your mouth without your interpretation," "as if they were gibberish."[19] This is not inconsistent with the "uninflected" delivery Mamet advocates, but it is important to make a distinction. Whether or not one accepts the argument, the words can be "gibberish" insofar as, for Mamet, the actor need not worry about interpreting what they signify. For the director, however, it is crucial to orchestrate the dialogue of the actors so that the poetic, aural connections between the words – the signifiers – are maintained. As Mosher says, "the process is discovering the correct rhythm and intonation,"[20] and with the work of a living writer, the rhythm of the playwright's own, everyday speech is often a vital clue as to how this should be done.[21]

Nevertheless, for Mosher "the paradox is [that] the play is not about text; it's about action" and "what you *direct* is the action."[22] For example, Mamet had told him that the subject of *American Buffalo* is "honor among thieves." This is a theme, however, and of little help to Mosher, because the director's job is to settle on what other directors might call the "through-line" or the "superobjective" to shape the action. What this is will differ from director to director, but it is important to distinguish it from simple plot. For Mosher,

> the action of *American Buffalo* has nothing to do with what the text would have us believe it is about, which is the robbery of a coin . . . For one thing, there *is* no robbery, and for another, the first and last ten minutes of the play don't have anything to do with a coin robbery. So the play gets onto the wrong track if the director's not doing his job. The story of that play is the destruction of a relationship between a father and son.[23]

Although Mosher and Mamet shared a common aesthetic, the director did turn down *The Water Engine*, a radically different play, as he "didn't quite get it" at the time, although he regretted it later;[24] conversely, he surprised the playwright in 1989 with his direction of *Bobby Gould in Hell*, settling on an English drawing room for the Devil's office. Asked if there is "a moment in one of your plays that you really didn't know was there," Mamet cited the moment when, as the Devil proves that some things are black and white by giving the example of a panda, "the assistant [held] up a picture of a panda, kind of pan[ning] it 180 degrees to the audience at the Vivian Beaumont Theater. That was the best moment I've ever seen in any of my plays."[25] By this time Mosher had long since moved from the Goodman to take the post of Director at New York's Lincoln Center, where he continued to champion Mamet's work with a double-bill of *Prairie du Chien* and *The Shawl* in 1986. However, in 1988 Madonna's presence in the cast of *Speed-the-Plow* led to the play opening directly on Broadway, one sign of Mamet's growing status in theatre and film which, together with the independent success of many of his collaborators, dissipated the company ethic, to be retained in part in the plays and films he would direct himself in the 1990s.

When Mosher directed *Speed-the-Plow* at the National's Lyttleton Theatre in London in 1989 it marked the end of Mamet's association with another company, run by Bill Bryden at the Cottesloe, that had presented the British première of *American Buffalo* in 1978 and the world première of *Glengarry Glen Ross* in 1983. Less at home with the American world of the plays, Bryden's company was perhaps even more attuned to the nervous anxiety demanded in performing them. No matter how close the working relationship between director, writer, and actors, this sense of danger remains a requirement. Some directors have discovered that it can even be produced by extreme familiarity with the material. André Gregory's workshops continued on and off for four years, the actors continually parting only to return to what actor Larry Pine describes as the "artistically safe" world of Gregory's *Uncle Vanya*, for which no production was envisaged.[26] Paradoxically, however, this demanded of his actors the courage in uncertainty that for Mamet is essential to honest performance. As Gregory says, "when you do it in five weeks . . . you figure out what you want to say ahead of time and then you find the best way to say it . . . [But] the interesting thing [is] to find out what you don't know. What you do know is not very interesting."[27] Certainly Gregory's methods enabled Julianne Moore, who played Yelena, to find a productive anxiety in the recognition that preconceived notions of "character" were being left far behind:

> It's liberating and absolutely maddening at different stages. Basically, he lets you go and go and go, until you run out of steam with one particular choice or a certain idea. It's intoxicating. And then you get to a dead-end, and you turn to André and say, "Well, now what?" And he asks, "Well, what do you feel like?" And you want to knock him to the ground, because you can't get out of

it. He forces you to find the way through it yourself. The result is you end up with a production and characterization that are intensely personal, where you really have created every little drop of it.

The result is seen in the performance in *Vanya on 42nd Street*, which gives the impression of demonstrating both the controlling intelligence of a director and the tensely spontaneous interactions of the cast. As Wallace Shawn remarks,

André doesn't seem to do much, while actually he's guiding everybody through his particular taste and interpretation of the play. There seem to be clear interpretations, certain choices that are made. Somehow, in some mysterious way, those are André's choices, although he never tells us to do those things. He never says, "Well, this is how I interpret the play."[28]

By contrast, Louis Malle shot the film in just two weeks, yet with the similar result that the actors were "filming without any safety net."[29] Such methods suit the work of a writer whose plays, lacking the security of exposition, do not provide any safety net themselves. Jack Shepherd, who played Teach in Bryden's *American Buffalo*, was still complaining at the end of the century that "I just wish that [Mamet] would give some handle . . . because playing it is like being on a rollercoaster without a ramp," but Bryden did not appear unduly distressed: "I just wish he would write another play!"[30]

Bryden had been brought to the National Theatre in 1974 by Peter Hall, who gave him responsibility for the Cottesloe, which was to open its doors to the public in 1977. Hall encouraged Bryden to take risks, one of the first of which was to stage *American Buffalo*. His ideas were in many ways similar to Mosher's at the Goodman: having worked with William Gaskill at the Royal Court, he counts himself a "Puritan" when it comes to respecting an author's work,[31] and he wanted a resident writer "who not only we admired, but who served the company as well. And there was no reason why it shouldn't be an American writer."[32] On receiving the script of *American Buffalo* from the agent he then shared with Mamet he immediately recognized a new voice, and secured the rights to stage the play in London after meeting the playwright in New York.

For this, the first play at the Cottesloe solely directed by Bryden, Grant Hicks designed a cluttered set that gestured towards realism in its metonymic representation of urban decay. The focal point, however, was a barber's chair, its peculiarity acquiring a sinister resonance when Donny (Dave King), whose faith in Bobby's story begins to evaporate in the second act, forced Bobby (Michael Feast) to sit in it.[33] The stage image conjures up scenes of torture from *King Lear* to *The Birthday Party*, and perhaps gestures particularly to

John Schlesinger's then-recent film *Marathon Man* (1976). Bryden brought out the simmering violence of the piece in other ways, too. Teach (Jack Shepherd) kicked out at one of the units on the set on his first entrance; when Bob returned in the second act, Teach dragged him into the shop and pointed a gun at his head; and when the violence finally exploded, the object Teach smashed over Bobby's head was a Coke bottle he had been nursing for some time, whereas the text calls for him to grab at a "nearby object" and assault Bob immediately.[34]

Although the production was well received, many critics felt that the actors had not yet mastered the accent. The question would be raised by reviewers of *Glengarry* also, although the director recalls Harvey Keitel coming over to confirm that "they're Yanks, right?" For Bryden, the accent is not the problem:

> The problem with the Mamet play is to learn it . . . because it's so repetitive . . . [But] by halfway through the rehearsals [for *Glengarry*] we were off the book, so then you could physicalise the characters and you can get the energy and the desperation and the speed . . . [which] makes them [appear] as if they've been together for a long time, and also makes the play travel like an express train.

If the actors' familiarity with the playwright, the play, and one another helped to generate the speed and rhythm that drive the play, it is less obvious that unfamiliarity with aspects of Mamet's world could also be turned to advantage. Evidence is provided by a scene from *Edmond* – a production of which was planned but never staged – that Bryden's company rehearsed for a documentary on the playwright broadcast in 1984.[35] Here, Bryden directs Kevin McNally on Edmond's bar-room encounter with a stranger:

> Here's a guy, David Mamet, trying to write an epic statement about, not his home town, but a strange town to him, New York . . . Who are we [the company]? Limeys, Paddies, right? What do we know? All we know is: observe the punctuation. When it says pause, pause. And during the course of the scene, the way it happens in bars, especially in David Mamet bars, [you get] what he calls "the blue hour," when people get the blues. You make friends, and you make the *best* friends. It's a hard thing to imagine, but during the scene, the man . . . will become your closest friend. And you'll never see him again as long as you live.

Edmond is in many ways a distillation of an American writer's feelings about New York, yet Bryden's direction indicates how Pinteresque is the playwright's conception of character and relationships. The company could exploit their ignorance of the world captured in the scene, because Edmond's own alienation is staged within it; but it is not simply the unfamiliarity of these particular characters that is important. In *The Pinter Problem*, Austin E. Quigley notes that "character," which implies a set of stable, immanent qualities, is a misleading term in connection with Pinter's plays. He prefers to speak of the "interrelational function" in demonstrating, by way of speech-act theory, the ways in which language does not refer to relationships, as it might if the plays were more conventionally expository, but constitutes them.[36] In Mamet's plays, too, character and relationships are indeterminate and ever-changing; and Bryden's direction of McNally indicates the importance of finding in each scene the connection between characters called for at that given moment.

The affinity between Pinter and Mamet emerged most strongly when, after an unsuccessful staged reading of *Glengarry Glen Ross* in New York, Mamet sent the play to the English writer, who knew a masterpiece when he saw it, urged Bryden and Hall to secure the rights immediately, and was an encouraging presence at several important rehearsals. The very things that had confused the New York auditors of this quintessentially American play struck a chord with Bryden:

> [Mamet] was insecure about the play at first, because he'd been told that the first act wasn't commercial, and the second act should be more like Neil Simon . . . whereas from our point of view the first act was a perfect Royal Court first act, where you don't know what's happening . . . And then at the end of the first Act, Roma says to Lingk, "this is a piece of land," and of course the audience goes ballistic: because not only have they learned the language, they've now got the dictionary, they can throw away the guidebook, they're hooked. And of course the second act is completely different.

During the rehearsals, Bryden asked Mamet if he had any notes for the actors, to which he replied: "I've got one note: These guys could sell you cancer." That is as far as "motivation" needs to go: the future-directed motivation of anxiety or desire, not the backward- or inward-looking "sense memory" of the Method. It also suggests that it is a mistake to regard the salesmen simply as losers in their profession, although it is an interpretation encouraged by the prologue Mamet added for James Foley's 1992 film, in which the über-salesman, Blake, humiliates the men in the office. Mamet's comments at rehearsals suggest the play should be seen differently. "Selling you cancer" is, in Mosher's terms, an action that the director can follow, while as Bryden says, "it's not difficult to motivate or find the backstory of the character. It's there, in the moment, the word is the action."

What happens when a director allows a character's "backstory" to replace the action is illustrated in different treatments of the vague references Shelly Levene twice makes to his daughter when speaking to Williamson, apparently in a hopeless attempt at emotional blackmail. Sam Mendes, who directed another celebrated production at London's Donmar Warehouse in 1994, felt that both men must have families, but he treated them quite differently. Williamson "must have another life, because of the way in which he performs within the context of the office." Recognizing, too, that Moss must have recruited Levene to commit the robbery after failing to recruit Aaronow, Mendes and his actors "spent a lot of time working out exactly what happened" to dramatize effectively Moss's unspoken anxieties in the second act.[37] With Williamson, Mendes was exploring the structure of the office relationships; with Moss, he was piecing together the necessary progression of seen and unseen actions. In each case he was not filling in hypothetical gaps in the story, but following the logic of the discourse – the ways in which the characters negotiate the here and now. For the same reason, the director need have no interest in discovering what ails Levene's daughter. In the film version, Foley literally loses the plot at this point. Bryden recalls that Mamet "insisted that Derek [Newark, who played Levene] didn't know what that was: decide what it is, and never tell us what it is. But Jack Lemmon knew what it was and sentimentalised this sick kid. That wasn't the intention when he wrote the play." There is a similar problem with Dustin Hoffman's Teach, endlessly scratching himself and fiddling with props in Michael Corrente's 1996 *American Buffalo*: the film becomes about a single performance, unintegrated with the work of the other actors or with any perceptible directorial interpretation, despite Mosher's work as producer on the film.

When Mamet, in interviews and in *True and False*, argues that there is no such thing as "character" but merely words on a page, interviewers and actors are often scandalized, but it reveals the writer–director's concern for coherence. It is, in fact, simply text-book structuralism: a character in a novel or a play does not possess inherent qualities (or "positive terms"); instead, the character's significance emerges from its differences from others within the structure. The point about Levene's daughter, for example, is that Levene is the only salesman who mentions his family; he has thereby contravened one of the unwritten rules of the office, and appears weak and unmanly. But as *American Buffalo*'s Don might put it, whether or not his daughter even exists makes no earthly difference in the world.

The temptation to sentimentalize Levene, and thereby throw him to the forefront of the drama, may arise because if one were to put a plot summary in *TV Guide* he would be the protagonist, just as Don Dubrow is the protagonist of *Buffalo*. However, the characters who leave the strongest impression in what are in any case ensemble dramas are Roma and Teach. Bryden is drawn to sporting analogies in explaining the problem with directing the relationship between the protagonist and what Mamet calls the "cufflink" part:

> The problem with actors [playing] Donny and Shelly is that you've got to work very, very hard, *knowing* the cufflink part's going to nick it in the end. But we didn't really know that in those days . . . David either knew it or discovered it by watching the plays . . . I kept that a secret during *Glengarry* because I knew. Same writer, same differential between the two leads . . . It's like defence and offence in American football, or midfield guys and forward players in soccer: the midfield works all the time, and somebody scores the goals. That's the cufflink part.

The analogy captures the kind of team spirit and fluid interplay that the director attempts to instill in his players, exploiting their competitiveness and mutual interdependence. With so much depending on correctly syncopating Mamet's rhythms, "[y]ou have to try to get the team together, on the field and all wearing the same strip by opening night."[38] The comparison acquires still greater resonance in performance, when the theatre audience becomes both the crowd and the opposition. If Mamet's early work was influenced by the crowd-pleasing demands of the Second City revue sketch, he was soon writing plays that, deliberately or not, embraced the oppositional function of the audience, claiming that businessmen who saw *American Buffalo* "were angry because the play was about *them*."[39]

The most notable example concerns Mamet's direction of *Oleanna* in Cambridge, Massachusetts, which he compared to staging "*The Diary of Anne Frank* at Dachau."[40] The play was widely seen as a polemic against "political correctness," although it was soon recognized that it also chimed with some of Mamet's own views about higher education. It certainly seems to be a play with a theme, unlike his earlier plays, which were tautologically "about" the characters and their actions. The notorious near-riots in Cambridge and at the Orpheum Theater in New York in 1992 revolved around the actions of Carol, whom most considered a hate figure, although many felt this was because Mamet had loaded the dice against her. This is some feat, because one of the many problems with *Oleanna* is that John quite plainly is guilty, first of offering Carol an A grade that her work does not merit, and second of assault at the end of the play; and in the words of David Suchet, who played John in Harold Pinter's London production, he is "arrogant, pompous, self-obsessed, in love with the sound of his own voice, always coming back to himself when discussing someone else's problems and never listening."[41] Yet it is almost impossible to direct the piece without making it appear, in Michael Billington's description of Mamet's New York production, "an intellectually loaded affair about a dowdy no-hoper getting her sadistic revenge on a perfectly pleasant prof."[42] The main reason for this is that Carol's wholly justifiable complaint about John's idiosyncratic approach to assessment procedures is lost amidst accusations of rape that are so ridiculous, not least in her abuse of language, as to make her appear unhinged. The inverted commas in the text indicate the absurdity: "I saw you [. . .] sit there, stand there and exploit our, as you thought, 'paternal prerogative,' and what is that but rape"; "You tried to rape me. I was leaving this office, you 'pressed' yourself into me. You 'pressed' your body into me."[43]

In Mamet's productions, both on the stage and in his 1994 film version, John was played by William H. Macy, whose endearingly open and boyish features help to create a presumption in favor of John's innocence. More subtly, the spatial fluidity of the film diminishes the claustrophobia of the single-set stage production, and thereby his control of the room. For example, he is able to retreat into his office to take the increasingly significant telephone calls; Carol waits outside, overhearing, but she can no longer be seen as the implied addressee of what are, on stage, presumptuous and potentially aggressive assurances that he is successfully dealing with her complaint. Mamet's direction of all three productions helps to explain the level of anger directed at Carol, and indicates the problems confronting any director aiming to find a balance between the characters.

Oleanna had secured a reputation for turning its audience into a mob of potential John Wilkes Booths by the time Harold Pinter came to direct the London production in 1993, first at the Royal Court and then on its West End transfer to the Duke of York's. Pinter did not think the play was a polemic, but a sense of strain can be detected in his discussion of how he approached the play, in which he found "the skein of sexual tension that seems to exist between father and daughters . . . The three of us, David Suchet, Lia Williams and me, have tried so hard to avoid hysteria . . . We have tried to find the wholeness of this girl."[44] This suggests an attempt to forestall the responses Mamet's productions had received, and perhaps a preconception of how to bring this about. Unlike the work of Mosher and Bryden, then, Pinter's direction of *Oleanna* was unusual in the degree of directorial input seemingly running contrary either to the playwright's wishes or to the apparent demands of the text, although the aim was clearly to do justice to the play rather than turn it into a showcase for the director.

Certainly, Pinter's decision to revert to the original ending led to a rift with Mamet. The published text is from the New York production, which ends with Carol huddling under the table after John's assault, muttering cryptically, "Yes. That's right" (80), bringing the play to a sudden halt after the climax of rage. Pinter wanted to use the Cambridge ending, in which a distraught John apologizes and reads from a statement Carol has prepared, in which he will accept "provisional employment" in return for agreeing that "I have failed in my responsibilities to the young." Punctuating his reading are the questions he asks of Carol: "What happened today?"[45] Mamet remained unhappy about Pinter's preference, but accepted a statement printed in the program that "the original ending is performed with the agreement of the author."

Pinter's decision allows for some reflection on the meaning of the violence. The ending recalls that of *American Buffalo*, as a parental figure suddenly recognizes that he has failed to protect a child, although John does not reach Don's level of empathetic insight, and whether it shows Carol in a better light than the published version is moot. Nevertheless, the choice of ending is consistent with Pinter's intention "to get the arguments as clear as possible."[46] Another way of doing this was by changing Carol from the fusty, repressed figure of the American productions. Instead, Lia Williams had long blonde hair and in the first act wore a T-shirt and jeans, and although Carol remained confused in this opening scene, her questioning of John's ideas appeared less the helpless mumblings of the bewildered and more an ironic puncturing of the pretensions of a man who barely knew what he was talking about himself. Already, her seemingly innocent interrogation of his book provided some balance to his annihilation of her essay.

With Carol a more appealing figure than in the American production, Mamet's dialogue, which usually operates according to the principles of seduction (as, famously, in Roma's sales pitch to Lingk), now took on more starkly sexual implications. Dejectedly looking at the floor during the opening telephone conversation with his wife, John repeatedly attempted to remove the phone from his ear; and at the end of her second call he held it away as if he were on the receiving end of a verbal hammering, and only then hung up on his wife, apparently cutting her off in mid-flow. Quite inappropriately, then, he drew Carol into an unwitting conspiracy with him against his wife; and towards the end of the act, in addition to putting his arm around her shoulder, he held her hand, whispered into her ear, and in a line absent from the published text told her to disregard the telephone when it inconveniently rang and broke the moment. At such moments he seemed torn between a boring marriage and an attractive young lover, delusions of sexual power heightened by the authority of his position, displayed, as in most stage productions, by Carol's lengthy spell of immobility in her chair at the start of the play, while John utilized all of the stage and sometimes perched on the edge of the desk, looking down on her. Establishing this attraction not only makes John potentially culpable, but also makes more sense of the sexual dynamic in the later acts. Carol's threat to leave at the end of the second act, and his insistence that she stay, had the sadness and repressed violence of the end of an affair; Act III became a squabbling, disastrous attempt at a reunion.

Directing the action as an unhappy love story gave a logic to the sudden changes in and irrational decisions of the characters that make little sense if the play is performed simply as a debate or a polemic. Indeed, words were continually undercut by action: Carol agrees to go after John discovers the rape allegation, yet, unlike in the printed text, here she makes no movement to leave. Moreover, Pinter inserted many lengthy pauses and silences that often served less to give emphasis to the words than to show the characters struggling over their meaning. A subtle example came when Carol asked the busy professor why he would stay with her, and then, on being told that he likes her, asked for an explanation. There was an unscripted pause during which Suchet's face registered a man searching for a reason, before he replied, "Perhaps we're similar" (21). It is an example of the way Pinter shifted the interest of the play away from thematic considerations and towards an examination of how, as Mamet had put it many years previously, "the language we use, its rhythm, actually determines the way we behave, more than the other way around."[47]

Pinter went some way towards redressing the balance between the characters, but at a cost. At almost two hours, this *Oleanna* was twenty or thirty minutes longer than other versions. In adding to or extending the pauses in the text Pinter, in one sense, rewrote the play; and while this is best explained by the need to combat the audience's preconceptions and to avoid a polemic, the slow tempo was also noticeable when Pinter directed his own *Ashes to Ashes*, the brilliant return to form of 1996. This is quite unlike the rapid delivery of the dialogue most have considered essential, and has the stamp of directorial authorship missing from the productions of Mamet's most regular collaborators.

This creative tension between the individual voice and the collaborative demands of theatre lies at the heart of directing Mamet's work. One of Carol's most telling criticisms of John is that he considers himself a maverick, yet shelters under the protection of the institution. The same could be said of many of Mamet's characters: his salesmen, criminals, and film producers think of themselves as rebels against the system; in practice they remain answerable to its demands. The drama plays itself out in anti-institutional energies and talents temporarily released in violence, anger, sexual desire, furious invective, an almost poetic creativity. The plays take on the quality of Bakhtinian carnival as the lowly are freed, it seems, to parody the pretensions of the powerful: Levene does his impression of a senior vice-president of

American Express; Don and Teach dream of the domestic sophistication of the bourgeoisie; *Speed-the-Plow*'s Fox imagines the uncountable riches of the studio head, all the time aping the status-ridden language of an elite that contrasts with his own obscenity-ridden urban argot.

The directors of the plays often find themselves in an uncannily similar situation. Mamet and Mosher evolved their own, brilliant productions at Stage Two, only to find that when they took *Lone Canoe* onto the main stage they took a critical pasting as "arrogant punks" from Chicago who had the temerity to stage a play full of "thees" and "thous";[48] Bryden's Cottesloe could only survive with a subsidy from the larger Lyttleton and Olivier theatres that Peter Hall took care to conceal,[49] while Sam Mendes's unsubsidized Donmar Warehouse required financial support from bigger players in the London theatre such as Maybox and Cameron Mackintosh. In staging Mamet's plays they have brought the "virtuoso of invective"[50] to Broadway and the West End; as administrators they have shown the loyalty of a Don Dubrow, while their theatres, like his resale shop, seem to exist in defiance of commercial logic. As for Pinter: "I can't be sacked, because I haven't got a job. Therefore, I'll continue to say whatever I like."[51]

NOTES

1. Oren Moverman, "Chekhov's Children – In Their Own Words," in John Boorman *et al.*, eds., *Projections 4: Film-Makers on Film-Making* (London: Faber, 1995), p. 229.
2. *Ibid.*, p. 222.
3. John Lahr, "The Art of Theater, XI: David Mamet," *Paris Review* 142 (Spring 1997), p. 64. See also Alisa Solomon, "The Goodman, the Organic, and the St. Nicholas: Resident Theaters in Chicago," *Theater* 10 (1979), pp. 75–81.
4. C. W. E. Bigsby, *A Critical Introduction to Twentieth Century American Drama*, vol. III: *Beyond Broadway* (Cambridge: Cambridge University Press, 1985), p. 65.
5. David Bradby and David Williams, *Directors' Theatre* (Basingstoke: Macmillan, 1988), p. 1.
6. David Mamet, letter to Christopher Hudgins, July 21, 1995; quoted in Christopher C. Hudgins and Leslie Kane, eds., *Gender and Genre: Essays on David Mamet* (New York: Palgrave, 2001), p. 3.
7. David Mamet, *True and False: Heresy and Common Sense for the Actor* (New York: Pantheon, 1997), p. 22.
8. Arthur Bartow, *The Director's Voice: Twenty-One Interviews* (New York: Theatre Communications Group, 1988), pp. 237–8.
9. Leslie Kane, "Interview with Gregory Mosher," in Leslie Kane, ed., *David Mamet: A Casebook* (New York: Garland, 1992), p. 245.
10. Mamet, *True and False*, p. 6.
11. Lahr, "David Mamet," p. 64.
12. Kane, "Mosher," p. 245.
13. *Ibid.*, p. 240.

14. Lahr, "David Mamet," p. 60.
15. Kane, "Mosher," p. 235.
16. *Ibid.*, pp. 233–4.
17. Bartow, *Director's Voice*, p. 235.
18. *Ibid.*, p. 236.
19. Mamet, *True and False*, pp. 12, 63, 62.
20. Bartow, *Director's Voice*, p. 233.
21. Mosher makes this point of Mamet's work in *ibid.*, p. 234; Peter Hall of playwrights generally in Peter Hall, "Directing the Plays of Harold Pinter," in Peter Raby, ed., *The Cambridge Companion to Harold Pinter* (Cambridge: Cambridge University Press, 2001), pp. 151–2.
22. Bartow, *Director's Voice*, pp. 233, 235.
23. *Ibid.*, p. 234.
24. Kane, "Mosher," p. 234.
25. Lahr, "David Mamet," pp. 66–7.
26. Moverman, "Chekhov's Children," p. 221.
27. *Ibid.*
28. *Ibid.*
29. *Ibid.*, p. 226.
30. Platform appearance, National Theatre, October 11, 1999; DAT recording in National Theatre Archive, London.
31. John Barber, "Sparkle of Northern Light," *Daily Telegraph*, October 25, 1975.
32. Unless otherwise noted, quotations from Bryden are from an interview with the author, April 28, 2003.
33. Details of this production are taken from the National Theatre's "Bible" production script, 1978.
34. Mamet, *American Buffalo*, p. 97.
35. *The South Bank Show*, London Weekend Television, 1985.
36. Austin E. Quigley, *The Pinter Problem* (Princeton, NJ: Princeton University Press, 1975).
37. Leslie Kane, "A Conversation: Sam Mendes and Leslie Kane," in Leslie Kane, ed., *David Mamet's "Glengarry Glen Ross": Text and Performance* (New York: Garland, 1996), pp. 255, 250.
38. Bill Bryden, "Bill Bryden on *Summerfolk*," *Guardian*, October 11, 1995.
39. Richard Gottlieb, "The 'Engine' That Drives Playwright David Mamet," *New York Times*, January 15, 1978, p. D4.
40. Richard Stayton, "Enter Scowling," *Los Angeles Times Magazine*, August 23, 1992.
41. Charles Spencer, "Bittersweet Battle of the Sexes," *Daily Telegraph*, September 15, 1993.
42. Michael Billington, *The Life and Work of Harold Pinter* (London: Faber, 1996), p. 351.
43. David Mamet, *Oleanna* (London: Methuen, 1992), pp. 66–7, 78. Subsequent page references are to this edition.
44. Steve Grant, "Pinter: My Plays, My Polemics, My Pad," *Independent*, September 20, 1993, p. 13.
45. Video recording of David Mamet, *Oleanna*, Duke of York's, 1993; Theatre Museum Library, London.

46. Grant, "Pinter: My Plays," p. 13.
47. Ross Wetzsteon, "David Mamet: Remember That Name," *Village Voice*, July 5, 1976.
48. Mosher, quoted in Kane, "Mosher," pp. 235–6.
49. Ronnie Mulryne and Margaret Shewring, eds., *The Cottesloe at the National: Infinite Riches in a Little Room* (Stratford-upon-Avon: Mulryne and Shewring, 1999), p. 41.
50. Guido Almansi, "David Mamet, a Virtuoso of Invective," in Marc Chénetier, ed., *Critical Angles: European Views of Contemporary American Literature* (Carbondale: Southern Illinois University Press, 1986), pp. 191–207.
51. Grant, "Pinter: My Plays," p. 13.

10

PHILIP FRENCH

David Mamet and film

Playwrights became involved in the cinema early in the twentieth century when the new medium was scarcely a decade old, and there are few dramatists who have not been courted by a film industry eager to adapt their work or employ them as screenwriters. At first theatre people condescended to the prestige-seeking movie moguls, and the results were frequently unsatisfactory. Just after the First World War Samuel Goldwyn lured the Nobel Prize-winning Maurice Maeterlinck to Hollywood with unhappy consequences, and he had no greater success with George Bernard Shaw who famously rejected his overtures ("There is only one difference between Mr Goldwyn and me. Whereas he is after art, I am after money"). However, Shaw's fascination with the movies was later to involve him in adapting three of his plays in collaboration with the Romanian charlatan Gabriel Pascal.

David Mamet, born in 1947, three years before Shaw's death, belongs to a generation that grew up after the cinema and television had decisively replaced the theatre as the dominant forms of public entertainment. His primary commitment may be to the stage, but since the early 1980s he has established a parallel career in the movies matched by no more than a handful of dramatists of comparable distinction. One thinks of Sacha Guitry and Marcel Pagnol in France (both chiefly interested in bringing their plays to the cinema-going public with the least interference); of Robert E. Sherwood in the United States (a distinguished film critic, a recipient of three Pulitzer Prizes for drama, an Oscar-winning screenwriter, a speechwriter for Franklin Roosevelt); and two British dramatists Mamet admires, Terence Rattigan and Harold Pinter. His range – as adapter, author of original screenplays, director, and reflective essayist on the craft of film – has been greater than any of those five, and on a different scale from his near-contemporaries in Europe and America. Sam Shepard, for instance, has worked extensively in cinema as an actor, but has only adapted one of his plays for the screen (*Fool for Love*), and his two movies as director are of little consequence. Alan Ayckbourn has had two stage plays filmed, Michael Frayn and Tom Stoppard one each, none of which attained any kind of commercial or critical success, and only Stoppard has directed a film (his own *Rosencrantz and Guildenstern Are Dead*), though he has written a fair number of screenplays and shared an Oscar for *Shakespeare in Love*. In the course of producing half-a-dozen collections of essays, articles, and lectures, Mamet has opined, briefly and at length, on subjects as various as hanging around while his first wife made a big-budget film in Canada,[1] and attending the Cannes Film Festival when he had a movie in competition starring his second wife.[2]

Excluding work written or adapted for television, Mamet has been involved in around thirty movies. Except for his limited contribution to Bob Rafelson's thriller *Black Widow* (1987), in which he is briefly to be seen at a poker table as a cigar-chomping player billed as Herb, his film work to date falls into three categories. First there are the movies adapted from his stage plays; second, the nine screenplays he has written (a couple in collaboration) for others to direct; and third, and cinematically the most significant, the series of films he has himself written and directed. There are, of course, thematic links between the three groups as well as apparent anomalies, and the quality of the films he has directed himself is more even than those tended by others.

His first two ventures into the cinema were adaptations of hard-boiled novels and clearly it was the reputation he established for eloquent, realistic dialogue with the 1977 Broadway success of *American Buffalo* that brought about the invitations. The first film was a version of James M. Cain's 1934 *The Postman Always Rings Twice*, directed by Bob Rafelson in 1981; the second was *The Verdict* based on a novel by Barry Reed and directed by Sidney Lumet. A dozen years earlier neither movie could have been made with such explicit depiction of sex or use of four-letter words. In 1966, however, the new President of the Motion Picture Producers Association of America, Jack Valenti, had replaced the rigid Hollywood Production Code by a series of guidelines, and this new freedom enabled a fresh generation of moviemakers who emerged in the 1970s to forge a cinema that visually and verbally reflected American life with a greater realism than hitherto.

The Postman Always Rings Twice had previously been filmed in France as *Le Dernier Tournant* (directed Pierre Chenal, 1939), in Italy as *Ossessione* (directed Luchino Visconti, 1942), and in Hollywood under its original title (directed Tay Garnett, 1946). In the 1981 version, Jack Nicholson (his fourth collaboration with his close friend Bob Rafelson) plays Frank Chambers, the Depression-era drifter, who is hired as an odd-job man by Nick Papadakis (John Colicos), the middle-aged owner of a Californian truck stop café. Very soon he becomes the lover of Nick's young wife Cora (Jessica Lange), with whom he plots to murder Nick.

Assisted by the atmospheric lighting of the great Swedish cameraman, Sven Nykvist, the movie has an elegiac bluesy atmosphere, drawing on both the sadness and manic exhilaration of the 1930s. The sex has an animal rawness uncommon in Hollywood, though it had to an extent been suggested in the sweaty embraces of Visconti's adaptation. Mamet and Rafelson greatly improved the opening of Cain's novel, re-wrote most of the often flowery dialogue, and wisely refrained from employing a tough *film noir* commentary. Surprisingly they decided not to use the celebrated scene in which Cora risks her life on a swimming expedition to test Frank's love, and the movie concludes after the couple's acquittal for Nick's murder, but before the arrest of Frank for the murder of Cora, a crime he has not committed.

As a result the movie drifts towards a somewhat sentimental ending that is inferior to Cain's mordant irony. Nevertheless it is a picture of some distinction and a good start for Mamet, whose *American Buffalo* Rafelson and Nicholson admired. With no heavy producer looking over their shoulders they apparently greeted the playwright as an equal partner,[3] watching movies with him and encouraging him to study François Truffaut's book on Hitchcock. An additional benefit for Mamet of an unusual, rather touching kind[4] was that Rafelson's uncle, the legendary Hollywood screenwriter Samson Raphaelson (1896–1983), read the script and, through his nephew, gave him notes on it. Raphaelson was the author of *The Day of Atonement*, the play on which the first talkie, *The Jazz Singer*, was based, and several notable Ernst Lubitsch movies.

For his second film as screenwriter, Mamet moved to the East Coast and the present day with *The Verdict*, one of Sidney Lumet's numerous pictures about the law. The setting is a gloomy wintry Boston and virtually all the characters are Irish-Americans. The plot centers on the redemption of the alcoholic ambulance-chasing lawyer, Frank Galvin (Paul Newman), through his involvement with a blue-collar couple who are suing a Catholic hospital for negligence after the administration of the wrong anaesthetic has left their sister a human vegetable. It is a David and Goliath story with Galvin standing alone against the Church, a biased Catholic judge, and a law firm headed by Boston's most ruthless advocate, the demonic Ed Concannon (James Mason). "Concannon's a good man," Galvin concedes in conversation with his ageing mentor (Jack Warden), who has pushed the case his way. "Good? He's the prince of fuckin' darkness," the man replies in a recognizably Mametesque manner. With its various twists (Concannon's daughter seduces Galvin, the final trial scene calls on the services of a surprise witness) and the moral contrivance needed to deliver a happy ending, *The Verdict* reveals that unabashed taste for melodrama that would become a characteristic of the numerous films Mamet was to make.

The actual shooting of the film was smooth enough. The problems had all come in pre-production. Having approved Mamet's script, Lumet offered the leading role to "a major star" who insisted that the part be "fleshed out more" but, Lumet says, "Mamet always leaves a great deal unsaid . . . so he refused to do it."[5] Another writer was brought in, then a third one, and, after five re-writes, Francis Galvin had become loveable. Lumet then declared he would direct only if the producers (Richard Zanuck and David Brown, the men responsible for *The Sting* and *Jaws*) agreed to revert to Mamet's original version. It was shown to Newman who immediately accepted. This must have been a valuable experience for Mamet. The movie did well at the box-office and attracted five Oscar nominations – for best film, direction, actor, supporting actor, and best adapted screenplay – which established Mamet's reputation as a screenwriter. He would be in demand for the next twenty years, his fees rising to $1m a movie.

His next Hollywood assignment was *The Untouchables* (1987), produced by Art Linson, an independent Hollywood moviemaker noted for off-beat projects, most recently Michael Mann's *Heat* and David Fincher's *Fight Club*. The film was inspired by the notoriously violent TV series of the same title starring Robert Stack as Eliot Ness, the federal agent who famously nailed the Prohibition gang boss Al Capone for tax evasion. The series, which ran for 117 episodes between 1959 and 1963, concerned the struggle for power that followed Capone's conviction, but it was preceded by a feature-length pilot called *The Scarface Mob* (1958), featuring Neville Brand as Capone, which was shown on American television and in cinemas abroad.

Linson approached Mamet because he greatly respected his stage work and thought that a subject so steeped in Chicago folklore would appeal to him. As Linson recalled, however,[6] their initial meeting did not begin with a discussion on art or urban history. "Dave, don't you think that the best career move for somebody who just won the Pulitzer Prize would be to adapt an old television series like *The Untouchables* for a *shitload* of money?" Linson asked. "Yes I think so," Mamet replied.

To Linson's amazement, Mamet came up with a workable script in a month, though he thought that the character of Capone, who had not appeared in the TV series because he was already in jail, needed to be enlarged to attract a major star. Paramount studio executives had some doubts about the screenplay – they found Mamet's elliptical style both stilted and unintelligible – but these were allayed when Brian De Palma agreed to direct. De Palma was a natural choice after his success with *Scarface*, the 1983 transposition to contemporary Florida (as an underworld feud between expatriate Cuban drug barons) of Howard Hawks's classic 1930s gangster picture based on the career of Al Capone.

Mamet's treatment is nearer to another Howard Hawks film, the 1959 Western *Rio Bravo*, than to *Scarface*, in being the tale of four upright men brought together to confront an evil enemy. They are the straight-arrow Eliot Ness (Kevin Costner in the role that made him a major star in the all-American Gary Cooper – James Stewart tradition), the middle-aged Irish-American cop Malone (Sean Connery in the Oscar-winning part that restored his flagging fortunes), the wimpish accountant in steel-rimmed specs Wallace (Charles Martin Smith), and the eager Italian-American rookie cop Stone (Andy Garcia). Except for Ness, Al Capone (a formidable menacing Robert De Niro), and the gangland hitman Frank Nitti (Billy Drago), the characters are Mamet's inventions, and apart from the central thrust of a US treasury agent bringing down America's most formidable gangster, the story is largely fictitious.

The movie's two chief motifs are blood and booze. The color red is associated throughout with Capone who, when not actually involved in bloodletting, is constantly surrounded by people dressed in red. The spilling of blood is, of course, caused by the trade in illicit liquor, and drink is part of the film's moral framework. The film's first victim is a child, blown up in a speakeasy while on an errand to buy beer for her parents. "We must be pure," the priggish Ness tells his team, and two of them are killed immediately after touching alcohol. When asked what he will do when Prohibition ends, Ness replies: "Have a drink."

The Untouchables is a stylish, operatic film with costumes by Giorgio Armani and a magnificent score by Ennio Morricone. It is at its best in a sequence shot largely in slow motion of a mother and a child whose pram is caught in the cross-fire between Ness and Capone gunmen on the staircase of Chicago's grandiose Union Station. This scene is a homage to Eisenstein's *Battleship Potemkin* and is without dialogue, as is the one in which Nitti whispers the news of Malone's death to Capone and De Niro's wordless close-up registers everything that needs to be said. These scenes are a tribute to Linson's and De Palma's integrity and good sense. When Mamet embarked on his first movie, *House of Games*, he refused to work further on *The Untouchables*. So they restricted their chief additions to scenes that did not involve trying to write dialogue in the Mamet manner.[7] Mamet appreciated the verbal economy; on several occasions he has quoted Hemingway's bon mot: "To write the best story you can, take out the good lines."

Mamet worked again with De Niro and Art Linson on his next Hollywood movie, a re-make of the 1954 picture *We're No Angels*, a version of a French boulevard comedy *La Cuisine des Anges*, by Albert Husson. The 1954 version starred Humphrey Bogart, Peter Ustinov, and Aldo Ray as three charming escaped convicts helping a distressed family in 1930s French Guyana. It was a labored sentimental comedy, directed with uncharacteristic clunkiness by Michael Curtiz towards the end of his prolific career, and is not improved by Mamet and the gifted Irish director Neil Jordan, whose first American picture this was. Their *We're No Angels* (1989) shifts the setting to the border between Canada and Upper New York State in 1935, and it begins as a heavy, not unamusing parody of an old Warner Brothers Big House movie with Ray McAnally as the warden of a brutal penitentiary. The convict heroes – now reduced to two, Ned (De Niro) and Jim (Sean Penn) – are minor crooks forced to join a psychotic criminal (James Russo) in an escape bid. At the heavily guarded Canadian border they are mistaken for a pair of innovative Catholic theologians by the clearly demented head of a local religious community, and they take refuge in his monastery disguised as priests.

They then decide to join a Catholic procession to a site of healing across the border, taking with them as cover the deaf-and-dumb daughter of a golden-hearted local prostitute (Demi Moore). In the subsequent imbroglio they are blackmailed by the crazy convict with whom they escaped, and Jim decides to remain with the monks while Ned crosses into Canada with Moore, whose daughter has miraculously regained her powers of speech. The Catholic aspect probably attracted Jordan, though what Mamet saw in the project – beyond some sad low-lifes trying to survive – is far from obvious. The result is little short of disastrous. De Niro and Penn perform in a moronic mugging manner redolent of the Three Stooges, and the film's jokes about Catholicism are heavily farcical and embarrassingly religiose. Demi Moore's resilient Depression-era heroine is the chief redeeming feature.

Mamet's next movie as screenwriter (and also associate producer), *Hoffa*, reunited him with Jack Nicholson, and was directed (his third movie) by the diminutive character actor Danny De Vito. Hollywood has always been wary of films about organized labor, not only because of the big studios' own involvement with unions, both honest and corrupt, but also because the public has invariably rejected them. The most recent example before *Hoffa* was Sylvester Stallone's *F.I.S.T.* (1978), a violent, fictionalized account of the corruption of an idealistic leader of the Truckers Union, clearly Jimmy Hoffa. *Hoffa* (1992) drops the fictional veneer. It is a direct biopic of Jimmy Hoffa, the ruthless head of the corrupt Teamsters' Union, who was sent to jail in 1967 for jury tampering, released by President Nixon in 1971 to help in his re-election campaign, and last seen in 1975. He is still officially a missing person, though presumed to have been buried by the Mob under some Midwestern flyover.

Undoubtedly Mamet, Nicholson, and De Vito were romantically drawn to this tough, amoral opponent of the American establishment. They were determined to present in a positive light a blue-collar outsider, a product of the Midwest and the ethnic melting pot, who has been demonized by the middle classes and idolized – whatever his depredations – by the rank-and-file truckers from whom he had emerged. The film is rather like *The Untouchables*, re-written so that Al Capone was the representative of the true American spirit and his upper-crust nemesis, crusading lawyer Robert Kennedy (played by Kevin Anderson as a twitchy neurotic), a vindictive do-gooder.

The film unfolds in flashback as the weary 62-year-old Hoffa (a heavily prostheticized Jack Nicholson) and his sidekick Bobby (De Vito) reminisce in the car park of a Detroit diner in April 1975 as they await a representative of the Mafia, who is clearly to be the Grim Reaper. The growth of Hoffa from trucker to leader is traced in an atmosphere of repression and violence that acknowledges Hoffa's courage and growing political savvy as it recognizes his arrogance and cruelty. The problem with this vivid movie is the way it skates over Hoffa's personal development and family life, ignoring entirely his wife's involvement as dubious director of phoney companies, and fudging the political and industrial context of a forty-year career. Ultimately what the picture suffers from is a tough-guy sentimentality that endorses the admiring statement of the De Vito character – "He built the union with a pair of balls and a billy club." This echoes the famous speech by the Chicago patrolman Malone in *The Untouchables* on escalating violence – "If he pulls out a knife, you pull out a gun" and so on. Mamet and his collaborators are merely bored by Hoffa's bland, conniving rival, Frank Fitzsimmons (J. T. Walsh), who succeeded him as boss of the Teamsters' Union.

Following *Hoffa* there were several aborted projects, most notably an adaptation of Michael Crichton's allegedly xenophobic novel about Japanese corporations in America, *Rising Sun*, which was eventually directed by Philip Kaufman, with a script attributed to Kaufman, Crichton, and Michael Backes. Mamet's next film as writer to reach the screen was *The Edge* (1997). As recounted in his second book of Hollywood memoirs,[8] Art Linson was in a fix at Twentieth-Century Fox where he had a new production deal and needed a sure-fire hit. He phoned his reliable colleague Mamet, and – reverting to the technique that began their relationship with *The Untouchables* – promised that there would be "lots of money" if he could come up with an idea, preferably an adventure movie. Their conversation was like something out of Mamet's Hollywood comedy *Speed-the-Plow*. Within minutes Mamet suggested "two guys and a bear." "It's a start," Linson conceded. Shortly thereafter Mamet called back with "a rather well worked-out wilderness story that promised big intrigue, betrayal, a fierce struggle for survival, and, indeed, a bear." After the usual arguments with studio executives and the customary casting problems (Linson originally courted Dustin Hoffmann to play the lead), the picture went into production under the working title "Bookworm" with Anthony Hopkins and Alec Baldwin (who had made such an impression in the film of *Glengarry Glen Ross*, of which more later) in the leading roles and the New Zealander Lee Tamahori (who had had a major art-house success with the fierce movie of Maori life, *Once Were Warriors*) as director.

The film is set in the wilds of Alaska where the billionaire business tycoon Charles Morse (Hopkins) is accompanying his wife, the model Mickey (Elle Macpherson), on a fashion shoot with the photographer, Robert Green (Baldwin). Robert is Mickey's lover and, as Charles suspects, the pair are planning to kill him, but during a short plane trip away from their base, Charles and Robert are stranded in the wilderness, and the other two people on the flight are killed, the pilot in the crash, the other passenger by a ferocious bear. Charles and Robert then engage in a fight for survival, Charles using his formidable intellectual gifts to solve practical problems of a sort he has never previously experienced. Gradually, though Charles has confirmed that Robert is an adulterer and a would-be murderer, the pair come to rely on each other, but Robert dies before they are eventually rescued.

The film is handsomely photographed on Canadian locations by the Australian cameraman Don McAlpine and there is a great feeling for the beauty of the awesome landscape and the fear it generates. The film, however, ends up as a *Boys' Own Paper* adventure yarn underpinned by Social Darwinism and buoyed up by some fancy dialogue sonorously delivered by Hopkins (e.g. "I once read that most people lost in the wilderness die of shame"). When the film was completed, the marketing department at Fox rejected the title "Bookworm" and offered Linson fifteen alternatives of which the least objectionable was *The Edge*. The picture attracted a mixed critical and box-office response, failed to go into profit, and was soon forgotten.

Mamet rapidly followed up *The Edge* with a low-budget ($15m) political comedy, *Wag the Dog* (1997), satirizing the connection between show business and Washington. It became startlingly topical by appearing just as the Monica Lewinsky affair exploded in Bill Clinton's White House, and in one scene a young woman wearing a beret as she stands in line to greet the President has an uncanny resemblance to "that woman". The fairly polished movie was directed in twenty-nine days by Barry Levinson during a hiatus in the shooting of his expensive SF picture *Sphere* and featured the star of *Sphere*, Dustin Hoffman, alongside Robert De Niro. Mamet and Hilary Henkin as screenwriters worked from a novel by Larry Beinhart called *American Hero*. It is really a one-joke squib, an extended *Saturday Night Live* sketch, centering on a pair of presidential spin-doctors (De Niro and Anne

Heche, anticipating characters from the TV series *West Wing*). Their task is to neutralize the effects of a revelation on the eve of an election that the President has sexually molested a teenage visitor to the White House. Together with camp, unscrupulous Hollywood producer Stanley Motts (Dustin Hoffman) they conspire to create a diversionary war with Albania to distract the public, using faked TV footage, the services of a country singer (Willie Nelson), and an expert on current fashion (Denis Leary). The result is rarely more than mildly amusing, a strained, toothless affair, low on genuine insight into the political process.

Mamet's next two professional assignments as screenwriter on Hollywood projects – his last to date – were lucrative tasks with which he could have felt little personal involvement. Both, however, involved working with actors he had previously written for and with gifted directors. Neither could have afforded him much personal satisfaction, though they must have swelled his bank balance by several million dollars. The first was *Ronin* (1998), a commonplace thriller involving an international team of ex-Cold War spies, hired by a woman with a suspiciously thick Ulster accent to steal a McGuffin from a gang of crooks on the French Riviera. The portentous title (the Japanese word for a disgraced samurai forced into a life of crime) was accompanied by pretentiously doom-laden dialogue. There were several elaborate car chases, and the big cast was led by Robert De Niro, his fourth picture written by Mamet. The director, John Frankenheimer, one of the great filmmakers of his time, had done his best work in the 1960s (most notably *The Manchurian Candidate* and *Seven Days in May*) and nothing of much significance since, except for TV. *Ronin* was his penultimate big-screen movie (he died in July 2002), and Mamet was so unhappy with the result that he shared a scriptwriting credit with J. D. Zeik using the pseudonym Richard Weitz.

The other film was an adaptation of *Hannibal*, Thomas Harris's third novel featuring the psychiatrist and cannibalistic murderer, Hannibal Lecter, and the long-awaited sequel to *The Silence of the Lambs* (1990), the film of which had brought Oscars to its director, Jonathan Demme, and its stars, Anthony Hopkins and Jodie Foster. Harris, after years of reclusive writing, came up with a bizarre novel of Lecter on the run in Italy, being pursued by one of his hideously disfigured victims. The producer, Dino De Laurentiis, and his Hollywood associates had paid millions for the film rights and immediately saw that the novel had problems, both in its horrendous climax and in offering a lesser role to the FBI agent Clarice Starling, the part played by Jodie Foster. Moreover, for the first time Lecter was out of jail and for the first time it was necessary to motivate his brutal murders.

Amid immense publicity in the trade press, Mamet was engaged to produce a script that would satisfy the producers, the director Ridley Scott (Jonathan Demme had disliked the new novel), and the stars. Hopkins had expressed doubts about the novel's morality; Foster was concerned about the prominence of her part (as well as the size of her fee – allegedly her agent demanded $20m and 15 percent of the gross). Hopkins liked Mamet's script, but apparently it did not please anyone else. As a result, another screenwriter, Steven Zaillian (who had won an Oscar for *Schindler's List*) was hired, also for a million dollars. Daniel O'Brien's book about the Lecter films, *The Hannibal Files*,[9] gives a convincing account of the complicated maneuvers surrounding the writing and casting of the picture and quotes Zaillian's tactful comment on Mamet's draft screenplay: "Good, but it wasn't the movie we want to do." Ironically, to write the script Mamet had broken off his preparations for his comedy about the vagaries of the movie business, *State and Main*.

The first Mamet play to be filmed was an adaptation of his early one-act piece, *Sexual Perversity in Chicago*, twelve years after its première in that city, and just before Mamet made his debut as a movie director. On stage it was a series of dialogues and monologues, mostly brief and occurring all over the North Side of Chicago one summer, involving four unmarried Chicagoans in their late twenties. They are Danny, a lecherous, foul-mouthed businessman; Debbie, an illustrator with whom he's having an affair; Danny's friend and fellow office worker, Bernard; and Debbie's roommate, the nursery teacher Joan. The movie, scripted by Tim Kazurinsky and Denise DeClue, stars Rob Lowe (Danny), Demi Moore (Debbie), James Belushi (Bernie), and Elizabeth Perkins (Joan), and was opened out. Numerous other characters were added, and the film was called *About Last Night . . .* It is less bleak, bitter, and verbally abrasive than the play, and because of the casting of Lowe and Moore, who had appeared together the previous year (along with Ally Sheedy, Emilio Estevez, Judd Nelson, and Andrew McCarthy) in *St. Elmo's Fire*, was categorized by most critics and moviegoers as an addition to the current series of "brat pack" pictures. Most of the pictures in this slick, knowingly observant cycle were written and produced by the Chicago-based John Hughes, and they featured up-and-coming Hollywood performers in tales of affluent, self-regarding young people starting out in the adult world.

About Last Night . . . is the directorial debut of Edward Zwick, who the following year was co-creator of *thirtysomething*, the highly regarded TV series about the personal, professional, and marital problems of seven well-off, self-centered middle-class Philadelphians. The TV series combined thematic boldness with cautious treatment in a manner that Zwick's movie anticipated. Within its limits, though, and for its day, *About Last Night . . .* is an honest comedy of manners and morals in a world where old problems of adjustment and commitment are joined by new ones produced by permissiveness and affluence. The characters are troubled by the new rules of co-habitation – "If he stops over three nights a week, should he pay half the rent?" They are also concerned about repeating the old patterns of their parents' lives – reviewing the domestication into which she appears to have slid, Debbie proclaims: "Well, it's official, I've become my mother." The film, of course, turns Mamet's pessimistic end on its head.

The next screen version of a Mamet play came six years later with Mamet's own adaptation of his Pulitzer Prize play *Glengarry Glen Ross*, directed by James Foley in 1992. The play is slightly opened out but retains the original's claustrophobia, with most scenes set in the office of a dubious company selling tracts of largely worthless real estate in Florida and Arizona to credulous purchasers. It is a triumph of ensemble acting starring as the four major salesmen Jack Lemmon (the burnt-out former sales champion Shelly), Alan Arkin (the resigned, ageing George), Ed Harris (the bitter, scheming Dave), Al Pacino (the young, confident new ace), and Kevin Spacey as Williamson, the cold, vindictive office manager. This is Mamet's cruellest commentary on the horrors of unrestrained capitalism and the shoddy, dark side of the American Dream. The movie, however, which clearly nods in the direction of Arthur Miller's *Death of a Salesman*, wins our sympathy for the salesmen whose resilience Mamet respects and whose language fascinates him. The audience is also made complicit in their schemes as we find ourselves guiltily hoping that they will pull off their confidence tricks.

Much of the film takes place at night under torrential rain that recalls the Flood (biblical references abound in Mamet), and the author created a striking new character for the opening scene, a sleek emissary from head office played unforgettably by Alec Baldwin. He is called Blake – the name evoking the author of *The Marriage of Heaven and Hell*, a work that reverses normal moral ideas and presents Satan as an angel – and he has come, he says, "on a mission of mercy." He is in fact there to tell them they are worthless, that the firm's only interest in them lies in the business they generate, and that only one of them will survive the current sales drive. He is the steel fist of capitalism, a man with contempt for community and compassion, and his baleful shadow is cast over the rest of the film.

At last, in 1996 – twenty-one years after its first production in Chicago – there was a low-key, somewhat under-powered screen version of *American Buffalo*, the play that put Mamet on the theatrical map. The screenplay is by Mamet, the film was produced by Gregory Mosher (who directed the original Chicago production of *American Buffalo*), and directed by the unknown

Michael Corrente. Dustin Hoffman plays Teach, the ferocious minor criminal who conspires with middle-aged junk store owner Don (Dennis Franz), and Don's feckless, young, drug-addicted gofer Bob (Sean Nelson) to steal a valuable coin (the eponymous American Buffalo) from a local collector. The trio are losers, self-deceiving low-lifes who believe themselves to be on the brink of the big time. Their ineffectuality is cloaked in a linguistic smoke-screen of gutter poetry. The pivotal, seemingly simple role of Teach has proved capable of many variations. On Broadway Robert Duvall gave him an air of palpable menace and stamping anger; in the 1988 revival Al Pacino played him in a skipping, balletic manner; on the screen Dustin Hoffman – less scary than Duvall, less sympathetic than Pacino – renders him as an ageing version of the pathetic, rodent-like Ratso Rizzo he played in John Schlesinger's *Midnight Cowboy* (1969).

Most of the action is set in Don's store which is both a realistic junk shop and a colorful museum of tawdry Americana. The play, though, is opened up onto the deserted urban streets and we get a glimpse of the calamitous poker game that takes place the night before the main action starts. Except for a pair of hands holding cards, however, we do not see Ruthie, the woman hated by the misogynistic Teach, and we see nothing of Fletch, the gambler and criminal who is hero-worshipped by the trio. The chief change, however, is in the casting of a black actor as Bob, which gives different, slightly uneasy undertones to the relationships and raises a problem over the way Bob's lines as written by Mamet relate to the rather different rhythms and language of working-class black speech. Mamet regards the play as a tragedy, but as directed by Corrente on the screen all that comes over is a general sadness.

In 1994 Mamet directed for the first time to date a film of one of his own plays, *Oleanna*, a controversial piece about feminism and political correctness and the damage their excesses and exploitation can cause. The play was first produced less than a year after the Clarence Thomas – Anita Hill affair (in which a nominee for the Supreme Court was accused of sexual harassment) and has remained highly topical. It is a two-hander set entirely in the office of a university teacher called John, and Mamet keeps the action between these four walls. William H. Macy reprises his Broadway role as John, a liberal arts professor, and Debra Eisenstadt is his disturbed pupil Carol, a part created on stage by Rebecca Pidgeon, who wrote the music for the film version. It is an intense, claustrophobic affair in which John, who thinks of himself as a decent, understanding teacher, discusses with the inarticulate, inadequate Carol her learning problems. He treats her sympathetically, possibly patriarchally, but in taking her into his confidence, and protectively putting his arm around her, John plays into her hands.

Complaining (off-stage) to a Tenure Committee that is considering John's future at this university, she levels a succession of deadly accusations against him – of sexism, elitism, telling offensive stories, embracing her against her will, and finally attempted rape. His career is destroyed and the seemingly weak have triumphed over the apparently strong. If *Glengarry Glen Ross* is Mamet's *Death of a Salesman*, *Oleanna* is his equivalent of Arthur Miller's *The Crucible* and, though not entirely convincing, it is a very frightening and depressing piece.

There had been nothing quite like *Oleanna* in the American cinema, though that same year Hollywood came up with the crude, melodramatic film of Michael Crichton's *Disclosure* which turns upon a bitter career woman, a vengeful Demi Moore, making false charges against professional rival Michael Douglas after he had spurned her advances. Demi Moore was the actress who gave as good as she got in *About Last Night . . .* , the film of Mamet's *Sexual Perversity in Chicago*, and *Disclosure* was directed by Barry Levinson who four years later was to collaborate with Mamet on *Wag the Dog*.

Although it is tangential to Mamet's career, there is a remarkable movie with which he was closely associated that deserves mentioning here – *Vanya on 42nd Street* (1994), the final film by the US-based French director Louis Malle. This apparently simple exercise, which draws on Malle's parallel careers as a documentarist and a maker of fictional films, purports to be a discreetly observed record of a run-through in rehearsal clothes of a version of Chekhov's *Uncle Vanya*. The legendary Off Broadway director André Gregory had been preparing this production with a dedicated cast of actors for four years, but never reached the point when he thought it quite right to put it before a public audience. The setting is the disused, dilapidated New Amsterdam Theater, a once magnificent turn-of-the-century auditorium, and the cast is led by Wallace Shawn (as Vanya), who had appeared with Gregory in Malle's film *My Dinner With André*. At the end of this fascinating, deeply satisfying film we are not quite sure whether we have seen the record of a work-in-progress, the definitive account of a production that never found a final form, or an original piece of cinema. David Mamet's unobtrusively American translation of Chekhov's text flows easily and never jars in an anachronistic manner. It is an essential contribution to the experience of the film.

In the late 1980s, David Mamet's debut as writer–director was excitedly anticipated by his admirers the world over. They wondered how he would bring together his taut, elliptical theatre texts with the three hard-nosed but fairly conventional screenplays he had written for mainstream Hollywood productions. It was clear from his chronicle of following his then wife, Lindsay Crouse, to remote Canadian locations when she was starring in Fred Schepisi's *Iceman*,[10] that by 1983 Mamet was straining at the bit; he needed to be the man in charge, the chief honcho on the movie set. He had also begun to rebel against the role of the producer. He subsequently, and with amusing vividness, recorded his reactions to the making of his first film in two essays – "A First Time Film Director" and "Film Is a Collaborative Experience."[11] "I like to make decisions, I like to be at the center of things," he wrote, and recalled how in September 1985 he had been on a panel in New York with Spike Lee, Alex Cox, Frank Perry, and Susan Seidelman, billed as "Directors Discuss Independent Films," and as he listened to his fellow speakers had "thought, enviously, 'I wish *I* could be a film director.'"

Mamet's directorial debut, *House of Games* (1987), proved an agreeable surprise – the surprise residing in the lightness of touch, the lack of strain. A witty, stylized thriller, it gave the star role to Lindsay Crouse, and featured several members of what was to become identified as his stage and movie repertory company – Joe Mantegna (who played Richard Roma in the Broadway production of *Glengarry Glen Ross*), Mike Nussbaum, J. T. Walsh, William H. Macy, and the actor/illusionist Ricky Jay.[12] Like five of his eight films to date it is a crime movie and, as in several subsequent movies and some of his plays, a seemingly innocent protagonist is sucked into a world of moral ambiguity where evil seems more attractive than good and right is not easily separable from wrong.

House of Games is about the milieu of itinerant con men, a constant subject of American literature from Herman Melville's *The Confidence Man* and Mark Twain's *Huckleberry Finn* onwards, and is probably influenced by *The Big Con*,[13] the classic book by the linguist David W. Maurer that inspired George Roy Hill's *The Sting*. The protagonist of the film is Dr. Margaret Ford (Lindsay Crouse), an unmarried psychiatrist in her thirties who has recently achieved financial success through her book *Driven*, a best-selling self-help work sub-titled *Obsession and Compulsion in Everyday Life*. This is probably the strongest role Mamet has written for a woman, the one least vulnerable to the charge of misogyny. The equivalent in his later work is the casting of his second wife as the feminist heroine of Terence Rattigan's *The Winslow Boy*.

Mamet has written[14] that he had originally conceived of the picture as a silent movie, and a strained sense is created around the cool, controlled Margaret by very deliberate camera movements and a stilted, theatrical dialogue that eschews the elisions of normal speech. She is having trouble distancing herself from the problems of her patients, and one of them, Billy, a suicidal compulsive gambler is threatened with death if he cannot settle a poker debt. This leads her to visit the eponymous "House of Games" run by Billy's creditor, the big-time crook Mike (Joe Mantegna).

The exotic "House of Games" with its one-armed bandits, pool tables, long bar, and poker parlor, is a romantic, enticing place. Mike emerges from a deep shadow to greet Margaret, and without realizing it she is hooked by this elegant alternative world. She is also the designated victim of Mike and his band of confidence tricksters, who draw her into a scheme to shake down a poker player from Las Vegas. Slowly, while thinking herself an accomplice, Margaret is drawn further and further into a world of deceit and murder in a manner that recalls another student of the criminal mind, the professor of criminology played by Edward G. Robinson, who is sucked under in Fritz Lang's *noir* thriller, *The Woman in the Window* (1944). She begins to lose her grip on herself and on the moral certainties by which she lives as she tries to maintain her bearings in a milieu where fate is manipulated and everyone seems to be a character in someone else's play. She ends up rather like the hero of Mamet's *Edmond*, who descends into the abyss of the big city, and *in extremis* achieves both damnation and salvation as a murderer. Unlike the stark *Edmond*, however, *House of Games* is brought off with a light touch that is almost exhilarating.

In his Spring 1997 *Paris Review* interview with John Lahr, Mamet spoke frankly about drama, crime, and movie-making:[15]

> I've always been fascinated by the picaresque. That's part of the Chicago tradition: to love our gangsters and con men, the bunko artists and so forth.
>
> It occurred to me while I was doing *House of Games* that the difficulty of making the movie was exactly the same difficulty the confidence man has. For the confidence man it is depriving the victim of her money; for me it is misleading the audience sufficiently so they feel pleased when they find out they've been misled, tricking them so that every step is logical, and at the end they've defeated themselves. So the process of magic and the process of confidence games, and to a certain extent the process of drama, are all processes of autosuggestion. They cause the audience to autosuggest themselves in a way which seems perfectly logical, but is actually false.

Mamet's second movie as writer–director, *Things Change* (1988), again featuring a cast of his regulars, appeared immediately after his tough Hollywood stage comedy, *Speed-the-Plow*, which centers on the production of a dumb buddy movie at a major studio. Not, one supposes, by chance is it a buddy movie, though kindlier, more amusing, and subtler than the one being confected by the play's cynics. It is surprisingly mild in its language with not a single four-letter word and was awarded a PG certificate by the censors. This deftly plotted movie is reminiscent of Gogol's *The Government Inspector*, Jerzy Kosinski's *Being There*, and Hal Ashby's *The Last Detail*. It focuses on a wholly innocent Italian-American, the quiet, elderly Chicago shoeshine boy Gino. He is played by the eighty-year-old Don Ameche, the former matinee idol, then enjoying an Indian summer career as a character actor, who picked up a Best Actor Prize at Venice for this role. Gino is a dead ringer for a Mafia hit man and is persuaded by a Mob boss to go to jail in his place. He is assigned a minder until the imminent trial, a not-so-bright minor mafioso called Jerry (Joe Mantegna), who takes him for a final weekend fling to Lake Tahoe, Nevada. There the genial Gino is mistaken for a leading Mafia capo, given carte blanche at the casino, feted by elderly syndicate chief Vincent (Robert Prosky, who played Shelly Levene in *Glengarry Glen Ross* on Broadway), and entertained by showgirls. After various complications, Gino and the decent, big-hearted Jerry get back to Chicago only to discover they are being double-crossed. Pitting an honorable thief against a dishonorable one, however, they call on Vincent in Nevada to help them, and Gino hangs on to his bribe and stays out of jail. So these losers turn up trumps, becoming happy survivors if not exactly winners.

Mamet's book *On Directing Film*[16] is based on a series of lectures and dialogues he had with Columbia University students just after directing these first two pictures, and modestly claimed that "there are some directors who are visual masters – who bring to moviemaking a great visual acuity, a brilliant visual sense. I am not one of [them]." Instead he claimed to see parallels between his two sides as a playwright in the theatre and the complementary roles of the writer and director in the cinema:

> a logical structure, an outline . . . is given to the other part of the dramatist – the ego of the structuralist hands the outline to the id, who will write the dialogue.
>
> This conceit is analogous, I think, to the case of the structuralist screenwriter who gives the dramatic outline to the director.
>
> I saw and see the director as that Dionysian extension of the screenwriter – who would finish the authorship in such a way that (as always should be the case) the drudgery of the technical work should be erased.

His next film as writer–director, *Homicide*, was his first to be shown in the official program at Cannes, his first to feature his second wife, the British actress Rebecca Pidgeon, his first to engage directly with the Jewish experience, and his third to star Joe Mantegna. The movie starts out as a police procedural thriller and has a harshness and urgency not to be found in *House of Games* and *Things Change*. This may be due to the presence of maverick, politically oriented producer Edward R. Pressman and the gifted camera-man Roger Deakins, an Englishman with a sharp eye for American life. In the opening scene a SWAT team in Baltimore storms a tenement in search of a black drug tycoon, and, when he has disappeared, detective Bob Gold (Mantegna) and his Irish-American partner (William H. Macy, the Mamet regular hitherto billed as "W. H. Macy") are assigned to pursue the drug baron's lieutenant. Along the way they discover the murder of an elderly female Jewish shopkeeper in the ghetto area, and the movie appears to be a highly topical confrontation between blacks and Jews.

In the context, Gold, the seasoned cop who has seen it all, is the innocent, about to be faced with unexpected challenges that will expose his compla-cency. A secular, non-practising Jew, Gold belongs neither to the Jewish nor to the gentile world, but has found for himself a role apart as a cop with a particular skill at gaining the confidence of suspects and witnesses. Now he finds himself torn between two sets of investigations – pursuing the black drug-dealer and finding the killer of the shop-owner, who influential local Jews believe belongs to a neo-Nazi organization. In *Homicide* Mamet explic-itly examines his own Jewishness at a time when there was a recrudescence of anti-Semitism, most especially among American blacks. He comes up with a paranoid conspiracy theory that puts the movie in a tradition stemming from *The Manchurian Candidate* in the 1960s. Through the troubled Bob Gold, Mamet is dramatizing, in extreme melodramatic form, his own position as an embattled, assimilated liberal Jew.

Gold's decency is exploited on both sides of the racial divide and he is crushed by the social pincers, leading to the most mortifying study of Amer-ican loneliness since the end of Francis Ford Coppola's *The Conversation* (1974). The movie turns on a linguistic clue in the form of a piece of paper bearing the word "GROFAZ," found on a roof from which a suspected sniper has shot. Gold is led to believe that this word is an acronym for Hitler, used by Nazis towards the end of the Second World War, that has been taken over by American neo-Nazis. In fact, at the end, it seems more likely that it is in fact "GROFAZT," a brand of food for pigeons.

In a highly critical piece on Mamet's view of the Jewish and black milieux, the American critic J. Hoberman speaks of "the absurd scenario" of *Homicide*. He accuses the film of dealing in racial stereotypes, and he quotes Mamet as saying, somewhat equivocally: "I am neither expecting people to call the film anti-Semitic, nor will I be surprised if they do."[17] I still think it Mamet's best film to date.

The gap between *Homicide* and *The Spanish Prisoner* (1998), the next original screenplay he directed, was broken only by his version of *Oleanna*, with which I have already dealt. Mamet has called *The Spanish Prisoner* a "Light Thriller":

> I cite *The Lady Vanishes* and *Young and Innocent*, both early Hitchcock, and films in which he was working out the balance between comedy and thriller. The paradigm of the genre, of course, is *North by Northwest* and, perhaps, Stanley Donen's *Charade*. In these the hero . . . must, through trial and disappointment, discover that supposed foes are friends and vice-versa, and will, at the end, emerge shaken and stirred to re-examine the benefits of a previous state of innocence. Good fun.[18]

The Spanish Prisoner (the title refers to a celebrated confidence trick) is an elaborate variation on *House of Games*, a Kafka-lite version of *The Trial*, in which a socially insecure, working-class inventor, Joe Ross (Campbell Scott), finds himself the victim of an enormous conspiracy that begins at a Caribbean resort and continues in New York. He has invented a valuable process of an undisclosed nature for his company, but feels unappreciated and suspects his boss (Ben Gazzara) and others are trying to wrest it away from him. A chirpy English secretary, Susan Ricci (Rebecca Pidgeon), and a rich playboy entrepreneur, Jimmy Dell (Steve Martin), seem to be on his side, but so do a couple of FBI agents who turn out to be unknown to the Bureau. "You never know who anyone is," Susan says; "People generally look like what they are," Jimmy claims. Mamet constantly wrong-foots us, but always keeps us involved with the lonely, guilt-wracked, vulnerable Joe. The film is full of witty detail, and has a lightness of tone that is emphasized by Gabriel Beristain's dappled cinematography and Carter Burwell's characteristically insinuating score.

Almost immediately after *The Spanish Prisoner*, which picked up a PG certificate, Mamet directed a "U" movie – a second screen version of Terence Rattigan's 1946 play *The Winslow Boy*, one of the biggest West End and Broadway successes of the 1940s and first filmed by Rattigan and his regular collaborator, director Anthony Asquith, in 1948. Rattigan dramatized the 1908 Archer–Shee case in which a middle-class Englishman challenged the Establishment when his fourteen-year-old son, a cadet at Osborne, a Royal Naval College on the Isle of Wight, was expelled after being falsely accused of forging a signature on a postal order. The great advocate Edward Carson took up the case and in the face of immense political and media opposition vindicated the boy.

Mamet might have gone to the original facts – which are far more interesting and ironic than those ironed out into Rattigan's well-made play. Instead he chose to be the faithful servant of a play he calls "a work of melodramatic genius . . . I love the play, and was thrilled to work on it."[19] The result is an enjoyable version of an enduring West End stand-by that is set on the eve of the First World War but does not have the feel of a period piece. Nigel Hawthorne's patriach Arthur Winslow is as impressive as Cedric Hardwicke's 1948 impersonation, and Jeremy Northam's suave advocate, Sir Robert Morton, is even better than Robert Donat's (and very close to the Wildean dandy outlined in Rattigan's stage directions). In the third of the play's leading roles, Rebecca Pidgeon gives her best performance so far as the feminist Catherine Winslow, a Shavian New Woman, who makes common cause with her proud, conservative father. One is perhaps not being over-fanciful in suggesting that Mamet was also attracted by the affinities between the evasive language of the Edwardian middle-class and that of his Chicago low-lifes. Old man Winslow starts out as a wry wit, punctilious in his choice of words and habitually interrogating others, but he lives in a world where people prefer to proceed by indirection, rarely saying exactly what they mean and veiling themselves in verbal obfuscation.

In an interview recorded while he was shooting the picture in Britain, Mamet was more forthcoming, claiming not to be interested in the immediate British context of the play.[20] "My main concern is another aspect of the story," he said: "When does a fight for justice become an arrogant pursuit of personal rectitude? Arthur is constantly asking himself that question. At what point does one give up the fight for an abstract principle?" Mamet's interviewer, Nick James (editor of *Sight and Sound*), pushes the conversation in another direction, suggesting that *The Winslow Boy* "fits a pattern of victimhood" in Mamet's work, and more or less attains his subject's agreement.

Before returning to his characteristic mode as writer–director – the elaborately constructed thriller – Mamet followed *The Winslow Boy* with *State and Main*. This *jeu d'esprit* about the movie business finds the writer in mellow mood and his picture lacks altogether the bitterness of *Speed-the-Plow*. There have been a number of films about movie crews on location disrupting and despoiling innocent townships, ranging from the savagery of Dennis Hopper's *The Last Movie* to the mildly barbed humor of Alan Alda's *Sweet Liberty*, both of them superior to Mamet's picture.

In his introduction to the published screenplay of *State and Main*[21] Mamet introduces the outsider to the concept of "van humor" – the jokes about movie-making exchanged by movie-makers during the hundreds of hours they spend cloistered in vans while scouting locations and making movies away from the studio. A particular example he cites as inspiring *State and Main* concerns a film crew shooting at dusk on a mountain which they consider has the most beautiful view in the world. The only flaw is an intrusive pine tree, which they promptly cut down to perfect their shot. On their way back they stop at a bar and the director speaks of having "just shot at the most beautiful vista I have ever seen." "Oh, you must have been up at Lone Pine Ridge," says the bartender. Sadly there is nothing as memorable as this in Mamet's genial movie.

The title suggests the archetypal American small town, the middle of which is predictably the intersection of State Street and Main Street. The town here is Waterford, Vermont, where frayed director Walt Price (Mamet stalwart William H. Macy again) has come to shoot a singularly unimportant costume movie. The film within the film is called *The Old Mill* and Waterford has been picked for two reasons – first because it has an old mill (though it transpires this ancient building was burnt down in 1960); second, because the production has been forced to retreat from a similarly idyllic New England town because the film's star, Bob Barrenger (Alec Baldwin), attempted to seduce an under-age girl. In Waterford there is predictably both conflict and fraternization between the inhabitants and the intruders. When local bookshop owner Ann (Rebecca Pidgeon) becomes friendly with the film's deeply serious screenwriter Joseph Turner White (Philip Seymour Hoffman), her fiancé, Doug (Clark Gregg), is driven into the opposition camp. The film people also hurt the feelings of Waterford's mayor (Charles Durning), and things come to a head when Bob, the star, once again surrenders to his weakness for under-age girls and crashes his car while in the company of a local teenager. Money however, changes hands and the movie proceeds.

By current Hollywood standards, *State and Main* is a film of some quality, but it is deeply flawed. The plot is overly predictable. The characters are all too familiar – the frantic director; his put-upon assistant; the sexy preening female lead; the troublesome technicians; that old warhorse the naïve writer, a newcomer to the industry, who is shocked to see his precious screenplay being mangled; and among the townsfolk the pompous mayor and sensitive literary young woman, who both seem to have stumbled into *State and Main* from *The Music Man*. Equally, *The Old Mill*, the movie they are making, does not ring true – it is unlike anything Mamet would be associated with, though reminiscent of the fustian dramas that he sent up in his sentimental, rather poor early play *A Life in the Theatre*, with which there are obvious affinities.[22]

For his eighth film as writer–director Mamet returned to the world of crime. His co-producer was Art Linson with whom he had worked on three Hollywood movies. Moreover he chose two fashionable young Hollywood figures to assist him – the production designer David Wasco, who worked on Quentin Tarantino's first three features as well as the first two movies of Wes Anderson, and the cameraman Robert Elswit, who lit Paul Thomas Anderson's *Boogie Nights* and *Magnolia*, and the Bond picture *Tomorrow*

Never Dies. The title *Heist* announces its status as a genre movie, a gesture confirmed by Mamet prefacing the film with a monochrome version of the pre-1960s Warner Brothers logo. He also, for the first time, cast three current Hollywood stars in leading roles – Gene Hackman, Danny De Vito, and Delroy Lindo – with two of his regular players, Rebecca Pidgeon and actor/illusionist Ricky Jay, supporting them. Hackman plays Joe Moore, an ace thief, who uses as a front for his operations a small boatyard in a port south of Boston. Moore is middle-aged, world-weary, violent, but essentially decent and honorable. He is reminiscent of the eponymous criminal played by Walter Matthau in Don Siegel's *Charley Varrick* (1972), who in his cover-job as a crop-duster advertised himself as "The Last of the Independents." Consciously or unconsciously Siegel's film is probably the model for *Heist*.

Like *Charley Varrick*, the movie begins with an ingeniously planned, briskly staged robbery that goes wrong. The target is a jewellery store in Boston and accompanying Moore are his young wife Fran (Rebecca Pidgeon), and his trusted henchmen Bobby (Delroy Lindo) and Don (Ricky Jay). Unfortunate Moore's face is caught on CCTV and he decides that this is the time to quit. However, his crafty fence, Mickey Bregman (Danny De Vito), forces him into taking on one last job – stealing a consignment of gold bullion from a Swiss cargo plane. Bregman also insists on Moore taking along on the job Bregman's handsome, dangerously unreliable young nephew Jimmy Silk (Sam Rockwell). This character inevitably brings to mind both Donny in Mamet's *American Buffalo* and the incompetent mafioso Sean Connery is forced to employ in Sidney Lumet's *The Anderson Tapes* (1971).

The film's second heist is superbly contrived, convincing in the meticulous detail of its planning and the sustained suspense of its execution. Indeed a year later it was copied for an equally successful robbery carried out at London Airport. Mamet, however, has complicated the affair by introducing significant elements of the con man movie into his picture so that it resembles a cross between Jules Dassin's *Rififi* and his own *House of Games*. Bregman, the dishonest fence, and Moore, the honest crook, become involved in a game of double-cross that is made more complicated by the real, or feigned, duplicity of Fran, Moore's wife, who is having an affair with Jimmy Silk. When we do not know who is deceiving whom, it is difficult to focus on character or concentrate on the subtleties of the heist. The climactic scene – set on the boat which Moore intends to sail into the sunset of retirement – involves a disappointingly conventional shoot-out and some familiar twists.

The dialogue is nearer to the well-honed material Mamet writes for Hollywood than the oblique, elliptical exchanges that characterize his more personal work. But it is well delivered and gets deservedly appreciative laughter. One of Moore's team, for instance, remarks admiringly that he's "so cool that when he goes to sleep the sheep count him." The malevolent Bregman (who at one point claims that his real name is Rumpelstiltskin) shouts into a phone: "Everyone needs money – that's why they *call* it money." The toughest exchange comes at the end when a dying victim says: "Don't you want to hear my last words?" "I already did," his executioner replies before finishing him off. The best lines, however, go to Hackman in a brief speech establishing, with affecting nostalgia, that he belongs to an older, better America that is vanishing, if not already gone, and linking small-scale crime to the capitalist process. Speaking about the preparation of a heist, he remarks (naming the baseball stadium the Brooklyn Dodgers played in before the club was sold and moved from New York to Los Angeles in 1957): "If you have the right getaway, you could steal Ebbets Field. Ebbets Field's gone. See what I mean?"

At fifty-five David Mamet has a great deal to give us on a number of fronts. Only a very glib, reductive commentator would suggest that the different aspects of his career were drawn together in *Heist*.

NOTES

1. David Mamet, *Writing in Restaurants* (London: Faber and Faber, 1988), pp. 142–60.
2. David Mamet, *A Whore's Profession* (London: Faber and Faber, 1994), pp. 84–98.
3. Patrick Gilligan, *Jack's Life* (New York: Random House, 1994), p. 313.
4. David Mamet, *True or False: Heresy and Common Sense for the Actor* (London: Faber and Faber, 1998), pp. 125–7. In this short essay Mamet establishes affectionate links with numinous actors from the theatrical past, e.g. playing cards with Roland Winters (of Charlie Chan fame), talking to Lillian Gish, working with Don Ameche.
5. Sidney Lumet, *Making Movies* (London: Bloomsbury, 1995), pp. 39–40.
6. Art Linson, *A Pound of Flesh: Perilous Tales of How to Produce Movies in Hollywood* (London: André Deutsch, 1994), p. 6.
7. *Ibid.*, pp. 74–5.
8. Art Linson, *What Just Happened?: Bitter Hollywood Tales from the Home Front* (London: Bloomsbury, 2002), pp. 25 ff.
9. Daniel O'Brien, *The Hannibal Files: The Unauthorised Guide to the Hannibal Lecter Trilogy* (London: Reynolds & Hearn, 2001), pp. 146–7.
10. *Writing in Restaurants*, p. 142.
11. David Mamet, *Jafsie and John Henry* (New York: The Free Press, 1999), pp. 69–71. Mamet remarks that "one of my best friends is a producer" (probably Art Linson), but says that the funniest joke about producers is to be found in a biography of David O. Selznick where a shot is described as "the most striking in all of Selznick's work": "The joke is that the film was *not* his work. To refer

to a producer's oeuvre is, at least to me, as ignorant as to refer to the oeuvre of a stockbroker."

12. Ricky Jay has been in six Mamet movies (as well as in the Bond film *Tomorrow Never Dies* and Paul Thomas Anderson's *Boogie Nights* and *Magnolia*). His major international reputation, however, is as a magician and conjuror, performing in clubs and theatres around the world and writing books on the history of his craft. His relationship to Mamet's own art is attested to by more than his appearances in the writer–director's films. Mamet directed Jay's one-man show *Ricky Jay and His 52 Assistants*, that toured the United States and played in London and Australia, and in 2002 directed the sold-out Broadway show *Ricky Jay: On the Stem*, described by the *New Yorker* as "the master magician's tribute to the flimflammery and weird entertainments that have cropped up over the years along the length of Broadway."

13. David Maurer, *The Big Con* (London: Century, 1999). First published in 1940 but out of print for half-a-century, this pioneer study of the art and language of confidence tricksters by a professor of English at the University of Louisville was for many years an underground classic. S. J. Perelman, an astute observer of, and contributor to, the development of the language, pressed copies of the book on Somerset Maugham and Raymond Chandler shortly after making their acquaintance. Maurer died in 1981, but not before he successfully sued Universal Studios for the unacknowledged use of his book by David S. Ward in his Oscar-winning "original screenplay" for *The Sting*. The case was settled out of court for a sum believed to be several million dollars.

14. David Mamet, *Some Freaks* (London: Faber and Faber, 1990), p. 117.

15. George Plimpton, ed., *The Paris Review Interviews: Playwrights at Work* (London: The Harvill Press, 2000), p. 376.

16. Mamet, *On Directing Film*, in *A Whore's Profession*, p. 350.

17. J. Hoberman, "Identity Parade," *Sight and Sound* (November 1991), pp. 15–16.

18. David Mamet, *The Winslow Boy and The Spanish Prisoner* (London: Faber and Faber, 1999), Preface.

19. *Ibid.*

20. Nick James, "Suspicion," *Sight and Sound* (October 1998), pp. 23–4.

21. David Mamet, *State and Main* (London: Methuen, 2001), p. v.

22. Mamet, *Writing in Restaurants*, pp. 103–6. Mamet calls the play "an attempt to look with love at an institution we all love, The Theater, and at the only component of that institution (about whom our feelings are less simple), the men and women of the theater – the world's heartiest mayflies, whom we elect and appoint to live out our dreams upon the stage."

11

CHRISTOPHER BIGSBY

David Mamet's fiction

Speaking in 1977, David Mamet remarked that, "I can't write novels . . . it's just not the form that touches a person . . . The play succeeds by exquisiteness, the novel by brute force, by repetition, by elaboration. It makes a different kind of impression."[1] By 1994, he had plainly changed his mind, though not entirely. When he turned to the novel he did deploy repetition and elaboration though scarcely brute force. He discovered – what surely he already knew from his voracious reading, particularly of nineteenth-century British and American fiction – that it, too, could succeed by exquisiteness, if we mean by that form and function in alignment, precise moral and linguistic discriminations.

Why reverse himself in the course of those seventeen years? It was, he explained, because "I always wanted to be a writer, and to me a writer was somebody who wrote novels. That's what a writer was . . . so I figured well . . . if you want to be one, why don't you try it."[2]

At the same time, to turn to David Mamet's fiction is seemingly to enter a different world from his drama. The style, the approach to character and narrative, the pace of the text appear radically at odds with expectations forged by *American Buffalo*, *Glengarry Glen Ross*, and *Speed-the-Plow*, though there are points of contact in an occasionally fragmented dialogue, a sense of the intransitive nature of relationships.

In a play, the setting provides whatever information he intends, virtually instantaneously and simultaneously. It may be that, as with a painting, the eye scans the set. It may be, too, that the implications of that set grow as a result of the unfolding action, but the place is there, entire, and most of his plays have no more than one or two sets. His first novel, *The Village*, by contrast, creates a world little by little. We are offered no overall description, no scene setting. The topography is not described. It only becomes apparent through the eyes of the characters who themselves only slowly come into focus.

The village is, we learn, an early eighteenth-century settlement with several stores, a post office, a garage, and a movie theatre, surrounded by hills covered with sugar maples, white pine, and birch, much of it secondary growth. Twenty miles away, for no reason that is ever made clear, is a church and its graveyard, though there are graves a deal closer than that. Each element of that description, however, is only disclosed gradually, almost inadvertently, in a book which seems to focus most directly on the inner lives of those who inhabit this place, remote from other places, contained and containing.

There is, we discover, though only indirectly as a character encounters it, a quarry, with giant blocks of rock. Nature, here, can be menacing. When the snow descends even long-time residents can lose their way in the hills, turned about as they search for home. The familiar is suddenly made strange so that we, like them, encounter this world anew, a world in which reassurance can be instantaneously transformed into threat (an experience that Mamet himself had when lost in the snows of his own Vermont settlement of Cabot and which he also dramatizes in an unproduced television play, *We Will Take You There*).

In the early pages of the novel we are offered no names for the characters. They are described as "the man" or "the girl." We encounter them in fragmentary bursts of prose. There is the hardware store owner, whose trade is failing not least because everyone buys on credit and few sales amount to much more than a few dollars or even cents. There is the Trooper, punctilious in his duty if not his private life. There is a man whose son must be protected from criticism but cannot finally be protected from the accident that sends him plunging to his death.

Even when names are given, they seem the least important thing about characters who have something of the archetypal about them. The names, however, are liable to disappear so that for readers there is a momentary sense of disorientation, like the vertigo felt by those lost in the snow of this isolated village, deprived of familiar landmarks.

By degrees, however, the characters come into focus. There is Maris, wayward, driven by instinct and with no sense of what her life might be. There is Henry, thoughtful, philosophical, seemingly in tune with the natural world and yet still isolated within himself. Indeed his internal life is more dramatic, more fulfilling, more real than the external one. A visit to an auction becomes a major event not because it has any meaning in itself but because he imputes meaning to it. The buying of a "Minnesota Fishing and Hunting Club" patch opens the door to fantasies of power, of secret knowledge that can be traded for advantage. The very triviality of the purchase says something about his life.

We enter the novel not from without but within, not with the clarity of an objective description but through an internal monologue deformed by fever and collapsing into dream. It is only the first of a series of such monologues which slowly constitute the village through a kaleidoscope of subjectivities.

The opening narrative then jumps so that it is unclear whether the character we next encounter, and whose mind we enter, is the same, though when he thinks, "I am sick of this life," the recurrence of the word "sick" seems to bridge the two scenes. This kind of echo becomes one of the means whereby Mamet stitches the quilt of the novel together. Discrete scenes do, it seems, interconnect even if the connections are established via mood, linguistic echoes, recurring patterns. The blurring of identities serves both to suggest their exemplary status and to imply that together these characters constitute the corporate identity which is the village, not so much a place as an experience, though one separately encountered and interpreted. It is a story told in short takes, some no more than a paragraph long, some a few pages. In the plays such a rhythm spoke of fractured lives, spiritually and morally discontinuous. Here, these are tessellations which slowly cohere into a larger picture. This is not, like *Sexual Perversity in Chicago*, an urban syncopation. The rhythms here are different. The past presses more clearly on the present. Lives are lived at a steady pace seemingly measured by habitual gestures, familiar rituals. A hand reaches for a pipe in the knowledge that it will be there, has always been there. A lost tool will come to light simply because time will eventually reveal it, and time is viscous here, flowing so slowly that people live within their minds, filling the vacancies and languors with speculation, mental possibilities, memories never challenged because they were never designed to make their way into words. This is *Under Milkwood* without the signalled poetry, the humor built out of the grotesque.

It is a world in which the texture of a piece of wood, the machined grace of a weapon, the tint of a Fall leaf seem of a piece with, and even in some respects more significant than, the daily events which otherwise seem to pace out the days. The world beyond the village penetrates in the form of memories of another place and time, the village war memorial acting as testimony to distant realities, literally now dead. Otherwise it is an address on a package returning faulty goods or strangers entering and leaving like ghosts. It is not that this place is sufficient in itself but that it is the place in which these figures live, life being essentially what it ever was, as young girls shock their elders and the store owner struggles to survive. There is a world elsewhere but it is not one to which they choose to set out or which exerts pressure on them.

In such a place small things gain significance. What others might disregard they make the center of their attention. The resonant events are animals seen out of season, strangers who appear without real explanation, the way a girl walks and does or does not meet the eye, a bank manager's tone implying problems to be deferred. People do die but in some sense we are never asked to stare their deaths in the face because those in the village choose not to do so either, accepting what comes as ordained. There is sex but it is presented as mere physiology, less described than noted obliquely. It is implied in the way a man folds his pants in a motel room or the thinness of a blanket casually draped on the bed of a truck as a girl watches herself and what happens to her as though from a distance, which is her protection from full knowledge of what she does and why she does it.

". . . to be *home* anytime?" a man asks a girl as he undresses and she sits, waiting, on the bed. "Do I Have To Be Home Any Time," she replies, supplying what is not there linguistically, beating out the time of the sentence with her right hand.[3] In that simple exchange is the story of their relationship as in her noting the rhythm of her reply there is a correlative of her abstraction, an indication that there is no relationship, only actions without moral content, an encounter taking place out of time.

This scene, cut off from what precedes and succeeds it, in which neither figure has a name or, seemingly, requires it, is followed by another in which one of the central characters, Henry, finds himself following behind an earth-filled truck from whose tailgate two lengths of chain dangle, dancing up and down. The rhythm provokes thoughts of literal dancers and a fantasy in which he is in Paris with a black dancer who offers him sex. The bridge between the two otherwise wholly separate scenes is thus provided by the sub-text of sex and by the sense of a rhythm to which each character responds. This idea of a defining rhythm itself recurs, rhythmically. A fan pans back and forth, swivelling regularly to the beating thrum of its blades; a car goes *Twaing twang* as it passes over the hose in front of gas pumps; a clock ticks, chiming regularly as a church clock does or does not chime. This is the beat of their lives: sometimes the habitual, sometimes the unexpected.

There is, a character observes, "great comfort in being part of a group; and it was, he thought, similar to the comfort of being alone. If you took the trappings off, he thought, it felt the same; and much of it was just the lack of need for speech" (101). The comfort, then, is expressed as a negative, and these characters are, indeed, sparing with their speech in a novel which appropriates something of Hemingway's aesthetic as if the process of simple description, as if an aesthetic of elimination, would leave truths exposed without the need for explication. As in a Hemingway short story, each action is separately described, given equal weight, almost, it seems, as a way of excluding sources of anxiety, the very obsessiveness of the detail implying what is thereby kept out of mind. For there is an undertow of anarchy resisted in the calculated slowing of events, each action performed with such care and precision that at times it seems as if this were a way of exorcising thoughts of dissolution.

These are all characters whose minds take them on associational journeys seemingly as real and affecting as the daily routines they otherwise enact. They inhabit not merely a place but imaginations stirred by memories, anecdotes, random events. Reality is fluid and internal as much as fixed and external. When Henry pulls off the road to go into a diner he enters in the middle of a story one man is telling another, just as a few pages before another man had entered a store as a story was being told, both stories featuring threatened or actual violence. There is, however, an etiquette to such interruptions as if the one entering threatened to disrupt a ceremony.

These are people who treasure their privacies: "Nobody knows what I'm thinking" (75) thinks a girl. It is where they live. Information is seldom shared. Withholding is a principle of existence in a place itself withdrawn from history, as it seems, as much as from a country which itself only becomes real when it reaches in and takes young men away to die in wars which seem as irrelevant as anything else beyond the surrounding hills.

These are not quite characters living lives of quiet desperation but there is despair here even if it is expressed indirectly in a place in which indirection constitutes a courtesy as well as a protective device. "That's the way it is," a character observes, "Time goes by" (232), and in a sense this is a novel about time, stretched out by the detailed description of objects, by internal monologues which extend actions and thoughts beyond the moment that provokes them. Sunrise and sunset, the slowly ticking clock are the measures of life. There is no frenzy, no sense of the need to rush through that life as if that were the evidence of its meaning.

In the village the past is the present. The old families are still there, in person and commemorated on the stones in the graveyard. This is a place of rusting signs, of stores which have scarcely changed with the years. Young girls have grown into women, boys into men, until they resemble those who had gone before them, their mutual memories as real as their daily lives. There is, surely, an echo here of Thornton Wilder's *Our Town*, a bittersweet account of passing time, of regrets fertilizing the soil, and Mamet has expressed admiration for a work which, he has suggested, celebrates the fact that people are born, love, grow old, and die. There is, to be sure, no knowing narrator, pulling the threads together, making the desired connections. In *The Village* the reader is in the same position as the characters, trying to shape separate experiences into some understandable form. The connection, though, is clear in the narrative strategy. As Mamet explained, "Wilder had the sufficient genius to abstract, in the same way Chekhov did, an experience of the community into vignettes, in such a way that the abstracted experience gave . . . the emotional totality of . . . a tragedy."[4]

There is a photograph of one of the village stores, taken in 1895: "it's about the same. The life's probably the same, too" (114). Generation replicates generation, mistakes being repeated, the same needs leading to the same conclusions, as if there were a comfort in repetition, even the repetition of error. If there is something tangible about this village there is also something of a fable about it. When they tell stories of the old days the characters are both announcing their own survival and confessing their mortality, the past they invoke being a measure of how far they have come but also an acknowledgment that they live within time, are subject to its depredations.

Nostalgia, then, offers its reassurances but also carries the smell of death which is what gives the novel its feel of melancholy. Those who were alive in the invoked past are now dead or dying and those who recall them are thus confessing themselves subject to the same logic. Yet there is a reassurance in the fact that the same stores still exist, the same trees, the same disordered passions giving way to stolid satisfactions and the ambiguous comfort of habit. These people live a life that is simultaneously real, specific to themselves, and mythic, part of a larger narrative expanding beyond the moment, in which each individual life forms part of a pattern, a narrative seemingly without end.

The inhabitants of the village may at some fundamental level be strangers to one another, never quite knowing the person to whom they hesitantly reach out, but there is an acceptance. Familiarity, at least, has long since filled in the silences. Anecdotes remain incomplete, stories half-told in the knowledge that other occasions will suffice to complete the thought. We overhear fragments of conversations, hinting at stories we will never know in their completeness except that we learn something of the tellers from what we do hear, from the tone of the voices, the disapprovals, remonstrances. Here a tightened mouth, a shake of the head betoken a shared knowledge, mutual suspicions if not necessarily shared truths. There is an underlying pattern even if this serves to underline the privacies that will never be addressed by casual words of greeting, familiarities which simulate a closeness for which the evidence is finally absent.

There is an incantatory quality to *The Village*, a listing familiar to American poetics. Despite a stress on continuity and recurrence, in another sense nothing is generic. Everything is particular, required to be in its place, respected for its qualities whether it be a tool or a gun. And the prose itself tends in the direction of simple declarative sentences laid one after another, controlled, just as a hunter places one foot carefully before the other the better to close on his prey. Indeed the rhythms of the prose reflect a community in which familiar rituals, minor ceremonies, are the essence of a daily life which thereby hints at some transcendent value itself always just out of reach but sought for. There is time, here, for thought even if this can lead to privacies which isolate, which serve to detach the mind from action.

If this place has a tactile reality it is also the sum of the sharp desires, the anxieties, the fogged hopes of those whose lives run in parallel, momentarily cross, and then diverge. Henry tends to see things in terms of their geometry, neat reiterated patterns conjured up by changes in the light or daydreams in which the boundary between the real and the imagined blurs. He seeks to organize his world, looking for that shape that would explain a mystery not even seen as such. This is a man who finds contentment in simple things in their right order at the right time: a cup of coffee, a home-made donut, a snake, but also a naked girl swimming in a pond at just the right moment in his adolescence to earth the energy then surging through him.

As a hunter he practices the hunter's lore with precision. It takes a page to describe the process whereby he lights a fire. This is a world of tools identified and used with exactitude, methods of work that are codified and exact. All of which proposes an existence in which everything has its place and there is a reassurance in routines which are rooted in something more than mere habit. There is a taxonomy to this world which seems to inhere in existence or if not then to be invoked against the fear that it does not. For this is not a world without violence, whether it be a beaten woman or even a possible murder. Doing things right, not appropriately but as is proper, in such a way as to show respect, is part of what pins experience in place; but it is also propitiation. A deer killed in the right way is a deer whose death carries no accusation or guilt.

Yet habit may mean something more than mere repetition. William James, Mamet has insisted, suggested that "it allows us to raise our thoughts and spirits from the mechanical – it allows our thoughts to wander."[5] These are characters who live most fully in the spaces provided by routine and whose thoughts do, indeed, wander. It is on their internal journeys that they often feel most completely alive, most fully themselves.

Henry is something of a philosopher, if we mean by that someone with a liking for playing with ideas, living with a consciousness of living, inspecting even the simplest action as though he were Thoreau aware that facts may simultaneously have an authority and power of their own and offer access to meaning. In bringing the maul down on a piece of maple "directly in the check," he is generating a metaphor as well as cutting wood. That is to say, he lives more than once, in each instant doing and interpreting, and giving each equal force.

Viewed externally, he is merely chopping logs for winter but much of *The Village* is not concerned to view the world externally. It is an attempt to give full value to an inner life, secret from others, but one which constitutes the core of such personal meaning as seems apparent. This is precisely what Mamet could not do in his plays, unless, like O'Neill, he had chosen to renovate the soliloquy. His fiction goes where his drama may not. It takes an inward track.

In his case, as Henry chops wood he is aware of comfort, but alert, too, to the fact that other things are thereby excluded, by virtue both of the activity, so precisely controlled, and of his own speculations. Indeed in the very emphasis on precision, on the need to shape his actions to some paradigm he never questions, he is excluding in particular an anarchic doubt about himself, his marriage, his situation in this village. Routine is a substitute for something else. It blots out an awareness of other possibilities.

When the young woman, Maris, charged with a sexual energy which makes her the source of moral anarchy, climbs into his truck, foul-mouthed, keeping her distance and yet drawing his eye as she draws the eyes of all the men, his thoughts ricochet around as he struggles to deny the disturbance she causes. This disturbance would not, he believes, be evident from his behavior but is evident to the reader not because we are told but because his denials are at odds with his confused and wayward thoughts.

The village has something in common with Lanford Wilson's portraits of rural communities, in which the details of daily life are piled up against the threat of despair. There are guns here, purchased for hunting or for the sheer pleasure of their construction and line, which may, it is implied, be used for something else. Indeed into the village comes a crude and seemingly brutal sexuality, a casual violence, sudden death, and the hint of abduction or worse.

Beneath the stillness, the matter-of-fact conversations, and seemingly inconsequential events, is a series of dramas, hinted at indirectly. An unmade bed and an upturned drawer signifies a man no longer there, a man who has left a woman with a bruised eye, a woman now taken away by a Trooper who eases the safety catch on his weapon against a threat that is never stated but which is implicit in the situation but still more in his simple action simply described.

There are the signature Mamet fractured sentences but this time not expressive of brittle sensibilities, social and moral discontinuities unraveling the very idea of community. These incomplete sentences, compressed words, turn on a mutuality that does not require redundant completions or are expressive of thoughts swept away by other thoughts or the interruptions which are themselves part of daily experience.

Each character is fenced around with privacies. Their stories may overlap but they never bleed into one another. *The Village* is in part the story of those privacies, so much of it taking place in the minds of those who confess to themselves what they would not to another, their thoughts running against their words and their actions like an invisible current, the one no more and no less true than the other.

There are fixed points which offer an anchor against the current of experience. These are simple things: a cord of wood stacked ready for the fire; the wood-burning stove ready to receive it; the coffee pot to start the day. The apples reach a point when they fall from the tree, their time come, and there is a sense of natural process about the book, a deeper rhythm than that provided by striking clocks. Certainly the characters seem to bow to what they appear to regard as inevitability, even though this thought is not sustained for long. Sudden death is accepted as part of the process. Two of the young of the village die in a fall from a cliff. Mamet no more describes the emotions of those who receive the news than does Hemingway describe the emotions of a crowd who watch as a bullfighter is gored in the glare of an unblinking sun. He itemizes the small gestures, the actions, the events which surround and contain but also express those emotions.

It may seem, at first, like a Norman Rockwell world, a *Saturday Evening Post* image touched with sentimentality, but that is not sustainable as the desperation, the randomness of experience becomes apparent. It is closer to Andrew Wyath's *Christina's World*, a painting which expresses the mute desperation of an individual trapped in herself as in a setting which echoes that sense of isolation. Certainly there is something reassuring in a community whose roots are sunk in another time, seemingly immune to the artificial necessities of modernity. Such reassurances, however – as in Arthur Miller's suburban world in *All My Sons* – serve to set the reader up for a fall. There is an anxiety, a desperation never fully neutralized by habit or the small change of daily life.

As a character called Dick observes in *The Village*, "he was frightened, for it had been proved to him that every certainty contained its opposite; and a goddess more wrathful than and immediate than Nemesis watched for the least sign of assurance on the part of Man" (56). Contentment inspires fear of its loss, awareness of its contingency quite as if entropy were the ultimate truth and everything an emblem of life given to be taken away. What is youth but an ironic commentary on age, perfection of form but a prelude to dissolution, just as, conversely, rain outside the door is a reminder of the warmth and the dryness within?

His characters, in other words, live within a tension usually denied but occasionally acknowledged, a kind of exquisite awareness of contingency. Indeed even as the hardware store owner plays with ideas of contentment and the perverse threat of dissolution, the telephone rings and we hear his fragmented answers to questions which we infer are about an extension to a loan which may or may not be forthcoming, his life either continuing as it has or coming to a stuttering end. We never hear the other side of the conversation.

There is a potential for both danger and violence. When two kestrel chicks are seen on the road, one is dead before the other can be rescued and the person who rescues it is aware that it may at any time attack him and tear his face, just as it had been a hunger for road kill that had drawn the chicks in the first place. When the Trooper stops a car at night, he eases the safety on his revolver. To step out into the snow is to step potentially into the unknown. The novel, indeed, is full of those who have been assaulted, betrayed, killed, even if the full force of this is muted in the telling. When the Trooper goes fishing and fails to net a fish, a scene which is an echo of Hemingway's "Big Two-Hearted River," there is a sense that some other tension lies behind actions so carefully described. This is a novel in which revolvers and rifles are admired, cleaned, directed at targets.

There is a solitariness about these characters. They share little in the way of conversation. They are grudging with words. Their most intimate truths are whispered within their heads. They come together for gossip, for simple transactions, for the occasional unfolding of a story but it is their privacies that are the most striking thing about them, the conversations they have with themselves. They live parallel lives. When one of them observes of his wife that "there is a *world* between what she is, and me" (174), he is identifying a ruling principle of relationships in this place just as his incomplete sentence, "It's the *small* things, that, if there is any meaning at *all* . . ." captures the truth not only of their lives but of the book's aesthetic.

Even when they do seem to celebrate moments of consonance there is liable to be a dark underside to it. The Trooper remembers the camaraderie of the gym but the occasion was a lesson in the use of calculated violence against assailants so that it is a tainted camaraderie. These thoughts, moreover, segue into the memory of his wife learning of his sexual betrayal, a tryst with the young girl called Maris in a hotel room described as if she had been the victim of a sudden assault and relationships were tenuous and provisional, as, indeed, they seem to be.

When Maris, object of much of the village gossip, has sex with a truck driver there is no intimacy, no sense that anything has been shared, that there has been a meeting of any kind. It is not the sex that matters to her but the conversation in her mind in which she expresses the contempt she feels for him and thereby the contempt she feels for herself, though this cannot be registered directly even in the privacy of her mind.

When we follow her home we are privy to her thoughts to do with killing her stepfather with a tire iron or a crowbar. She develops her own fantasy of beating him, dragging him to a mineshaft, and listening to his screams as she tortures him. To others she is a young woman, attractive if no better than she should be. In her own mind she is a calculating killer and it is that self to which we are introduced. On one level she is what they take her for, offering sex to truckers, perhaps as a revenge against her mother, though this is not a novel in which the author gives direct guidance, motives being unclear even to the characters themselves, but she is also something that they could never guess.

Maris's stepfather smells of sweat. In the next section of the book Henry insists that he can smell something bad, this serving as a bridge between the two sections as a film-maker will cut from one scene to another via a visual or aural homophone, and, indeed, there is something cinematic about the construction of *The Village*, a Robert Altman choreography of seemingly insignificant moments whose significance grows from accretion.

"So many things to do," says the owner of the hardware store to himself, who has so little to do because not enough people come into his store to enable him to survive. So much is this so that when the bank manager calls he has to stage a piece of theatre, like the salesmen in *Glengarry Glen Ross*, pretending to serve a non-existent customer, evidence that his store remains busy. When one does enter it is to buy seventy-three cents' worth of nails and even this is a debt written down to be paid later. Another purchase costs twenty-nine cents, precisely the price of a postage stamp. In fact virtually all the sums of money mentioned in *The Village* are small, just as are most of the incidents.

The significant acts are never described directly, merely inferred from their effects. We do not see Mrs. Barnes being beaten by her husband, only register her bruises and a disordered room to match a disordered life. These are people who have learned to read the signs, the tracks of animals, character expressed through a sideways glance, a swish of the hips. Mamet encourages his reader to do much the same.

Asked to characterize *The Village* he described it as a "laconic, stoic, Northern novel."[6] So it is. It asks the question, he helpfully adds, "how does one live in a harsh climate . . . People have to figure out a way to do it better, to make do or do without. The tradition survives up there. How do you get along in the woods, how do you get along in nature?"[7] The harshness, however, consists of something more than the climate. Speaking of his Vermont settlement, Mamet has said that it is a very "social place to live because people need each other . . . the person's born, that person died, so you need to help with something . . . People are legitimately dependent on each other in a way we, in the cities, have forgotten."[8]

The Village contains such needs and acknowledges such dependencies but need does not always find its satisfactions. Solitariness may have its context, resilient individualism its triumphs, but there are some spaces that cannot, seemingly, be closed as there are moments when even a promised sense of community is not enough, indeed may carry a threat, corrosive gossip being as likely to characterize a coming together as is a comforting conviviality. Nature can turn from benign environment to deadly threat as a gun can turn from admired artifact to lethal weapon. These are a people who live within the tension of alternative and co-existing possibilities, within the tension of an internal and external reality thankfully or disturbingly often not in alignment.

Given his commitment if not to rediscovering then to reclaiming his Jewish heritage, a fact reflected in a number of his plays and in *Homicide*, as in the instructional stories for children, *Passover* and *Bar Mitzvah*, he might have been expected to present the central character of his next novel, the historical figure Leo Frank, falsely convicted of rape and murder and lynched in 1913, as no more than an innocent man destroyed by bigotry, the American Dreyfus case. He is certainly that but Mamet's concern, in *The Old Religion*,[9] cuts deeper than a mere celebration of a victim defined by his religion, while innocence may lie as much in wilful naïveté, a refusal to acknowledge reality, as in a lack of responsibility for crime. Mamet has said that, "It's a book about race hatred." So, in a sense, it is, but that hatred is not addressed directly. It is registered in terms of its impact, particularly on those who absorb the fact of that hatred and respond to it with subtle, even unconscious appeasement as if such hatred could be deflected by denial, by implicitly acceding to those whose contempt is in fact implacable.

Part of the fascination of the novel, indeed, is what it is not, as part of the fascination of the character is what he has not allowed himself to be. This is the story of a man who believes he wishes to belong, to claim his part in a suspect identity, and who believes, for much of his life, that decorum, fastidiousness, a certain balance between a quiet success and self-abnegation will achieve this aim. He is a man who seeks to turn denial into the basis for a tentative assertion, who, despite his continuous self-interrogations, fails to realize the extent to which he has accommodated himself to what he should have resisted.

He is a Jew who has seemingly believed that the price of incorporation into community and nation is the establishment of a discrete distance from an identity which he suspects, but cannot confess, earns him the contempt of those with whom he wishes to claim true kinship. It is the story of a man who has lost his way, who has come close to not living at all, and becomes most himself in the losing of his life, though even then not fully restored to himself as that self is finally forfeit. This is not an angry book about southern violence, though that violence inheres in the attitudes and assumptions of a society that defines itself by exclusion. The anger, transmuted into a kind of cold dismay, is directed at the victim. It is the story of a man's collaboration in his own irrelevance and hence a vulnerability in which he colludes by refusing to acknowledge the hostility which confronts him. It is the story of a man who fails to grant full force to the reality of other people's lives because he is so concerned to reconstruct himself into an acceptable figure. Like George F. Babbitt or Willy Loman he wants to be included, if not to be well liked (which would draw undue attention to him) then at least to be respected, though less for what he is than for what he is willing to become. To that extent his is an American story, but it is also a Jewish story, the story of a man who in forgetting his history has cut himself adrift from meaning.

He recognises his "basic . . . need to be accepted by the community," a need which he is ready to characterize as "savage": savage because elemental, fundamental. But he recognises, too, that such a need can be turned to advantage in his advertising which should appeal to "the fear that one is to be excluded," seemingly not recognizing the degree to which this savagery goes beyond a social preference, exposing his vulnerability: the degree to which this axiom applies to himself.

The portrait Mamet draws is of a man imprisoned within the language, the ways of thought, the strategies that he has allowed to distance himself from the meaning he believes himself to pursue. His problem is in part that he believes he can inhabit the mind, find security in his reconfiguring of the world, detach himself from what he will not confess he fears, must not confess he fears, if he is to achieve his objective. There is a level on which he knows that the apparent good-fellow society of the South conceals a crude historic and contemporary contempt for himself and those like him. However, he pushes such thoughts away with self-deprecating ironies, rituals of thought and action which seem to establish an alternative order not subject to the anarchy which on some level he registers even as he is anxious to press it beyond the boundaries of thought.

This is a novel, though, that we enter by way of a dedication to a rabbi, a Hebrew inscription, and a quotation from Proverbs. The process of the novel is one by which the protagonist himself moves out of one language into another, rediscovering what he had believed should be set aside. Punished as a Jew he becomes a Jew once more not just in his fate but in his shifting loyalty. He hears a different drummer and begins to march to a different beat, so that at least he may die as the man he once refused to be. Indeed, the book, which we enter as though into an inconsequential world, is actually the protagonist's attempt to trace back through his recent life as if he could thereby discover a clue to a fate to which the reader is not at first privy. In other words, the reader, like Leo Frank, begins in a state of some bafflement, only gradually coming to an understanding of his fate and hence his life. The questions the man tries to answer are "What does it mean? What is justice? What is God? What is reason? What can a man reasonably accept? Is he a good man? What is the definition of a good man?"[10]

It is not that Leo Frank has purged all signs of his Jewishness. Indeed the book begins with his preparation to visit a friend for Passover. More precisely it begins with his noting, in the process of preparing, an old newspaper, dating to 1868 and glued inside his collar box, which contains an account of a petition for the recovery of a Jewish boy seized by the Catholic church following a forced conversion. The paper is one that confronts him each time he opens the box but it is not its content that seemingly concerns him but the manner of its preservation, an act of displacement, a method of evasion which it emerges typifies his approach to experience. He sees what he wishes to see and has devised strategies of distraction designed to preserve him from what he would not.

That displacement rests not simply on the process whereby he stages internal debates with himself, turning down intellectual byways, but on certain linguistic rhythms which extend out into the narrative voice which in turn recapitulates, reflects, and extends that rhythm. Consider the opening few sentences:

> The newspaper lined a bandbox. He opened the bandbox to get a fresh collar. He wondered, as he often did, at the appearance of the newspaper. It had been glued into the sides and bottom of the box, and the date showed, April 10, 1868. But the newsprint had not yellowed. "Obviously the glue is a preservative," he thought. "We might think that there is in the glue to preserve the clarity . . ." (1)

The words "newspaper" or "newsprint" are repeated three times; the words "box" or "bandbox," "glue" or "glued" likewise; "preserve" or "preservative" twice. There is an incantatory quality to the passage which slowly emerges as a reflection of the protagonist's mode of thought, a central tactic of a man whose life consists of such minor stratagems. Consider, for example, a later passage: "The fan fluttered the bookmark off his desk. He watched the bookmark, flat, climbing, and falling, as the fan swivelled to the other corner of the room. As it returned, the bookmark fluttered again, as it rose as if to fly. Then it fell back" (64). It is not simply that words are repeated but that the description is of repetition, as the fan slowly pans back and forth. A prosaic world is reconstituted as poetry, down to the alliteration. The rhythm has a mesmerizing quality as Leo Frank seizes on details which serve to lift him out of the immediacy of concern, as a drug will distract, deflect meaning onto irrelevancies, discover a new logic to the sensibility.

Nor is this process wholly restricted to Frank. When he and his family join a friend, Morris, the latter tells a story of Klansmen requiring the Jews of a town to leave. They prepare to do so only to be told that the injunction does not apply to them since they are "our Jews." The anecdote is offered as a joke but behind that reassurance is also an acknowledgment of fear. The joke is a means of deflecting anxieties. They are all, it suggests, similarly immune. Frank's wife, we are told, "Slowly, in the rhythm of his speech," sank down into her chair.

Frank's language is not naturalistic. Its curious formalities are simultaneously an expression of his sense of his own superiority and of a desire to contain and to formalize. Watching Morris perform a card trick, he thinks, "It is all a play, capitalizing on my human instinct to respect the portentous. There is that in the ordering of his features which apes the solemn and momentous. So it is natural I would pay homage to it with still concentration" (28). The structure of his thought and expression is formal, even archaic. The portentousness and solemnity that he ascribes to Morris is no less a feature of his own life. He stares out at the world from a place whose securities are constructed partly out of language, a language freighted with the authority of the past.

It is partly this, however, which will make him vulnerable as another rhetoric (or rhetorics) confronts him with a world made strange. Language, in the end, has no power to protect him, but it does have the power to destroy. The man who offers himself as southerner and American is treated as a Jew and words have the power to kill.

There is something of the actor in Frank, as in Morris. They both perform, play out the roles in which they have cast themselves. Acting has its own pleasures but, like Morris's magic trick, it deals in deceit. Frank performs the self he believes most acceptable but performance is also falsehood and depends on the acquiescence of an audience. Frank ultimately discovers that that is precisely what, calamitously, he lacks.

There is something almost Jamesian in the pleasure Mamet takes in distinguishing the nuances of moral attention, the etiquette of social behavior, like James slowing down the action the better to appreciate the shifting valencies of thought. This is a world, it seems, in which ethics and aesthetics seem intimately connected, in which people have devised versions of themselves to send out into the world.

There are other strategies, however, that are more disturbing, not least because they are not acknowledged. As the story of Jews menaced by Klansmen is unfolding we are told that "The colored girl was coming in with a new pot of coffee" (10), as later a "large black man" (24) is summoned from the kitchen. The Jewish family of the story, meanwhile, is called Weiss "White". As the novel unfolds so it becomes apparent that the Franks have easily and casually absorbed southern attitudes to blacks, as though that were an avenue to acceptance, an attitude that will later prove deadly as a jury refuses to grant sufficient intelligence to the actual murderer because of his race.

It is the "colored girl" who brings forward the Passover tray, the Passover being a celebration of survival, the victory of Jewish slaves over their oppressors. The irony is left to express itself with no further urging from the narrative voice.

The black servants are not invisible to Frank, merely irrelevant. He is capable of acknowledging their situation – "It must grow tiring. To heft the tray, immobile in his palm, like that; though, perhaps, they grow used to it" (29) – but this seems no more than an expression of a sensibility acutely aware of its own procedures, form, and generosity. As he watches the large black servant, close to stereotype, so he congratulates himself "that he found no admixture of superiority in the thought" (35), in thinking such revealing the superiority he denies. He offers indulgence but at the heart of this, uninspected, is the casual assumption of his own status. Later, we discover that his wife, too, is large, and register his fear that she will be seen as a stereotype by those on whom he suddenly relies to see him, and that wife, in their particularity. There is little sense, however, that he registers anyone else's experience and reality except in so far as he incorporates them in his own refined considerations.

His attitude to those who work with their hands is scarcely different. He thinks, with some amusement, of the laborer with his "round of beers" (38). Everyone, he believes, has his place, and his wealth, like others' poverty, constitutes no more than a description of two conditions sanctioned by differing abilities and heritages. Each has his rightful position, this in some way providing evidence of the order he requires. There is, he feels, a natural hierarchy.

He sees not so much a person as a performance. He projects thoughts, feelings, attitudes onto Morris as he performs his card trick, quite as if the visible world, like the trick itself, were a deceit, pleasurable or not, an appearance preferable, in its way, to the merely mundane, the banal, which has to be charged by the imagination, gifted significance by the mind.

Frank notes that the waiter has "reconfigured" himself, but not in any way other than to withdraw himself from other people's attention. He is simply awaiting the appropriate moment to resume his function as a waiter, suspended for the duration of the card trick, quite as though he existed only in the moments when he was required, even if that implied a muted and never to be expressed sense of irony. The waiter is, Frank muses, "quite cognizant – to the limits of the intelligence authorized to him" of the excellence of the trick. The condescension is carried in the language of this unspoken observation as in the role in which the waiter is cast. The word "cognizant" is as much a claim to authority as the observation itself.

Like the prosecutor later in the novel, Frank aspires linguistically no less than socially, reaching for a language which seems to confer status on its user: "absent their obeisance," "surpassing my adoption." The same voice, however, seems to invade the narrative. The "voice of inanition," we are told, "informs him." It is as if the membrane between narrative voice and character had collapsed. Frank was, we are informed, "Happy to be possessed of a liberality sufficient to allow contemplation of the free-spirited art of philosophy" (40). Whose voice is this except a narrative projection of Frank himself as though he were framing the story of which he is the subject, a man in love with the arabesques of language as if it were itself a reality independent of any referent?

He plays with language, as, in a sense, he does with life. Nothing seems to cut deep. He works hard but seemingly lives most fully in the interplay of internal debates, his contemplation of the significances which give him the illusion of abstraction from the world. The reality of that world, however, becomes suddenly and shockingly apparent. Somebody dies. He is accused. He watches almost like a figure from Kafka as his life rapidly and unaccountably unwinds, but even then it is the external world that seems the phantasm and the internal dialogue, in which he continues to fret over insignificant details, that seems the more real.

His sense of the irrelevance of others leads him to fail to acknowledge their agency. Without wholly registering the fact, he subscribes to a southern view of the Negro which refuses to grant to him the independence of being which will ultimately prove to be his own undoing. He is vulnerable not only to their prejudices but to his own. When he is sitting on the back porch of his cabin his friend Morris remarks, "Waal, Jedge . . . if you was oncet a nigger on a Saady night, you'd never wan' to be a white man ev'again" (32). Frank makes no reply. The joke is an invitation to assimilate through shared prejudice. It is a claim to security which turns on becoming part of the community which at some level they both fear. Others may be vulnerable; they are not. Others may claim licence; they do not.

Sitting in the backyard at night, indeed, Frank contemplates what it is to be a citizen of a country. He plays with the idea of failure, the loss of certainty, only to reassure himself of his grasp on the world and his place in it. The frisson of concern serves only to emphasize both his right to and his possession of security. He stages debates in his mind, one voice expressing doubts which the other lays to rest. Yet uncertainty is never far away. Thus he smokes a cigar, a symbol of his status, yet "hated the fact of the Big Cigar being associated with the Jew" (36).

Frank situates himself uneasily in terms of his faith. He confesses his ignorance of the details of Jewish lore, not wishing to "arrogate" to himself such knowledge on the "mere precedent of blood" (13). Not anxious to "disclaim" a relationship, he is equally unwilling "to suggest a greater than accidental liaison between himself and that tradition." His is a balancing act, as he invokes a seemingly scrupulous distinction which in effect lacks both scruple and distinction. He takes pleasure and comfort, however, precisely in such discriminations and differentiations which seem to locate him between two traditions to which he wishes to lay claim, albeit on his own terms. So they discuss the dietary rules of Judaism with a sense of irony and detachment that betokens the space that Frank in particular wishes to maintain.

There is something over-precise, self-conscious, fastidious about him. He conducts his personal life according to principles of limited equity rather than passion. His is a measured life. The problem is that he uses a suspect measure. His internal dialogue betokens self-concern. Even his supposed humility is a matter of pride. He cedes power only when it has no significance. His wife is "just a woman" (47).

He watches himself live, inspecting his own actions and status for signs of betraying aspects of himself that might be thought inappropriate. He lives most fully within his own mind. The external world impinges but it is not where he seeks out meaning. There is little suggestion of intimacy between his wife and himself. "I have my place and she has hers," he tells himself as if this pattern were itself the source of reassurance. She is in turn a badge of his achievement and the source of embarrassment, depending on the response of others.

He believes himself secure but the mere assertion of security, the elaborate mechanisms for sustaining it, hint at a fear of something else. As he, his family and friends sit on the back porch of their lakeside cabin, "hidden from the road," he tells himself "we have the right to be here . . . We are not screened off from them . . . how could they take umbrage . . . we are not *sequestering* ourselves" (20). The assertion of fact contains its denial. Each statement is self-cancelling; the question not as rhetorical as it seems.

There is, indeed, a current which runs against the tide of confidence which he and others exude. In the context of a discussion of Wells Fargo and the death of a dog, Frank contemplates what it might be to be hunted, quite as though it had no relevance to him or to those from whom he comes. At this moment, however, there is a sudden intrusion into the text of another story, another time frame, as, quite unprepared for it, the reader is confronted with the sentence: "In the courtroom, Frank heard the judge drone on" (26). What courtroom? This is the first mention of this other reality and, for the moment, mention is all it is.

It is not that he denies his Jewishness. Indeed, he likes to believe that it is that which gives him a sense if not of consanguinity then of shared presumptions with the South, living contentedly within its own myths. In one of those debates with himself that characterize this man drifting towards a proximate danger, he argues himself into accepting the South's rationalizations of slavery and celebrations of survival. His conservatism he sees as a bond. This man who is most himself in his internal debates convinces himself, of his fellow Jews, that "the savagery they feared was not in the world, as they thought, but in their minds" (44), only to discover that at the limits of the mind is an implacable world for which such intellectual notions are wholly without meaning. The "problems of the world," are not, finally, "a diversion" (45).

Suddenly, into this seemingly inconsequential narrative, this contemplation of the minutiae of daily experience, words and phrases begin to obtrude – "courtroom," "judge," "trial" – hinting at a master story not yet wholly disclosed, the reason for these rambling reminiscences. Slowly it becomes clear that this man, who wryly notes that a prosecutor "does not *pause* so much as *inflect*, and . . . does not *inflect* so much as *signify*," is fighting for his life and beginning to understand that distinctions, linguistic, racial, are precisely "what they're going to kill me for" (49).

His own deliberate and fine distinctions, his own love of inference, it seems, have merely replicated those of a culture which he had persuaded himself he admired and which, had he paused to think, was predicated on the worthlessness of his life. The very time he had squandered in meaningless distraction and which had seemed evidence of contentment, an untroubled mind, had actually mirrored that of a society seemingly content to live with its fictions, its apparent reverence for style over substance, until the stakes were raised and an innate violence lay exposed.

Sitting in his office he contemplates the bookmark blown by the wind of an oscillating fan and in a passage lasting some four pages finds in this a focus for a contemplation of time and its effects, the rise and fall of civilizations, a drift of thought finally ended as he writes the date in a ledger, a trivial enough gesture but one which pulls him back into history, a history about to become precise, something more than abstract speculation. So it is that his contemplation of a paper-clip and its metaphysical implications suddenly stands exposed as the narrative is taken over by rape and murder. Thus Mamet springs his fictive trap.

What is at one moment an account of an obsessive, filling the vacancies of life with trivia, is, it now seems, the portrait of a man under pressure, summoning up memories to be pitched against an accusation of random violence. It is his very vacancy, indeed, which seems to have invited someone to fill it, to project on the blankness of his life images born not out of his own actions or predispositions but out of the prejudice of those for whom his passiveness and interiority invite accusation and assertion.

To this point his life has been a triumph of small ceremonies, of trivial calculations invested with metaphysical dimensions which in truth they lack. He is guilty of moral myopia. Other people's lives barely seem to have registered. They are so much background noise, mere material to trigger the interior speculations which are evidence of his failure to engage more significant truths. He is a man who, consciously or otherwise, has constructed invisible barriers, choosing to live within the redoubt of his own mind, the nuanced world of fine judgments, of actions contemplated rather than performed. He looks for order and affects to find it in the details of office life, the calculated habits which constitute the rhythm of his existence. When the crude facts of irrational accusation crash into his constructed world, however, he has no resources with which to respond, indeed scarcely any understanding of a world so unsusceptible to the subtleties of thought or an ordered inner life.

He is suddenly the focus of something more than his own sensitivities and minor scruples. He is the object of others, re-invented without his leave and in ways he finds impossible to confront. This is a man who has learned to discipline even imagined passion yet is here accused of a passion beyond imagining. Until this moment his anxieties had been no more than minor tremors, indulged precisely to be set at rest, so many minor victories over a disorder that he presumes is merely a race memory or a shared but unexpressed sense of imminent threat.

The trial, when it comes, disables him because he has no recourse. His usual strategy, passive, unresponsive, is no defence. He is what they choose to make him. Only now does the earlier discussion of the kidnapping of a Jewish child become relevant. The inverted logic, earlier a matter for dinner-table discussion, now reaches out to Frank as he discovers that reason and justice are to play no part in his trial.

In the trial, for all his assumption of inclusion, his Christian accusers now become "Your," "They," "Their." He can no longer include himself in their number and since this is what he had most assiduously sought he has nowhere to turn. As the false accusations are rehearsed so his inner assurance crumbles. Perversely, life begins to seem real in the face of the unreal accusations. For the first time he acknowledges to himself the furtive nature of his life. He is, in effect, one of the "brotherhood of Jews" (85) who, in his mind, he accuses others of being, this man who never kept the sabbath.

The prosecutor's speech is marked by the rhetoric of the racist, seemingly elevated by biblical cadences, the admittedly suspect linguistic presumption of one seeking to impress by claiming a language not legitimately his own. Bizarrely, it is a performance in part admired by Frank as if the man were giving him an unwarranted attention. A performer himself, he admires other performers. Yet at the same time the trial seems in some way irrelevant to him. His mind again drifts towards irrelevancies.

The irony of the trial, which is not played out in any detail, is that the real murderer escapes conviction because, a black man, he appears to confirm notions of black incapacity. He is so completely what they fear that denial is an ultimate protection; and if not he, then who but "The Kike. The 'Nigger to the nth degree?'" (95). His apparent status in the community, as he should have known, was purely provisional. All it required was an accusation for that status, such as it was, to be rescinded. He was not their Jew after all.

Under pressure of the trial he is now inclined to separate himself from those whose company or identity he had sought. The "they" is intensified as he is forced to acknowledge the contempt which he had mistaken for acceptance or at worst toleration.

Even as he sits in jail, the prejudice is there in the books he reads. Bone-deep hostility, he now realizes, could never be propitiated by mere acquiescence, by discretion, silence, by living in the mind. Thoughts of Jewishness now begin to replace his other obsessions as he sets himself to recover what was lost, to learn Hebrew, rediscover an identity he had sought to deny. Slowly, he has a sense of belonging, if not within the parameters of a faith then within a culture, a history, a way of being.

In the Hebrew he catches the feel, the sound of poetry, a sense of assonance and harmony; and with that comes a feeling of membership. Yet he can still misread the world. When he thinks he is being accepted by his fellow prisoners it is as if he had learned nothing for one of them takes him aside and dispassionately cuts his throat.

The lynching which concludes the book is hurried through in barely a page. We are told that a photograph of the event is made into a postcard and sold throughout the South; but that is not the irony that lies at the heart of the novel. That has to do with a man who drifted away from one faith and community in a quest for acceptance in another which in part defined itself by his rejection. It has to do with the process whereby reality is reconstituted in a desire for significance. Leo Frank, for much of his life, staged an internal drama at a tangent to those around him, to history, to a sense of the immanent meaning he suspects subsists in the smallest of details. In thinking to read the code of his being, however, he looks in entirely the wrong place.

This is not a novel about a victim of American anti-Semitism, though Frank is plainly that. It is a novel about the price of being part of a society whose values are not one's own, the price of not being at all. It is about the belief that detachment is a virtue and accommodation the route to true being. Leo Frank kills himself long before the lyncher's noose is fitted around his throat, though at the end he has glimpsed a meaning he had forgotten, an identity he had been ready to trade for something as insubstantial as what the protagonist of Edward Albee's *The Zoo Story* called "solitary free passage."

The Old Religion is a considerable achievement, a work of great subtlety from a man often assumed, in his drama, to shock with his language and disturb with his portraits of characters morally deformed by a socially aberrant environment. Yet there are connections to be made. He has always had a fascination with the figure of the confidence trickster, the spinner of tales, the fraudulent self. Leo Frank, destroyed by those trapped within their own self-justifying fictions, is not so remote from them, proposing that he should capitalize on other people's fears. Yet the principal victim of his deceits is himself. In his quest for becoming, he forgets to be, opting for a qualified invisibility only to discover that he was already the thing he sought. He simply gave it the wrong name. His unambiguous death nonetheless contained an ambiguity as he began, at least, to assume the identity he had so assiduously fled. His suffering is not without its residue. In the words of the book's epigraph: "A crucible for silver, a furnace for gold, and the Lord tries hearts."

As in many of his plays, Mamet draws a portrait of a society bereft of the human values to which it nonetheless wishes to lay claim. He presents the strategies by which his characters struggle to deny the reality of their fears, their sense of the absences in their lives. In *The Old Religion*, however, there seems at least the possibility of reconstituting what was lost, even on the very brink of apocalypse.

Mamet's third novel, *Wilson: A Consideration of the Sources*,[11] was rejected by his agent and publisher. He failed to take the hint. At well over 300 pages it is the longest of his novels and the one, it is tempting to feel, that least needs length. It is a parody of an academic treatise, complete with suspect footnotes, and seems to have given him considerable pleasure. For the reader, perhaps, the pleasure is more muted. Certainly the virtues of his first two novels seem significantly absent here, as well they might in a book which, with his usual irony, he has described as "an autobiography . . . about a psychotic's vision of his own mind."[12]

This is not a book that turns on reticence, understatement, the oblique. It signals its effects, as the kind of academic study he mocks tends to signal its scholarship. Like its model, it delights in the abstruse as he plays postmodernism at its own game. It is the kind of book that a writer harassed by critics with agendas of their own would doubtless be tempted to write. Like Oscar Wilde, he plainly sees no virtue in not succumbing to temptation. He has said, "there are more things in heaven and earth than are dreamt of by those with an academic bent."[13] *Wilson* enumerates a few of them. What does he think of critics? "Fuck 'em . . . that, I think, sums up my feelings about critics."[14] It certainly seems to sum up his attitude in this parody, pastiche, self-destroying treatise.

The word "novel" is perhaps not entirely appropriate. It is certainly a fiction, set in the future but looking back to the present, that distance being the authority for judgments about a general decay of literature, literacy, and humanity. The central conceit is that, following a "great destruction," historians, cultural archeologists, and simple self-serving and self-regarding students of the past endeavor to reconstruct what was lost, filling in the spaces with guesswork, fantasy, prejudice, anything that comes to hand. This process results in bizarre presumptions whose distortions, however, are not always devoid of at least parodistic truth.

In an essay called "Poll Finds," Mamet quotes Edward Gibbons as observing that "A cloud of critics, of compilers, of commentators, darkened the face of learning, and the decline of genius was followed by the corruption of taste."[15] He seems to have written *Wilson* in much the same spirit.

The text is scattered with ironic references, jokes (good, poor, downright bad), signalled ironies. This is a text almost entirely constructed of sub-text, with references leading down multiple blind alleys. There are moments in which a single sentence seemingly requires a full page of exegesis, of footnotes that are often neither notes nor at the foot.

It is, in truth, a little difficult to know why it goes on at the length it does unless exhaustiveness is to be part of what is parodied, the idea that the more extended a study, the greater its truth, or at least its plausibility. In *Wilson*, scholarship crushes and deforms, or simply ironizes what it affects to address, its scientific or pseudo-scientific assumptions resulting in laughable affectations and still more laughable conclusions. *Wilson* is about the elephant promulgated by a blind man from the feel of its tail.

The book is full of momentary shocks of recognition, if not always with respect to the most profound of subjects. It is hard, for example, not to respond to the statement that "The populace had of course long suspected that all ethnic food was cooked in one vast kitchen and then trucked out and doused in that sauce that would identify it as Chinese or Indonesian," and still more to the proposition that much the same is true of the Democratic and Republican parties. And this despite the fact that this means our associating ourselves with a narrator whose own judgments are often disastrously wide of the mark.

The problem is that some of the jokes are too easy (footnoting a Bernard Shaw quotation to Irwin Shaw), have too short a half-life (the invoking of Hillary Clinton in connection to a reference to effect and stimulus), or are, one hopes deliberately, excruciatingly poor, as when we are told that a doctor who, wishing to visit a dying man only to fall down a cistern, is told to care for the sick and not the well. *Wilson* is an excuse for a scattergun assault on a whole filing cabinet of accumulated targets.

The problem is that the very clogged prose and distracting academicism he satirizes may clog and distract the reader. In replicating procedures he is at risk of replicating effects. If his other works are pared down, here redundancy is part of the strategy. In truth it is not hard to see why agent and publisher were tempted by the Delete button.

Wilson is best treated as a treasure house, a distorted reference book in which nothing is to be trusted. It is the antimatter of scholarship, though doubtless there are already worthy Ph.D. students, immune to irony, digging themselves in to wage a critical war of attrition on this self-aware, self-mocking text.

Wilson is not so much a stage in his career as time out from it, the *jeu d'esprit* claimed on the dust jacket, itself an integral part of the book. And yet, of course, it does share something with his other works. It is a confidence trick, a sleight of hand, a conspiracy. It is a book aware of the absurdities of scholars as elsewhere he is aware of the absurdities of Hollywood. It expresses that same fascination with the power of language not so much to communicate as to persuade us of a suspect reality. This is David Mamet, trickster, once again, as it is David Mamet, mordant observer of a civilization blind to its own inanities.

This is vaudeville, Second City revisited, the Marx Brothers crossed with Derrida, cultural studies building theoretical castles from broken bricks; this is *reductio ad absurdum*, a sawdust barrel from which we are invited to pick surprise after surprise. It is David Mamet between takes jotting down whatever strikes his fancy and finding that the jottings can be extended into a Lewis Carroll world in which things are simultaneously strange and, oh, so familiar.

To offer a critical reading of *Wilson* would be to enter an Escher-like journey less to fundamentals than to fundament. The job of exegesis has already been accomplished at the level of parody. It is, in fact, disturbingly close at times to the ever-continuing snowstorm of academic treatises produced in quest less of knowledge than promotion. At a time when clarity is frequently dismissed as naivety, and reflexivity and deconstruction seen as sure paths to canonization (even if the canon itself is by definition suspect), *Wilson* is at moments so close to its originals that only pastiche and not parody can suffice.

The novel adopts the same shake-and-bake approach to knowledge that characterizes so many graduate schools. *Wilson* is Mamet's invitation to take out a card in a Borgesian library which is growing exponentially even as its volumes turn brittle and their pages blow away.

The David Mamet who once believed that to be a writer was to be a novelist has demonstrated, then, that he is a writer, that is to say he takes pleasure in writing. What form that writing takes depends less on his subject than the approach which that subject demands. Certainly *The Village* and *The Old Religion* can stand beside any of his plays while taking us in a different direction. As for *Wilson*, as Joe Gargery says in *Great Expectations*, "What larks!"

NOTES

1. Leslie Kane, ed., *David Mamet in Conversation* (Ann Arbor: University of Michigan Press, 2001), p. 35.
2. *Ibid.*, p. 153.
3. David Mamet, *The Village* (New York, 1994), p. 68. Subsequent references will appear parenthetically in the text.
4. Kane, ed., *David Mamet in Conversation*, p. 154.
5. David Mamet, *Jafsie and John Henry* (London: Faber & Faber, 1999), p. 71.
6. Kane, ed., *Mamet in Conversation*, p. 153.
7. *Ibid.*, p. 155.
8. *Ibid.*, p. 156.

9. David Mamet, *The Old Religion* (London, 1998). Subsequent references will appear parenthetically in the text.

10. Kane, ed., *David Mamet in Conversation*, p. 185.

11. David Mamet, *Wilson: A Consideration of the Sources* (London, 2000).

12. David Jenkins, "England of his Dreams," *Sunday Telegraph Magazine*, August 22, 1999, p. 16.

13. David Mamet, *Writing in Restaurants* (New York: Viking, 1986), p. 94.

14. Kane, ed., *David Mamet in Conversation*, p. 79.

15. David Mamet, *Some Freaks* (New York: Viking, 1989), p. 165.

12

DAVID SAUER AND JANICE A. SAUER

Misreading Mamet: scholarship and reviews

> That is why "realistic" acting rings so false. "Realism" – the concern
> with minutiae as revelatory of the truth – was an invention of the
> nineteenth century, when The Material seemed to be, and, perhaps,
> was, the central aspect of life. Our own time has quite understandably
> sickened of The Material, and needs to deal with things of The Spirit.
> – David Mamet "Some Lessons from Television,"
> in *Some Freaks*, p. 64.

After reading 1,200 reviews and 200 articles and book chapters on Mamet
for *David Mamet: A Resource and Production Sourcebook*, our sense is that
reviewers, and many scholars as well, have misunderstood Mamet – from his
first productions to the present. By Mamet, we mean the playwright/director
David Mamet, not the playwright alone. Most reviewers fault Mamet's direction of his own plays. It certainly is possible to fault a playwright as director,
but the objection is that his theory of drama is at fault in his directing. But it
is the same theory which underlies the construction of the plays. What is at
issue is the idea of realism which critics expect in Mamet's plays, but which
he seems not to deliver.

In "Mamet vs. Mamet" Todd London argues, in *American Theatre,* that
Mamet the theorist and director is Mamet the playwright's "own worst
enemy." The argument is straightforward – Mamet is a realist, but he refuses
to direct his plays realistically. London's words provide a good starting
point on realism: "Whereas many of the playwrights of the '60s and early
'70s experimented with fluid characters who transformed before our eyes,
Mamet's creations have always been essentially fixed beings, defined by their
actions, limited by their native tongue" (18).

This idea of "fixed" character, however, does not accord with Mamet's
staging, nor with his style of acting, both of which are minimalist rather
than realistic; such production elements send signals which conflict with
the idea of consistent, seamless characters. His earliest plays, written in a
blackout style often linked with Second City improvisations, provide a disjointed rather than smoothly consistent view of characters. Like London,

when reviewers find pieces they do not expect, or which conflict with a conventional view of the real, they blame Mamet rather than their mistaken expectations.

Reviewing reviewers

In the very first notices on *Squirrels* (1974), critics spend most of their reviews attacking the program notes which articulated Mamet's new approach. Both Roger Dettmer in the *Chicago Tribune* and Jon Ziomek in the *Chicago Sun–Times* ridicule the idea of a new approach to acting. Ziomek takes particular exception to the idea of presenting "real life on the stage," a play with "[i]nteresting and clever parodies that make a point about the way people often talk meaninglessly. But parody, none the less. Would that the real life human comedy were that funny." The critic's problem with expectations of "real life" is fully evident from the outset.

Comparing a Yale production by Walt Jones in 1977 with a 1979 New York revival with the same actors, Mel Gussow complains of Mamet's direction: "All three plays [*Reunion, Dark Pony* and *Sanctity of Marriage*] have been directed by the author, and, especially in the two brief opening episodes, he seems to have an infatuation with his own words (too few) and with his pauses (too long)." He also criticizes the set as "too spare to be called scenery," and so Mamet's minimalism "is a bit like a child's coloring book; someone has forgotten to fill in the spaces." There is no recognition here that those "spaces" are designed for the audience to fill in, and to recognize that it is filling them in, closing gaps in the narrative.

Also in 1977, Richard Christiansen, Mamet's most ardent Chicago supporter, took exception to his direction of *The Woods* because "the production frequently undercuts the text." By production he seems to mean the mix of "mythic" with "non-poetic" writing, "the stripped-down dialog ('This is not good, Nick.'), approaches the banal and ludicrous range of a soap opera." Linda Winer ("Clickety Clack") questions the setting of the play by Mamet's designer: "Michael Merritt's plain porch isn't pretty – as though Mamet wanted a neutral set in which the characters can see what they want." Shelly Goldstein is baffled by the peculiar lighting: "I wonder why after specifically entitling the play's three scenes 'Dusk,' 'Night' and 'Morning,' Mamet chose stark, bright front lighting for the entire play." Sherman Kaplan notes what critics for the next twenty-five years would continue to descry in Mamet's direction: "Patti LuPone as Ruth and Peter Weller as Nick are directed by playwright Mamet in a style which seems almost stilted. The characters speak at each other rather than to each other. They don't use contractions;

each word is spoken as if it had been clipped from the printed page and pasted into their working script. [. . . Mamet's] language and style are too self conscious." Since the lighting, setting, and acting all work counter to what the reviewers expect, it seems fair to ask – why did they demand realism rather than accept that the production deliberately sought to undercut realistic responses?

The Woods is simply an early instance where the critics are upset that the actors do not emote. John Lahr later observes of *Oleanna*:

> Both Mr. Macy and Ms. Pidgeon are a bit under wraps here, at once awed and cowed by Mamet's authority, which takes some of the acting oxygen out of the air. In this Mamet joins the likes of Samuel Beckett and Harold Pinter, whose literary touch was always much surer than their directorial hand. Mamet keeps his show clean and crisp, but leaves a lot of production values still to be explored in the many other versions that *Oleanna* will certainly have.
>
> (232–3)

Michael Coveney prefers the more "realistic" approach of Pinter's production, in contrast to the New York production in which Carol "is pretty much of a zombie." He explains, "Lia Williams does not wear spectacles and allows her long hair to fall sensuously below her shoulders. David Suchet adds a leavening of vanity to John, a thin smile, an ineradicable air of smugness about his book and his son and his career. This restores equilibrium to the drama." Evidently Pinter's version provided much more detail to the characters, much more fullness in realistic characterization, and was much preferred by critics.[1] But this does not appear to be Mamet's aim, as his own production revealed – though it is what audiences are most used to seeing.

Linking his dislike of Mamet's minimal set for *Oleanna* with similar complaints about acting, Clive Barnes remarks:

> The physical production (it took 13 producers to raise the money for this!) looks so Spartanly bare (even chintzy – and not in the English sense) that it appears more suitable for a read-through than a staging. Adding to the antitheatrical chill Mamet himself has directed his actors [. . .] into a stylized ritual, effetely artificial in phrase and pause, halfway between debate and conflict but irreversibly frozen.

Hersh Zeifman, reviewing Pinter's London production, notes that Mamet's direction was "badly misconceived" while "Pinter's production uncovered the true heart of the play." Zeifman describes Pidgeon in New York as an "automaton. Who could possibly care anything for a robot [. . .]?" (3). Knowing exactly who to "care" for and how much is another key to realism that Mamet continually subverts in his writing and his direction – and it became evident when he became the New York director of his own plays, beginning with *Oleanna*.

As if in refutation of the critics who seek to read Mamet purely realistically, and who fault him for not making audiences care for his characters, Arthur Holmberg reports that at the *Oleanna* première in Cambridge, Massachusetts, when an audience member objected, "your play is politically irresponsible," Mamet replied, "I have no political responsibility. I'm an artist. I write plays, not political propaganda. If you want easy solutions, turn on the boob tube. Social and political issues on TV are cartoons; the good guy wears a white hat, the bad guy a black hat. Cartoons don't interest me" (94).

In some sense the critics who attack Mamet for misdirecting his plays are complaining that, as London argues, "[his] reductive thinking has the opposite effect: that of making less out of more, until it appears that he has turned against himself. The plays are getting the worst of it" ("Mamet vs. Mamet," p. 18). The "more" in this case is the text, which is read as realistic. The "less" Mamet makes out of the script is the minimalist production in terms of set, lighting, and acting. But since Mamet has operated this way from the outset, it seems possible that the "more" critics think should be there is their invention. There are no stage directions in the published texts to give the illusion of reality which reviewers seem to expect.

Reviewing the scholarship: realists vs. minimalists

When one turns from reviewers to scholars, it is not surprising to find that many gloss over the difference between realistic and fragmentary staging. William Worthen, for example, argues there is no difference in effect:

> The bizarre and unexpected turn of plot, unusual mises-en-scene, or oblique and refractory language of David Mamet, Harold Pinter, Sam Shepard, Maria Irene Fornes, and other playwrights like them often seem to signal an effort to reshape the project of realistic theatricality. In many respects, though, this drama capitulates to the categories of meaning and interpretation found in earlier realistic modes, especially the classic dialectic between character and environment, still visible in the drama, in production practice, and in the figuration of an audience. In the contemporary theatre, a determining offstage order no longer needs to saturate the visible space of the stage with objects in order to be realized.
> (*Modern Drama*, pp. 82–3)

As a result of dismissing the unrealistic plots, mises-en-scene, and language, Worthen, like London, contends the characters of postmodern playwrights are constructed essentially as realists constructed them.

Though Worthen does not pursue this argument, his approach is reflected in those scholars who take Mamet as a pure realist. There is another group, however, who see his three ingredients, "bizarre" plot, "unusual" mises-en-scene, and "refractory" language as signaling an approach which subverts realism. Christopher Bigsby, in his foundational work *David Mamet* (1985), makes the point directly when he reflects on The *Disappearance of the Jews*: "plays that might be thought to work with almost equal effect on the radio; what would be lost, however, is the contrast between an expansive and some-times confident language and a manifestly reductive physical setting" (43). Bigsby's perception is crucial for scholars who may not have seen the play in production. In that case, all that remains – because Mamet gives minimal stage directions – is the dialogue as if delivered on the radio.

As Bigsby argues, treating the text as radio drama distorts the play because the minimalist "reductive physical setting" is not available to serve as a counterweight to imagined realistic staging.[2] Without seeing the near-Brechtian A-effects which subvert realism in staging, one might consequently miss the similar effects Mamet uses in the play's language:

> Within the apparent harmonics of conversation are dissonances that suddenly expose the extent of alienation, the nature and profundity of personal and social anxieties. The plays exist for those moments. The reassuring worlds which his characters construct prove predictably fragile; the sound of their fracturing provides the background noise against which they enact their lives. Mamet has something of the artist's eye for creating painterly tableaux where realism is subtly deformed, as it is in art by the photorealists whose own portraits of urban vacuity combined realist aesthetics with self-conscious techniques that destabilize the reality they seemed to embrace.
>
> (Bigsby, *Mamet*, p. 44)

For Bigsby the language of the text in its disjunctions is reflected by the theatrical set in its "deformed" realism. Taken together, these techniques "destabilize" the realism the play purports to present.

William Demastes makes a similar point in *Beyond Naturalism*: "Mamet has found his own unique way of dramatizing that experience, again by beginning with realism to present surfaces and working to illustrate the cracks in those surfaces" (67). Writing of *Oleanna*, Harry Elam similarly notes that "theatrical performance has become an increasingly potent site for the examination and destabilization of the real and for the renegotiation of American identity. By destabilization of the real I mean the ability of the theatre to move beyond the representation of actuality to challenge, critique, and even subvert it" ("only in America," p. 152).

Edward Esche takes this idea of performance further, by arguing that the audience is needed to complete the gaps, but when it does complete them it discovers its completion problematic. In his analysis of *Reunion* Esche focuses on Carol's declaration that she's "entitled to" a father:

> As she stands in front of us claiming her right to have a father, and as we agree with her, we know, by the very depth of our desire, that she is simultaneously demonstrating the impossibility of reclaiming her father in that lost past. The play then presents a dilemma of profound moral dimensions; and our unsureness, the problem of the play, lies in the final irreconcilability of desire with fact. ("Mamet," p. 175)

This conclusion points to the purpose of the disjunctions in plot, language, and staging. As with Brecht's techniques, the purpose is to make the audience recognize the disharmonies, fill in the gaps, and then recognize its own complicity, its own experience of "the final irreconcilability of desire with fact."

As a consequence of the split between scholars who interpret Mamet as a realist and those who do not, there are deep divisions in approaches to his works. Those who see him as a realist tend to see him as a misogynist; those who do not, see him as problematizing gender issues. Those who see him as a realist tend to take his language as descriptive of reality; those who do not, see his characters as constructed by the language they use. Those who take him realistically see the center of his plays as emptiness; those who do not, see the void as implying, somehow, a need for community. Only when one looks at critics whose starting point is theatrical performance, and who as a result ignore the view of conventional realism, is there no similar binary split.

Realist = misogynist?

Scholars who denounce Mamet for antifeminism are upset when characters say things demeaning to women because words are taken literally. That seems to be the case with Marcia Blumberg's "Staging Hollywood, Selling Out" and Katherine Burkman's "The Myth of Narcissus: Shepard's *True West* and Mamet's *Speed-the-Plow*." Burkman acknowledges that some scholars have constructed Karen in very different ways, but she asserts that such differences are evident only in performance: "the ambiguity of Karen as virgin/whore that the director sought [as argued by Ann Hall] such ambiguity seems to be sadly missing in the script" (117). All such ambiguities are missing in her interpretation. Karen is "just another kind of whore" (117). Thus the text, independent of performance, exists with an unambiguous meaning in Burkman's view.

Curiously, she makes the opposite argument in "The Web of Misogyny in Mamet's and Pinter's Betrayal Games" where she finds that Pinter's direction of *Oleanna* fits her conception of the play better than Mamet's does, and therefore performance becomes a norm. Others who construct Mamet as a misogynist include Stanton B. Garner, Jr., "Framing the Classroom"; Dorothy H. Jacobs, "Levene's Daughter: Positioning of the Female in *Glengarry Glen Ross*"; Carla J. McDonough, "Every Fear Hides a Wish: Unstable Masculinity in Mamet's Drama"; Daniel Mufson, "The Critical Eye: Sexual Perversity in Viragos"; Jeanne Andrée Nelson, "*Speed-the-Plow* or Seed the Plot? Mamet and the Female Reader"; and Marc Silverstein, "'We're Just Human': *Oleanna* and Cultural Crisis."

Those who defend Mamet against such charges see him as exploring issues of power. Such critics include Karen Blansfield, "Women on the Verge, Unite!"; Verna Foster, "Sex, Power, and Pedagogy in Mamet's *Oleanna* and Ionesco's *The Lesson*"; Ann C. Hall, "Playing to Win: Sexual Politics in David Mamet's *House of Games* and *Speed-the-Plow*"; Christine MacLeod, "The Politics of Gender, Language, and Hierarchy in Mamet's *Oleanna*"; and Steven Price "Disguise in Love: Gender and Desire in *House of Games* and *Speed-the-Plow*." Price's article examines how Mamet's plays deconstruct the power position: "ostensibly privileged ideology (respectively capitalism, free will, psychoanalysis, Hollywood, and academic discourse) is undermined and ironized from within. This newly weakened ideology enters into competition with an alternative: pastoralism, determinism, the confidence game, high art, political correctness. By the end, this alternative has also been discredited" (45). Hall too uses poststructuralists, Lacan and Irigaray, to conclude that the "male characters view women dualistically: they are either Madonnas or whores. The female characters, however, persistently violate such codification" ("Playing to Win," p. 137).

Janet Haedicke's defense begins with a re-examination of the issues of Mamet and realism. Her study of *The Cryptogram* reverses the usual objections concerning realism (a "foundationalist ideology of linearity, transparency of language, and stability") finding that Mamet instead "exposes the mythologized, politically capitalized Family as a system providing a prototype for the economic system" ("Cipher Space," p. 2). In her earlier study of *American Buffalo* she attacks realistic interpretations; she notes that Mamet's early plays were episodic, and that later, more linear narratives might imply a realistic inscribing of women. But Haedicke counters that argument by asserting that: "As the language cracks under its excess, so, too, does the realism as Mamet's characters frantically strive to perform into existence a stable, objective reality in which identity is fixated or gendered and such binaries as male/female, professional/personal, and rich/poor remain reassuringly hierarchical" (29).

(Un)Realistic language

Other scholars have focused on the issues of language which Haedicke raises, particularly as a means of questioning the construction of Mamet as realist. Dialogue expert Ruby Cohn notes that Pinter's *Betrayal* and *Speed-the-Plow* "function on realistic sets, the shaped language and its resonance lift them beyond realism into wider significance" (91). Gerald Weales explains the basis for this language-based approach – it is Mamet's theory from the outset, as he told Ross Wetzsteon in the *Village Voice* (July 5, 1976):

> "that words *create* behavior . . . our rhythms *prescribe* our actions." It is not simply that the young men, permanently on the make, use the most reductive words to describe women, but that the vocabulary itself precludes seeing the women as complex human beings; the women, in their own turn, use catch words and attitude-producing jargon in a way that not only defines the men as types but fixes their own roles in relationship to the men. (11)

In Mamet's postmodern view, language constructs reality, rather than describing some existent reality, and the descriptions used form the way the characters interact with the world and each other.

Scholars who concentrate on language usually see it as reflecting the kind of gaps Weales and Bigsby initially observed. Examples include Park Dixon Goist and Alain Piette. Similarly, Guido Almansi argues: "A comic character can never be the writer's mouthpiece. [. . .] A character says 'soft things with a hole in the middle,' but someone somewhere thinks that it is a rather eccentric definition of women. Yet with the most alert modern playwrights, say from Harold Pinter onwards, this voice is kept as muted as possible" (*"Virtuoso,"* p. 194). He recognizes that the delight in language itself opens a gap, and functions as an A-effect undercutting the literal interpretation of the lines. Kevin Alexander Boon goes further as he examines *"Glengarry Glen Ross,* where much of the dialogue among the characters is clearly unethical. Yet the screenplay itself is not without ethics, inviting us to examine how a screenplay in which all characters are unethical manages to construct an ethical point of view" ("Dialogue," p. 51). His answer is that "We provide the moral critique of the discourse" (51). As with the examination of scenic gaps, or blackouts between scenes, here again is a recognition that Mamet requires a greater participation by the audience than is often recognized.

There are, however, more literal treatments of language – like John Ditsky's: "People really do speak as Mamet's characters do; the sound of his plays has the fascination of an overheard phone conversation" ("He Lets You See," p. 26). Poet Barry Goldensohn, who once team-taught Shakespeare with Mamet, rebuts this nicely, contending that his language is "entirely imbedded in the action of the character and the play. It is realistic dialogue of stunning *dramatic* precision – as opposed to simple tape-recorder accuracy" ("Poetic Language," p. 148). Ryan Bishop also argues against the idea of Mamet as recorder. And Anne Dean notes "Mamet's characters speak in words that sound absolutely authentic and believable and yet contain the essence of true poetry with all of its compression, rhythm, and artificiality" (*David Mamet*, p. 17).

More theoretically, language is seen as a site of conflict constructing alternate views of reality. Roger Bechtel approaches *Oleanna* this way, as does Richard Badenhausen, who examines it in terms of the "difficulties of acquiring and controlling language" ("The Modern Academy," p. 2). Thomas King uses a dualistic Saussurean approach, arguing that Teach's approach to language in *American Buffalo* is fundamentalist, based on an assumed connection between words and things. Donny, by contrast, is more of a semiotic relativist ("Talk," p. 541). Jonathan Cullick also employs a binary system of oppositions: "The discourse of community is transactional, comprised of speech acts that communicate and invite responses. It is a language of mediation, negotiation, and cooperation – an open discourse. On the other hand, discourse of competition is adversarial, the language of manipulation, deception, self interest" ("'Always Be Closing,'" p. 23). Jeanette Malkin's dualistic approach to language is grounded in the work of Basil Bernstein. "Elaborated and Restricted Codes are used to distinguish two classes: one of which uses language fluidly, the other of which is imprisoned by it" (*Verbal Violence*, p. 150).

Others simply find the language open rather than closed, and therefore ambivalent. Speaking of *The Cryptogram*, Jill Gidmark observes, "Speech is evasive or elided or aborted; no one knows how to interpret the codes of another" ("Violent Silences," p. 187). For John Heilpern this is a source of frustration because he is unwilling to fill in the gaps, "Everything's there, you just can't see it. It's all hidden in the coded subtext! You may wonder what's hidden there, exactly. And the answer is, a projection of yourself. Where, then, is the drama? It's up to you" ("*The Cryptogram*," p. 224).

Emptiness vs. community

With Mamet's structural minimalism, gaps, and blackouts, thematic critics tend to split into those who accordingly see only emptiness in his plays, and those who fill the gaps with meaning. William Herman considers the ending of *Sexual Perversity* and finds "some saving grace has been savagely anni-hilated" ("Theatrical Diversity," p. 136). Hersh Zeifman similarly observes in "Phallus in Wonderland" that "The homosocial world of American busi-ness so wickedly critiqued" becomes "a topsy-turvy world in which all values are inverted by characters who think with their crotch" (125–6). Matthew Roudané also takes this view of "a world from which Mamet eviscerates any moral balance between public virtue and private self-desire. From such a theater of disruption has grown Mamet's unique and disturbing, cultural poetics" (*American Drama*, p. 161). Bigsby, in *David Mamet*, tends to find emptiness in the early plays, as he finds parallels in the Absurdists: "Mamet writes of a world in which alienation is a fundamental experience; he creates plays in which that fact is reflected in the linguistic and theatrical structure. They are, indeed, episodic for more than structural reasons. Discontinuity, disjunction, a disruption of coherence at almost all levels is fundamental" (109). This bleak vision appears in the section on *Edmond*.

Later, with the advantage of seeing Mamet's post-*Glengarry* work, Bigsby's *Modern American Drama, 1945–2000* offers a much more positive vision: "Yet there is redemption. It lies in the persistence of need, in the survival of the imagination, in the ability to shape experience into performance and in a humour born out of the space between the values of the characters and those of the audience" (205).

This view of "redemption" found in the cracks and gaps and "spaces" left in the plays is also part of Dennis Carroll's vision: "Contact ripening into communion is the salvation that Mamet hints at" (*David Mamet*, p. 21). Each chapter of Carroll's book is grounded in performance. In the setting for *The Woods* he reads symbolic duality: "The summer-home porch set suggests intersection between the spheres of the natural world and human domesticity; it also suggests openness, vulnerability, lack of protection" (60).

Carroll's view of "communion" as the implied aim of Mamet's plays, however, is gleaned not from what is said, but from what is left unsaid: "The potential for positive contact tends to be manifested less in the text of dialogue than in nuance, implication, pause and silence; and in the will and intent that the rhythm of words, more than the word-choice itself, portends" (27). Finding "communion" as Bigsby finds "redemption" is pretty startling where so many find emptiness. Michael Hinden goes further, using Victor Turner's *communitas* as the object of Mamet's characters who "care less about sexual conquest and still less about business (the topics that preoccupy them) than they do about loneliness and their failure to construct a satisfying context for emotional security" ("'Intimate Voices,'" p. 34).

Others, too, have found meaning amidst the failures to communicate. John Russell Brown seeks to fill *The Woods* with meanings found in Greek mythology. Leslie Kane's whole book, *Weasels and Wisemen*, argues for a fully developed Ethics grounded in Judaism in Mamet's plays where others have found realistic depictions of a world without values. Her book is particularly valuable for the inside information she has about Mamet and his personal background. Her approach through ethics places it in the middle of a whole debate which focuses mainly on *Glengarry Glen Ross* and often finds a home in MBA programs. Jason Berger and Cornelius B. Pratt, Ruby Cohn ("'Oh, God, I Hate This job'"), Jonathan S. Cullick, Eugene Garaventa, and Deborah Geis have all contributed to the debate over the values, or lack of them in that play. Geis, for example, argues that the business plays are "all preoccupied with the connections between narrative (especially monologic) language and deception" (*Postmodern Theatric[k]s*, p. 99).

In contrast with these studies are those grounded not in Marxism/capitalism, but rather in Baudrillard. Thus, Linda Dorff who follows the imagery of money in *Glengarry Glen Ross* and finds that there is no real cash in the play – Levene does not have enough to bribe Williamson, the Nyborgs have none to pay Levene, the salesmen are detectives trying to find out who has money and where it is hidden (in socks and government bonds). Elizabeth Klaver and Tony Stafford similarly argue that the "leads" become the currency of the play, though they have no real cash value.

Uniquely theatrical scholars

A few scholars have developed an approach that is unique to a play or a set of plays, grounded in a theatrical rather than a thematic approach to text. For example, Varun Begley does excellent work in examining the differences between play and film in examining *Sexual Perversity in Chicago* on stage and its film adaptation. He observes "The film thus begins to flesh out the bare semiotic bones of a play which uses metonymic shorthand – a few barstools, a desk, and a bed – to denote the range of public and private space, so that the stage itself acts as a metaphor for a fragmented, denatured, urban world" ("On Adaptation," p. 167). The film, by contrast, fills in the gaps, smooths the landscape, and creates realistic characters in a real physical world. Another outstanding work is Andrew Harris's *Broadway Theatre* which traces the evolution of *American Buffalo* from its earliest Chicago productions through to Broadway. Harris claims that Ulu Grosbard, the Broadway director, was influential in getting Mamet to revise the script through six drafts in the four months before the opening. The result was that in "the rewritten script, Teach was unpredictable, uncontrollable, and psychotic" (106). According to Harris, Mamet saw the play with Donny as tragic hero; a few Chicago critics saw this, none did in New York.

Oleanna in particular has prompted a wide variety of approaches. Robert Skloot grounds his in Frière's theories of teaching, but filters his perceptions through examining the play in the theatre, taking particular note of costuming. Focusing on acting, David Sauer approaches Carol from the point of view of an actress who is not trying to negotiate modernist ambiguity, but rather postmodern indeterminacy. Sandra Tomc has similarly grounded "David Mamet's *Oleanna* and *The Way of All Flesh*" in performance theory. Another interesting new direction is Deborah Geis's examination of metatheatrics in Mamet; her work has been extended by M. L. Quinn and Howard Pearce.

Reviewers' recognitions and reversals

Intermittently, especially with recent revivals of the plays, reviewers have seemed to grasp Mamet's style as something other than simple realism. Perhaps it took Mamet's UFO/ESP play of the supernatural, *No One Shall Be Immune*, to make clear that his work is more concerned with the interface between inner and outer worlds than with the outer alone. David Rasche, featured actor in that play in 1995, next performed the Atlantic Theater revival of *Edmond* which prompts Ben Brantley to rethink Mamet:

> When "Edmond" opened at the Provincetown Playhouse in 1982, much of the critical reaction was bewildered and even hostile. [. . .] But the playwright has also always insisted that this story [. . .] of an empty man driven to murder was a fable, and hence beyond the standards of psychological realism. Mr. Gregg's production, anchored by Mr. Rasche, doesn't disguise a certain sanctimoniousness in "Edmond." But here the actors and the director, trusting in the dislocating rhythms of Mr. Mamet's dialogue, do indeed make a sinister, Grimm-like forest out of a New York that the playwright described as having "lost its flywheel," adding, "It's spinning itself apart."
>
> ("In Mamet's *Edmond*," p. C13)

This recognition that Mamet is not a naturalist but a writer of fables is best conveyed by the settings which are so often ignored, or are puzzling, as well as by the "dislocating rhythms of Mr. Mamet's dialogue."

In *Boston Marriage* the setting clearly is sending a signal which is not fully understood by realistic interpreter M. S. Mason, who only begins to see its connection to the language:

> To underscore the contradictions and confrontations, Mamet, who directed the play himself, has chosen a strangely cartoon-like set (by Sharon Kaitz and J. Michael Griggs). The walls are done in stripes of red, orange, pink, and black, a kind of post-modern mockery of the late Victorian period. A

goofy lavender settee with zebra stripes dominates the stage. All the furniture is mismatched, ugly, and absurd. Absurd, too, are the crude, contemporary idiomatic expressions that break out every once in a while, disturbing the graceful surface of Mamet's language – albeit, always to reveal something about the mental state of one of the women: the vulgarity of the maid, the predatory selfishness of the lovers. *("Boston Marriage")*

The set's evolution is traced by the designers with sketches and photos (www.people.fas.harvard.edu/~jmgriggs/portfoliopages/bostonmarriage. html). This is no haphazard cartoon, however; Mamet is extremely careful about the set design, a point David Barbour makes in *Theatre Crafts International* when discussing the design of *The Old Neighborhood*.

British reviewers similarly may be coming to understand Mamet anew. The revival of *Speed-the-Plow* in 2000 elicited some very different responses from those of the original reviewers who were simply mystified by the figure of Karen. In New York they blamed what they saw as the inadequacy of the character on Madonna's failure as an actress. They were then puzzled that an accomplished actress, Felicity Huffman, replacing Madonna, failed to rectify that inadequacy. When Rebecca Pidgeon played the role at the National Theatre a year later, British reviewers were a little more gentle with her, simply blaming Mamet for underwriting.

Kimberly Williams offers a quite different appreciation. Georgina Brown, in the *Mail on Sunday*, for example, observed that "As the biddable, beddable temporary secretary, the stunning young American actress Kimberly Williams brilliantly manages the shifts from girly faux-naivete, through knowing manœuvres, to shattered defeat." This recognition of the twists and turns in the role, and acceptance of the seemingly ambitious transformation between acts, is also commented on in Kate Kellaway's review in the *Observer*:

> The second act, at Gould's house, is fascinating because Mamet never oversimplifies. He gives Karen the right words, set to the wrong music. She argues for quality and passion, but with the help of a lousy book. She is dazzled by it. Williams is superb: her nervous posture has gone. It is as if she had melted between acts; she is translated by her own enthusiasm. Her rapture is described as "naïve," but there is – even so – a sense that Gould's cynicism might actually be in the balance. There is a big, predatory painting of a snarling tiger behind the sofa (*The Jungle Book* gone oriental). The question that hangs fire is: is it possible to be seduced by an idea?

Although the setting and direction is not Mamet's, there is here a recognition of his techniques in constructing the character, "the right words, set to the wrong music," and hence of his leaving gaps which the audience must fill on its own, if it is to grasp the play's power.

A map of misreading

The audience, the amateur, the critic – *their* job, in the face of this new vision of reality, is to *resist*, to the point where the determination of the artist overcomes their resistance. This is the scheme of aesthetic natural selection.
Mamet, "Stanislavsky and the Bearer Bonds," in *Some Freaks*, p. 72

In Mamet's view, critics are performing their function as they "*resist*" his "new vision of reality," especially as articulated in his direction of his own plays.

The first level of resistance, or misreading, comes from those critics who expect the play to be self-explanatory, conveyed by text and actorly sub-text. When this does not happen, they react as did David Sheward to Mamet's direction of *The Cryptogram*: "But we don't learn enough about this odd trio to really care about what happens to them. Nor do the actors provide enough subtext to pique our interest in what the playwright has left out. They're merely talking in stylized and cryptic Mamet-ese" (review in *Backstage*). He had agreement from Jonathan Kalb ("actors who either cannot or have been told not to animate his mannered language" – "Crypto-Mamet"); Donald Lyons ("Words here are as dysfunctional as people, with everybody repeating, interrogatively, what they've just heard" – "To Paris and Back"); and John Simon ("About language, then? Yes, if you like rambling monologues that, merely because they occasionally connect, pretend to be dialogue – and don't even connect so much as encroach on one another" – "Verbal Mastication"). Such critics clearly recognize that language is the center of the play, but it washes over them, and does nothing more than become a parody of itself, Mamet-ese.

A second variant of misreading comes from those who take all the words quite literally. For Howard Kissel, "At a certain point, we sense instinctively to what unhappy purpose the knife will be put, but it is a measure of the sheer tedium of the evening that we want it to be put to that purpose sooner" ("Mamet's Musky *Cryptogram*"). John Heilpern thinks that he similarly understands all too well: "Mr. Mamet infuriates us knowingly. His psychological power plays, the repressed undercurrents of anxiety and simmering violence, the oblique, disjointed Mametspeak that has become his signature style, are meant to dislocate and disturb us" ("*The Cryptogram*," p. 220). Thus he complains at the conclusion of the review that, while Donny says "the meaning is not clear," "the meaning of *The Cryptogram* is all too obvious, and my frustration is with Mr. Mamet's portentous play, rather than with the abandoned child" (224). It is always fascinating to find some reviewers who find the whole experience "too obvious" while so many others complain that it is too cryptic.

A sub-group of this kind of reading takes the play positively, but as real because it is autobiography. Linda Winer ("Emotional Puzzle") notes that it has "undeniable sorrow and power" but attributes that, reluctantly, to Mamet's "working from the misery of his own parents' divorce. While we're indulging in the dangerous world of psycho-dramatic interpretations, we may as well note the suggestion of the playwright/director's own ex-wife in the strong physicality of Huffman's Donny." Clive Barnes complains that Mamet's direction undercuts the realistic center of the play which was better done in London, "the playing was altogether more naturalistic, which added to the story's poignancy, and the sense of a child looking back mostly into his life and finding, if only vaguely, that defining point of character ('A Tale of the Cryptic')" Such a reading gives a very fixed center to a play which seems ideally to work better when it is more ephemeral.

There is a middle group, therefore, for whom the experience of the play itself is almost beyond language, rather than solely consisting of language. Jeremy Gerard concludes, for example, "what's overwhelming about that final scene is how Mamet's signature speech rhythms – the halting staccato delivery, the half-finished sentences, the constipated emotional outbursts – seem completely natural, pouring forth from a confused, hurt boy, the fitful patterns of a child who cannot – who will never be able to – comprehend why he has been treated so cruelly" (review in *Daily Variety*). Giving the play a different center, Michael Feingold observes "The play's emotional weight rests on Huffman, whose fierce, precise assurance on every elliptical line makes you marvel even while she's wrenching your heart out" ("Codehearted") Vincent Canby centers on Mamet: "His direction is as cool and formal as his intricately designed dialogue. [. . .] It's as if Mr. Mamet were deconstructing language to make us think more clearly" ("Attempt to Decode") It is hard to imagine that this last set of critics are misreading, though they all read the play differently. The common denominator is that all three take the style to be the substance.

Matter and spirit

The direction in which Mamet is heading is implied by the epigraph to this article, where he asserts "Our own time has quite understandably sickened of The Material, and needs to deal with things of The Spirit."

Reviewers and critics who have misread Mamet force him into the category of nineteenth-century realistic writers for whom "The Material seemed to be, and, perhaps, was, the central aspect of life." When he is forced into this category, the audience sees nothing at the center, finding his plays to depict meaningless materiality, a junkshop assemblage out of *American Buffalo*. Or worse, they discover negative messages, like the sexism found by those who assume he is represented by his on-stage characters, who are misogynistic. At its most neutral, reviewers complain at what they characterize as Mametspeak, language detached from any reality, a parody, they often say, of everyday language.

More damaging are readers who see the gaps and fill them in to make a seamless, realistic narrative. Readers often do this with *Oleanna* where Carol's "group" is given all sorts of constructions by different interpreters – none of which are in the text. Mamet seems to suggest as much with the *Playbill* covers for the New York production, half of which featured the figure of a man with a target on his body, the other half featuring a woman with the same target. The motto on the film poster for *Oleanna* made the same assertion – "Whichever side you choose, you're wrong." In Washington, at the National Theater, where he moved the New York cast of Macy and Eisenstadt (later the film cast), there was a blackboard erected in the lobby after the play to register the audience's votes – "he was right," "she was wronged," and "this could really happen." Emerging from the theatre the audience recognized, as they had during the performance, that responses to this play are divided, and not solely along expected lines of gender or age. These extratextual devices problematize the response itself.

The difficulty of avoiding misreadings of Mamet is clear. It is often hard to navigate between the Scylla of under-reading, to find little or nothing there, and the Charybdis of overreading, finding one's own reflection in the critical mirror. To maintain balance, it helps to see the play in a theatrical context rather than as a reader.

Examples of critics who approach Mamet from a broader context, working as both reviewers and scholars, include Leslie Kane, Christopher Hudgins, Robert Vorlicky, and Toby Zinman. Kane makes clear that she places *The Old Neighborhood* in a wider cultural context in order to discover values that most others miss: "Thus the trilogy, Mamet's first, merges the minimalism of *Goldberg Street* and the dazzling language that we identify as Mametic, its clear articulation of a culture encompassing the double-bind of legacy as blessing and burden in a teaching moment that envisions an ethical contract between individuals within or outside the margins of family, both seminal and communal" (*Weasels and Wisemen*, p. 259). Filling in Mamet's minimalism with Jewish culture leads Kane to her view of the ethical basis to his work.

Vorlicky's argument places Mamet's plays in the context of 500 published male-cast plays, and these lead to perceptions which separate him from the more materially oriented critics:

> The world of *American Buffalo* is not, finally, as Hersh Zeifman suggests, "literally ruthless and graceless" (129); it is a world in which charity and responsibility can be, and are, present. [...] Don's and Bob's talk is finally based in self-awareness. It is open and sincere, and not "pointless words of apology and forgiveness," as Malkin argues (154). Their attempt through language to fill a "missing intimacy" (Bigsby 1985, 22) is an uncommon feature in male-cast drama. (*Act Like a Man*, p. 227)[3]

Vorlicky's vision of "charity and responsibility" is a unique perception – but it is not just a solipsistic vision of his own. It expands an implication of the ending of the play itself, as he places Mamet's play in the context of all the other male-cast plays he has examined.

Like Vorlicky, Christopher Hudgins demonstrates an aspect of Mamet's plays often missed by readers – though not by reviewers who frequently are surprised by the laughter evoked in performance. Mamet's comedy and humor are "moralistic," but it is a subtle, ambiguous moralism, not overly didactic. That we laugh, with him, at his characters, and at ourselves, is a huge part of our enjoyment in response to a Mamet play, and that laughter points towards the celebration of life at the core of all Mamet's work ("Comedy," p. 225).

Finally, Toby Zinman strings together six Mamet works dealing with Bobby Go(u)ld, notably, *Speed-the-Plow,* "Bobby Gould in Hell," and *Homicide*, to discover "a gaudy and deeply outraged parody of Dante's *Divine Comedy,* a kind of Diabolical Comedy for our times, with Los Angeles, the City of Angels, as Inferno on earth" ("Hollywood," p. 103). Her conclusion is that "Mamet has made a career out of the inspection of America's spiritual trashheap and like his Bobby Goulds, he knows that the most glamorous ruins and the most ruinous glamour is Hollywood" (111). This is not quite the positive view of the other three scholars, but invoking Dante implies the possibility that this is not all, that *Paradisio* may yet await.

Where others stressed the negative aspects of his plays these critics see something more, perhaps because of their experience of viewing these plays in multiple productions. As a result, they have a larger sense of a play's potential effects on audiences. And so they are able to recognize greater implications of spirit in the silences, gaps, and minimalism of Mamet's plays.

NOTES

1. This was not a unanimous view. One reviewer did prefer Mamet's direction to Pinter's – Blanche Marvin:

> The London production does not match New York. Lia Williams, who plays the bogus girl, has long blonde hair and is gorgeous. The girl must be a sexless spinster or the play is thrown off balance. [. . .] The first act clipped along, being 15 minutes shorter than in New York without changing a word. So much for the Pinter pauses Mamet directed in New York. The girl's frustration and her backwardness as a college student is much clearer here. Her support from the woman's group that leads her onto this aggressive behaviour is also much sharper. But one loses sympathy with the wimpy weak professor of David Suchet who tries ingratiating himself to the girl, not out of sympathy, but patronisingly. One believes her accusations of his need for power, called passive aggression these days. (Review in *London Theatre Reviews*)

2. London's objection to Mamet's staging uses the same word that Bigsby uses. His opposition to Mamet as director is that his "reductive thinking has the opposite effect" instead of creating "essentially fixed beings." But Bigsby's point is that this is precisely Mamet's purpose in using a "reductive physical setting." The same minimalism upsets Heilpern who complains of *The Cryptogram* that the set shows "no evidence that a child lives here, no toys, no sign of anything but alienation" ("*The Cryptogram*," p. 222).

3. "Literally," of course, Zeifman is right – the characters of Grace and Ruth do not appear in the play. His point, though, is what leads to the quotation Vorlicky cites: "In the brutally macho and materialistic dog-eat-dog world of American business, values like compassion and spirituality – implicitly inscribed as 'feminine' and therefore, in the figures of Ruth and Grace, devalued and excluded – are totally lacking. The world of *American Buffalo* – the world of American business – is thus *literally* ruthless and graceless" ("Phallus in Wonderland," pp. 128–9).

MAJOR SECONDARY WORKS

Almansi, Guido. "David Mamet, a Virtuoso of Invective," in *Critical Angles: European Views of Contemporary American Literature*, ed. Marc Chenetier (Carbondale: Southern Illinois University Press, 1986): 191–207.

Badenhausen, R. "The Modern Academy Raging in the Dark: Misreading Mamet's Political Incorrectness in *Oleanna*." *College Literature* 25.3 (1998): 1–19.

Barbour, David. "You Can't Go Home Again." *Theatre Crafts International* 32.2 (1998): 10–11.

Barnes, Clive. "Mamet with a Thud." *New York Post*, Oct. 26, 1992. Rpt. in *New York Theatre Critics' Reviews* 53.19 (1992): 359.

"A Tale of the Cryptic." *New York Post*, April 14, 1995. Rpt. in *National Theatre Critics' Reviews* 56.7 (1995): 212.

Bechtel, Roger. "P. C. Power Play: Language and Representation in David Mamet's *Oleanna*." *Theatre Studies* 41 (1996): 29–48.

Begley, Varun. "On Adaptation: David Mamet and Hollywood." *Essays in Theatre /
Études Theatrales* 16.2 (1998): 165–76.
Berger, Jason, and Cornelius B. Pratt. "Class and Power: Exploring with College
Students the Ethics and Class Conflict Messages in the Films of David Mamet," in
*The Image of Class in Literature, Media, and Society. Selected Papers. Conference
of the Society for the Interdisciplinary Study of Social Imagery*, ed. Will Wright
and Steven Kaplan (Pueblo: University of Southern Colorado, 1998): 298–304.
"Teaching Business-Communication Ethics with Controversial Films." *Journal of
Business Ethics* 17.16 (1998): 1817–23.
Bigsby, C. W. E. *David Mamet*. Contemporary Writers (London: Methuen, 1985).
Modern American Drama, 1945–2000 (Cambridge: Cambridge University Press,
2000).
Bishop, Ryan. "There's Nothing Natural About Natural Conversation: A Look at
Dialogue in Fiction and Drama," in *Cross-Cultural Studies. American, Canadian
and European Literatures: 1945–1985*, ed. Mirko Jurak (Ljubljana, Yugoslavia:
English Dept., University of Ljubljana, 1988): 257–66.
Blansfield, Karen. "Women on the Verge, Unite!" in *Gender and Genre: Essays on
David Mamet*, ed. Christopher C. Hudgins and Leslie Kane (New York: Palgrave,
2001): 126–42.
Blumberg, Marcia. "Staging Hollywood, Selling Out," in *Hollywood on Stage: Play-
wrights Evaluate the Culture Industry*, ed. Kimball King (New York: Garland,
1997): 71–82.
Boon, Kevin Alexander. "Dialogue, Discourse & Dialectics: The Rhetoric of
Capitalism in *Glengarry Glen Ross*." *Creative Screenwriting* 5.3 (1998):
50–7.
Brantley, Ben. "In Mamet's *Edmond*, a Man on Empty." *New York Times*. October 2,
1996, C13. "Victorian Women? From Mamet? Well, #@%*!" *New York Times*
June 16, 1999, E1.
Brown, Georgina. Rev. of *Speed-the-Plow*. *Mail on Sunday*, March 19, 2000. Rpt.
in *Theatre Record*, March 11–24, 2000, p. 323.
Brown, John Russell. "The Woods, the West, and Icarus's Mother: Myth in the
Contemporary American Theatre." *Connotations* (Munster, Germany) 5.2–3
(1995/6): 339–54.
Burkman, Katherine H. "The Myth of Narcissus: Shepard's *True West* and Mamet's
Speed-the-Plow," in *Hollywood on Stage: Playwrights Evaluate the Culture
Industry*, ed. Kimball King (New York: Garland, 1997): 113–23.
"The Web of Misogyny in Mamet's and Pinter's Betrayal Games," in *Staging the
Rage: The Web of Misogyny in Modern Drama*, ed. Katherine H. Burkman and
Judith Roof (London: Associated University Presses, 1998): 27–37.
Canby, Vincent. "David Mamet's Attempt to Decode Family Life." *New York Times*,
April 14, 1995, C3. Rpt. in *National Theatre Critics' Reviews* 56.7 (1995): 209–
10.
Carroll, Dennis. *David Mamet*. Modern Dramatists (London: MacMillan, 1987).
Christiansen, Richard. *Anglo-American Interplay in Recent Drama* (Cambridge:
Cambridge University Press, 1995).
"Mamet's New Play in Uneven Debut." *Chicago Daily News*, Nov. 17, 1977, B9.
"No Words Wasted in Mamet's *Cryptogram*." *Chicago Tribune*, Feb. 21, 1995,
Sec. 1, p. 14.

Cohn, Ruby. "'Oh, God I Hate This Job,'" in *Approaches to Teaching Miller's Death of a Salesman*, ed. Matthew C. Roudané (New York: MLA, 1995): 155–62.

Coveney, Michael. Rev. of *Oleanna*. *Observer*, July 4, 1993, p. 56. Rpt. in *Theatre Record*, June 18 – July 1, 1993: 744.

Cullick, Jonathan S. "'Always Be Closing': Competition and the Discourse of Closure in David Mamet's *Glengarry Glen Ross*." *Journal of Dramatic Theory and Criticism* 8.2 (1994): 23–36.

Dean, Anne. *David Mamet: Language as Dramatic Action* (Rutherford, NJ: Fairleigh Dickinson University Press, 1990).

Demastes, William W. *Beyond Naturalism: A New Realism in American Theatre.* Contributions in Drama and Theatre Studies 27 (Westport, CT: Greenwood, 1988).

Dettmer, Roger. "Squirrels: Overrun with Obscurity." *Chicago Tribune*, Oct. [12] 1974: n. pag.

Ditsky, John. "'He Lets You See the Thought There': The Theater of David Mamet." *Kansas Quarterly* 12.4 (1980): 25–34.

Dorff, Linda. "Things (Ex)Change: The Value of Money in David Mamet's *Glengarry Glen Ross*," in *David Mamet's Glengarry Glen Ross: Text and Performance*, ed. Leslie Kane (New York: Garland, 1996): 195–209.

Elam, Harry J., Jr. "'Only in America': Contemporary American Theater and the Power of Performance," in *Voices of Power: Co-operation and Conflict in English Language and Literatures*, ed. Marc Maufort (Liège: English Dept., University of Liège, 1997): 151–63.

Esche, Edward. "David Mamet," in *American Drama*, ed. Clive Bloom (New York: St. Martin's, 1995): 165–78.

Feingold, Michael. "Codehearted." *Village Voice*, April 25, 1995, p. 97. Rpt. in *National Theatre Critics' Reviews* 56.7 (1995): 208–9.

Foster, Verna. "Sex, Power, and Pedagogy in Mamet's *Oleanna* and Ionesco's *The Lesson*." *American Drama* 5.1 (1995): 36–50.

Garaventa, Eugene. "A Tool for Teaching Business Ethics." *Business Ethics Quarterly* 8.3 (1998): 535–45.

Garner, Stanton B., Jr. "Framing the Classroom: Pedagogy, Power, Oleanna." *Theatre Topics* 10.1 (2000): 39–59.

Geis, Deborah R. *Postmodern Theatric[k]s: Monologue in Contemporary Drama* (Ann Arbor: University of Michigan Press, 1993).
    "'You're Exploiting My Space': Ethnicity, Spectatorship and the (Post)Colonial Condition in Mukherjee's 'A Wife's Story' and Mamet's *Glengarry Glen Ross*," in *David Mamet's Glengarry Glen Ross: Text and Performance*, ed. Leslie Kane (New York: Garland, 1996): 123–30.

Gerard, Jeremy. Rev. of *Cryptogram*. *Daily Variety*, April 17, 1995, p. 45. Rpt. in *National Theatre Critics' Reviews* 56.7 (1995): 211–12.

Gidmark, Jill B. "Violent Silences in Three Works of David Mamet." *Midamerica XXV: The Yearbook of the Society for the Study of Midwestern Literature* (East Lansing, Michigan) (1998): 184–92.

Goist, Park Dixon. "Ducks and Sex in David Mamet's Chicago." *Midamerica XXV: The Yearbook of the Society for the Study of Midwestern Literature* (East Lansing, Michigan) (1998): 143–52.

Goldensohn, Barry. "David Mamet and Poetic Language in Drama." *Agni* (Boston) 49 (1999): 139–49.

Goldstein, Shelly. WNUR Radio (Evanston) Nov. 17, 1977. (Typescript held by the Chicago Theater Collection of the Harold Washington Center, Chicago Public Library.)

Gussow, Mel. "Stage: *Reunion*, 3 Mamet Plays." *New York Times*, Oct. 19, 1979, C3.

Haedicke, Janet V. "Decoding Cipher Space: David Mamet's *The Cryptogram* and America's Dramatic Legacy." *American Drama* 9.1 (1999): 1–20.

"Plowing the Buffalo, Fucking the Fruits: (M)Others in *American Buffalo* and *Speed-the-Plow*," in *Gender and Genre: Essays on David Mamet*, ed. Christopher C. Hudgins and Leslie Kane (New York: Palgrave, 2001): 27–41.

Hall, Ann C. "Playing to Win: Sexual Politics in David Mamet's *House of Games* and *Speed-the-Plow*," in *David Mamet: A Casebook*, ed. Leslie Kane (New York: Garland, 1992): 137–60.

Harris, Andrew B. *Broadway Theatre* (London: Routledge, 1994).

Heilpern, John. "*The Cryptogram*: More Mametspeak, More Provocation." *Observer*, April 24, 1995. Rpt. in *How Good Is David Mamet Anyway?* (New York: Routledge, 1999): 220–4.

Herman, William. "Theatrical Diversity from Chicago: David Mamet," in *Understanding Contemporary American Drama* (Columbia, SC: University of South Carolina Press, 1987): 125–60.

Hinden, Michael. "'Intimate Voices': *Lakeboat* and Mamet's Quest for Community," in *David Mamet: A Casebook*, ed. Leslie Kane (New York: Garland, 1992): 33–48.

Holmberg, Arthur. "Approaches: The Language of Misunderstanding." *American Theatre* 9.6 (1992): 94–5.

Hudgins, Christopher C. "Comedy and Humor in the Plays of David Mamet," in *David Mamet: A Casebook*, ed. Leslie Kane (New York: Garland, 1992): 191–230.

Jacobs, Dorothy H. "Levene's Daughter: Positioning of the Female in *Glengarry Glen Ross*," in *David Mamet's Glengarry Glen Ross: Text and Performance*, ed. Leslie Kane (New York: Garland, 1996): 107–22.

Kalb, Jonathan. "Crypto-Mamet." *Village Voice*, Feb. 28, 1995, p. 83.

Kane, Leslie. *Weasels and Wisemen: Ethics and Ethnicity in the Work of David Mamet* (New York: St. Martin's Press, 1999).

Kaplan, Sherman. Rev. of *The Woods*. WBBM Radio. (Typescript held by the Chicago Theater Collection of the Harold Washington Center, Chicago Public Library.)

Kellaway, Kate. "Cynics of the Best." *Observer*, March 19, 2000, p. 10. Rpt. in *Theatre Record*, March 11–24, 2000, pp. 324–5.

King, Thomas L. "Talk and Dramatic Action in *American Buffalo*." *Modern Drama* 34 (1991): 538–48.

Kissel, Howard. "Mamet's Murky *Cryptogram*: Is a Puzzlement." *New York Daily News*, April 14, 1995. Rpt. in *National Theatre Critics' Reviews* 56.7 (1995): 212–13.

Klaver, Elizabeth. "David Mamet, Jean Baudrillard and the Performance of America," in *David Mamet's Glengarry Glen Ross: Text and Performance*, ed. Leslie Kane (New York: Garland, 1996): 171–83.

Lahr, John. "Dogma Days." *New Yorker*, Nov. 16, 1992, pp. 121–6. Rpt. in *New York Theatre Critics' Reviews* 53.19 (1992): 351–3.

"Talk of the Town: 'David Mamet's Child's Play.'" *New Yorker*, April 10, 1995, pp. 33–4.

London, Todd. "Mamet vs. Mamet." *American Theatre* 13.6 (1996): 18–21.

Lyons, Donald. "To Paris and Back in a '20s Dream." *Wall Street Journal*, April 14, 1995, Sec. A, p. 7. Rpt. in *National Theatre Critics' Reviews* 56.7 (1995): 213.

MacLeod, Christine. "The Politics of Gender, Language, and Hierarchy in Mamet's *Oleanna*." *Journal of American Studies* 29.2 (1995): 199–213.

Malkin, Jeanette R. *Verbal Violence in Contemporary Drama* (Cambridge: Cambridge University Press, 1992).

Mamet, David. *Some Freaks* (New York: Viking, 1989).

Marvin, Blanche. Rev. of *Oleanna*. *London Theatre Reviews* (June/July 1993): 17.

Mason, M. S. "*Boston Marriage*: Barbs beneath Victorian Propriety." *Christian Science Monitor*, June 18, 1999, Sec. Arts & Leisure, p. 20.

McDonough, Carla J. "Every Fear Hides a Wish: Unstable Masculinity in Mamet's Drama." *Theatre Journal* 44.2 (1992): 195–205.

Mufson, Daniel. "The Critical Eye: Sexual Perversity in Viragos." *Theater* (New Haven) 24.1 (1993): 111–13.

Nelson, Jeanne Andréc. "*Speed-the-Plow* or Seed the Plot? Mamet and the Female Reader." *Essays in Theatre / Études Théâtrales* (Canada) 10.1 (1991): 71–82.

Pearce, Howard. "Illusion and Essence: Husserl's *Epoché*, Gadamer's 'Transformation into Structure,' and Mamet's *Theatrum Mundi*." *Analecta Husserliana* 73 (2001): 111–28.

Piette, Alain. "The Devil's Advocate: David Mamet's *Oleanna* and Political Correctness," in *Staging Difference: Cultural Pluralism in American Theatre and Drama*, ed. Marc Maufort. Theatre Arts 25 (New York: Peter Lang, 1995): 173–87.

Price, Steven. "Disguise in Love: Gender and Desire in *House of Games* and *Speed-the-Plow*," in *Gender and Genre: Essays on David Mamet*, ed. Christopher C. Hudgins and Leslie Kane (New York: Palgrave, 2001): 41–61.

Quinn, Michael L. "Anti-Theatricality and American Ideology: Mamet's Performative Realism," in *Realism and the American Dramatic Tradition*, ed. W. W. Demastes (Tuscaloosa: University of Alabama Press 1996): 235–54.

Roudané, Matthew C. *American Drama since 1960: A Critical History* (New York: Twayne, 1996).

Sauer, David Kennedy. "*Oleanna* and *The Children's Hour*: Misreading Sexuality on the Post/Modern Realistic Stage." *Modern Drama* 43.3 (2000): 421–40.

Sauer, David K., and Janice A. Sauer. *David Mamet: A Resource and Production Sourcebook* (Westport, CN: Praeger, 2003).

Sheward, David. Rev. of *Cryptogram*. *Backstage*, April 21, 1995, p. 52.

Silverstein, Marc. "'We're Just Human': *Oleanna* and Cultural Crisis." *South Atlantic Review* 60.2 (1995): 103–20.

Simon, John. "Verbal Mastication." *New York*, April 24, 1995, pp. 76ff. Rpt. in *National Theatre Critics' Reviews* 56.7 (1995): 209.

Skloot, Robert. "Oleanna, or, the Play of Pedagogy," in *Gender and Genre: Essays on David Mamet*, ed. Christopher C. Hudgins and Leslie Kane (New York: Palgrave, 2001): 95–109.

Stafford, Tony J. "Visions of a Promised Land: David Mamet's *Glengarry Glen Ross*," in *David Mamet's Glengarry Glen Ross: Text and Performance*, ed. Leslie Kane (New York: Garland, 1996): 185–94.

Tomc, Sandra. "David Mamet's *Oleanna* and *The Way of All Flesh*." *Essays in Theatre / Études Théâtrales* (Canada) 15.2 (1997): 163–75.

Vorlicky, Robert. *Act Like a Man: Challenging Masculinities in American Drama* (Ann Arbor: University of Michigan Press, 1995).

Weales, Gerald. "The Mamet Variations." *Decade* (Promotional Issue) 1.1 (1978): 10–13.

Winer, Linda. "Clickety-Clack of David Mamet's Typewriter Is Heard through Woods." *Chicago Tribune*, Nov. 17, 1977, B6.

"An Emotional Puzzle from Mamet." *New York Newsday*, April 14, 1995. Rpt. in *National Theatre Critics' Reviews* 56.7 (1995): 210–11.

Worthen, William. *Modern Drama and the Rhetoric of Theater* (Berkeley: University of California Press, 1992).

Zeifman, Hersh. "Phallus in Wonderland: Machismo and Business in David Mamet's *American Buffalo* and *Glengarry Glen Ross*," in *David Mamet: A Casebook*, ed. Leslie Kane (New York: Garland, 1992): 123–36. Rpt. in *Modern Dramatists: A Casebook of Major British, Irish, and American Playwrights*, ed. Kimball King (New York: Routledge, 2001): 167–76.

Rev. of *Oleanna. David Mamet Review* 1 (1994): 2–3.

Zinman, Toby Silverman. "So Dis Is Hollywood: Mamet in Hell," *in Hollywood on Stage: Playwrights Evaluate the Culture Industry*, ed. Kimball King (New York: Garland, 1997): 101–12.

Ziomek, Jon. "Squirrels Lacks Subtlety." *Chicago Sun–Times*, Oct. 12, 1974, n. pag.

INDEX

Works indexed by title are by Mamet (as director in the case of films) unless otherwise stated. Literary/stage works by other authors are listed under the author's name. Entries in **bold italic** type denote detailed treatment. 'DM' = 'David Mamet'

CAMBRIDGE COMPANIONS TO LITERATURE

CAMBRIDGE COMPANIONS TO CULTURE